THE CATHOLIC LEFT

The Catholic Left

THE CRISIS OF RADICALISM WITHIN THE CHURCH

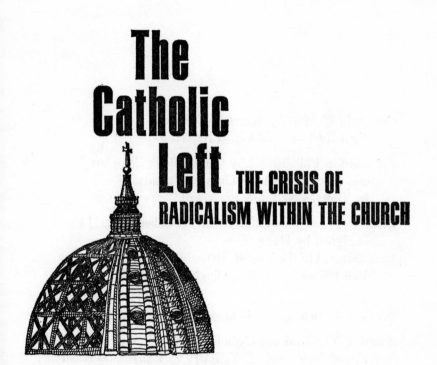

by James Colaianni

INTRODUCTION BY DONALD J. THORMAN

Chilton Book Company

PHILADELPHIA · NEW YORK · LONDON

Copyright © 1968 by James F. Colaianni
First Edition   All Rights Reserved

Published in Philadelphia by Chilton Book Company
and simultaneously in Ontario, Canada,
by Thomas Nelson & Sons, Ltd.

Library of Congress Catalog Card Number 68-29313
Designed by Harry Eaby
Manufactured in the United States of America by
Vail-Ballou Press, Inc., Binghamton, N.Y.

Special acknowledgment is made to the following:

America, The National Catholic Weekly Review, 106 West
56th Street, New York, N.Y. 10019 © 1967-61-66 America
Press, Inc., to quote from "Groppi's War on Milwaukee" by
Paul J. Weber (September 30, 1967), "God Bless America"
by Rev. George H. Dunne (June 17, 1961), and "Controversy within the Church" by John O'Connor (April 9,
1966).

Farrar, Straus & Giroux, Inc., New York, to quote from
What I Believe by François Mauriac, translated by Wallace
Fowlie. Copyright 1963 by Farrar, Straus & Co.

The Bruce Publishing Co., Milwaukee, to quote from *Church
and Revolution* by Peter Riga. Copyright 1967 by The
Bruce Publishing Co.

To my wife, and to Father Edward,
good Christian and true friend.

To my wife and to fellow Physician,
good Nutrition and free from

CONTENTS

INTRODUCTION

The most serious misjudgment the reader of this book could make would be to dismiss and reject the author as an angry, impatient man with nothing to communicate to the Church. Let me be the first to admit that by his own words, illustrations, and selection of materials Mr. Colaianni assuredly does not come across to the reader as a Catholic Casper Milquetoast.

His writing is tough and aggressive, and at times he uses a pickax when a scalpel would seem to be more appropriate. No reader, including me, will agree with everything he criticizes or proposes or suggests, though I feel certain he does not expect or want complete agreement.

Nor does he always succeed in achieving the purpose of his book, which he describes as "a positive manifesto of the religious attitudes of the Left, as I perceive them, and more concretely, as I find them meaningful in my own religious experience—a series of reflections, not a sociological study and not a theological tract."

But if his approach is not always completely positive, this fact is in itself a further symptom of a basic deficiency of the Catholic Left and Catholic progressives today: they know more what they are against than what they are for. The conservatives have had centuries to build up a rigid, static, closed view of what the world should look like; they have a world view, a program, a clear set of agreed-upon goals.

The Left, on the other hand, has never held real power within the Church (at least certainly not since Trent), and so its orientation is understandably more anti and negative than either we would like or the Church desperately needs. Without ecclesiastical power and responsibility, the Left will always find itself a kind of opposition party.

(This seems to be the author's approach to the business community as well as to the Church, if I may judge from the chapter dealing with Father Riga, in which there is little tolerance or understanding shown for management. I confess that as one who has responsibility for meeting a payroll, who has been associated with the National Conference of Christian Employers and Managers, and who is a member of the American Management Association I would like to debate some of the slashing statements and broad charges made by both the author and Father Riga. But then the author did not write this book to make us feel comfortable!)

My point, however, remains to be made: do not make the mistake of allowing Mr. Colaianni's general forthrightness and his style of calling a spade a spade to stand in the way of hearing his message—for he does have a message.

What is he attempting to communicate? In historical perspective, he is one of a long and honorable (though thin) line of American Catholic radicals, one who has been disenchanted by the institution and its authorities but who fervently loves the Church as the Body of Christ, as the People of God. I guess you could say he has had it with the institution. But the Church he loves is not institutional only, and for that reason he is not opting out in frustration, disappointment, or disbelief.

Instead, he has chosen to express himself in this book basically to give his views as a member of the Catholic Left on the inadequacies of the institutional Church and some of her less lovable authorities. True, there are times in the author's writing when you get the feeling that he believes insensible mediocrity to be the norm for Church authorities, and you must keep reminding yourself that heroic, charismatic Pope John was for most of his lifetime a faceless member of the Vatican Establishment. Things are not so simple and black-and-white as they often appear, even though they are black-and-white on occasion.

We must remember at all times that the Church is not the hierarchy, the chancery, the pastor, the rectory *alone*. (But again, in simple justice, though I have known Church officials of all degrees who were asses and boors, I must also acknowledge that some of the finest Christian men and women I have been privileged to know have been bishops, chancery officials, pastors, and sister superiors.)

I hope these remarks are not prompted by my preconciliar habit as a Catholic editor of always leaping to the defense of the institutional Church. What I am really trying to do is to put this volume by Mr. Colaianni into perspective. To use a more homely example: you can hold up your 50 percent-filled martini glass and, depending on your mood, say it is half-full or half-empty. In effect, this book says the Church is half-empty, but to say that does not mean the Church is not half-full at the same time. A Church which is completely empty without hope of improvement or redemption would scarcely be worth writing about.

A friend, a priest who would certainly be regarded as progressive, if not Left in the author's sense, proposes that in our criticism of professional religious functionaries such as the hierarchy and priests, we keep in mind that these are men of the people. They come from the people and they represent, generally, the level of the people from whom they come. Even bishops and priests, he maintains, are sensitive to public opinion and live up (or down) to the expectations of their constituency.

His point is that the professional comes from the People of God and is a kind of gauge of the mediocrity or superiority of the People itself. To effect a long-range change in the level of the professionals would require as much work changing the standards and expectations of the People as of the hierarchy or priesthood. Obviously this view has some immediately apparent limitations, but it also provides some insights.

My points are twofold. First, the author cannot be dismissed as a malcontent. Even though he writes impatiently, almost angrily, at times, he is writing about something with which he is emotionally involved, something he loves and wants to be better—he passionately desires the Church of Jesus Christ to live up to her heritage.

And, although the author does not say so in so many words, it seems to me apparent between the lines that he understands the complexity of upgrading the level of leadership within the official Church and that far more is involved than a broadside attack on the weaknesses of our official leaders. And yet, leaders are always highly visible, and since they are the first to benefit from the system, it is not unjust that they also stand ready to be the first to be shot at when the system is under siege.

I said earlier that Mr. Colaianni is one of a long—though thin—line of American Catholic radicals. In order to understand him and the present situation better, it would be instructive to take a brief look back at some other Catholic dissenters in recent history. First, however, a few preliminary observations.

The Catholic Left today as described by the author is greatly different from the Left, or radicals and dissenters, we knew in the past. Those in the past were fiercely dedicated to the institutional Church and generally wanted only to improve and patch up the structure. There was never any question of the so-called phoenix theory sometimes discussed today of burning the Church down and letting a new structure rise from the ashes.

The single most common characteristic of Catholic radicals in the past about whom I've read or of those I've known in person has been their deep loyalty to the Church as an institution and as the Body of Christ, even at times when they were rejected by both the authorities and the People for their views.

This is no longer true. Within the ranks of the Catholic Left today are included those who are ready to ignore the institution rather than bother with it. They feel no great loyalty to the institutional Church and for the first time—and this is an essential difference between them and dissenters of the past—they are raising questions about the validity of the institution itself. I refer you to the words of the author in Chapter 2 on the Church when he states:

. . . I, for one, have little confidence in the trustworthiness of the magisterium; I am deeply resentful of its misguided, arrogant, and often forced articulation of truth, with little or no respect for consultation and dialogue with the whole Church (that is, the rest of mankind). I believe I am justifiably suspicious of a teaching authority whose record for yielding to the temptation to overstate is clearly discernible through centuries of its history. I believe I am rightfully wary of a teaching authority whose effort to preserve itself in a certain mold has, for centuries, been a source of inordinate distraction from the central message it purports to bear with unwavering fidelity.

But enough. This is sufficient to make my point. I submit that seldom is such open, frank, and even harsh comment about the Church made by someone who still regards himself as a member of the institution. And the author is but representative of an admittedly small (but growing) group with similar ideas and sentiments. It is this questioning of the very essence of the institution itself that marks a vast gulf between the dissenters of the past and those of today.

Taking "radical" and "dissenter" in a broad sense, we might examine some of our history for a better understanding of where the new Catholic Left stands in perspective.

It is interesting that since the turn of the century much, if not most, of the Catholic Left leadership has come from the clergy. For example, Msgr. John A. Ryan, whose name is little known today, published his doctoral dissertation, *A Living Wage,* in 1906. He was a prolific writer, speaker, and social actionist for more than three decades after this book was published, but he always remained well within the ambit of the Church as an instructor at Catholic University and as head of the Social Action Department of the National Catholic Welfare Conference. For his progressive economic and social views he was almost always regarded as a "left-winger" or Socialist, though in the light of history he can hardly be classified as either.

Another widely known figure for many years was also a domestic prelate, Msgr. Luigi Ligutti. He was a leader, especially during the 1940's, in the National Catholic Rural Life Conference who promoted the ideas of family farms and the development of a meaningful rural culture of a religious and secular nature.

Then during the 1930's and '40's there was Bishop Bernard J. Sheil and his imaginative approach in Chicago to such diverse problems as delinquency and adult education (the Catholic Youth Organization and his Sheil School for Social Studies, with its heavy emphasis on the support of unions and interracial and ecumenical activities).

A priest-social scientist at Catholic University, Father Paul Hanly Furfey, also took a radical spiritual approach to the social problem, which he spelled out in three influential books: *Fire on the Earth* (New York: Macmillan, 1936), *Three Theories of Society* (New York: Macmillan, 1937), and *The Mystery of Iniquity* (Milwaukee: Bruce, 1944). Father Furfey recently published *The Respectable Murderers* (New York: Herder & Herder, 1966) on the Christian ethic and violence, linking him in at least one way to the Catholic Left of the present.

There are other names which must be mentioned, the Jesuit racial radicals La Farge, Heithaus, and Dunne, the latter two of whom were on occasion shuffled around and out of the way in the boondocks for their troublemaking. And in more recent times there are the names of Msgr. John J. Egan in Chicago and Father Groppi in Milwaukee. (Both of whom have received at least the tacit support of their bishops.)

Let's pause for a moment. Look at what has happened. I started out to talk about putting the new Catholic Left into perspective and almost immediately two things occurred:

First, with the exception of a few I deliberately withheld, all the names that popped up were those of clerics, including a bishop—officials of the institutional Church. True, they were not always appreciated and on occasion some of them suffered for preaching and acting on the message of the Gospel. But they were never excommunicated for their efforts.

I think it would be true to say that these men were universally inspired by the social teachings of their Church. Without exception they all seemed to have accepted the Church as given and were or are willing to work within that framework.

Secondly, I ended up giving something of a history of the Catholic social action movement in the United States since the turn of the century, for without a doubt most of the radical (broad sense) thinking in the Church has been in terms of social action, with some oblique liturgical connotations. In sum, most of the issues with which the Catholic Left of the past has been concerned have been the traditional problems of race and labor and social philosophy generally. And compared to the Catholic Left of the present (at least as exemplified by Father Riga and the author in Chapter 6), they have really been rather traditional and conservative in their social and economic views—not a real Socialist in the crowd, I would judge.

Let's take a look now at some of the lay persons who might be called members of the Catholic Left of their day.

In response to the trauma of the Great Depression, the 1930's generated a number of movements which helped provide outlets for the abilities and talents of many outstanding

lay men and women. Friendship House, and its many deriva-
tions since then, was begun by Baroness Catherine de Hueck,
a refugee from Russia. This apostolate of being present,
particularly among the Negro poor, began in Toronto; the
second house was in Harlem, and the third on Chicago's
South Side.

The greatest link between the past and the present Catholic Left is undoubtedly Dorothy Day and the Catholic Worker
Movement. Dorothy Day's great love for Christ and for
mankind has always made pacifism and conscientious objection a part of the Catholic Worker philosophy, and, indeed,
many of today's Catholic Left received their commitment at
the Catholic Worker House in New York City or through
the pages of the *Catholic Worker,* which has long espoused
conscientious objection.

Dorothy Day has had a profound influence on the lives of
many, as she has helped make it possible for Catholics of
two generations to meet the reality of poverty and love in
the Catholic Worker soup line. As Sister Corita has said
about Mary, the great thing is how well her son turned out.
We may note the same about Dorothy Day's spiritual children, including names such as John Cogley, until recently
religion editor of the *New York Times,* and Jim O'Gara,
editor of *Commonweal,* to name but two from the 1930's.

When he died in 1967 at the age of seventy-nine, George
K. Hunton had logged some thirty-six years in the fight for
interracial justice largely in association with Father La Farge
and the interracial council movement both in New York City
and on the national level. His quiet and effective work laid
not a little of the groundwork and foundation on which many
of today's Catholic Left tread.

Many other lay groups with more or less radical views
have existed since the 1930's in various parts of the nation.
In Chicago, for example, Ed Marciniak (not to mention
Father Daniel Cantwell, the original chaplain) helped spear-

head the Catholic Labor Alliance and the Catholic Interracial Council.

In South Bend, Indiana, men like Julian Pleasants, Eugene Geissler, and Burnie Bauer and their wives have been active for almost three decades (along with their friend and chaplain, Father Louis Putz from nearby Notre Dame) in many works, such as their joint family farm community, a house of hospitality and, not least of all, the Christian Family Movement.

For a few years beginning not long after the end of World War II, Ed Willock and Carol Jackson put out a delightfully influential magazine called *Integrity* from New York. In economics distributism was their principle, and they seemed to want to scrap the entire social and economic order as it existed and start over again. It might seem an anomaly to today's generation to learn that one of the magazine's most popular articles of its career (and remember, the audience was largely liberal) was an anti-birth-control-of-any-kind article called "Rhythm—the Unhappy Compromise," written by a priest.

It is important to observe that in recent years the emphasis has not been so much on individuals as on movements: the Christian Family Movement, the Confraternity of Christian Doctrine, the National Liturgical Conference, the Grail, the National Catholic Social Action Conference, the National Catholic Conference for Interracial Justice, the Cana Conference, and the National Councils of Catholic Men and Women. In most cases the personnel comes and goes, but the movement continues. This assures continuity and efficiency, but not always daring and charismatic leadership.

Let me again make the point I have made before—namely, that these members of the Catholic Left I have been discussing were, so far as I know, without exception noted for their devotion and unquestioning loyalty to the institutional Church and her authorities, especially the Pope.

The situation has been modified today, with the concept of loyalty changing into something more like loyal opposition. Further, the membership of the new Catholic Left, despite its open and declared independence of the institution, is not restricted to the laity. More and more clergy are joining the club. The author's interview with Father Eugene Schallert and his frank response in Chapter 8 is unique evidence of my point. Perhaps it would be instructive to think a little more about some of the things Father Schallert said.

I think one of the most important points he made—or at least I think he made—is that there is no question of his loyalty to the Church, but it is a loyalty on *his* terms rather than the Church's traditional terms of obedience of an inferior to a superior. He is, in other words, democratizing his loyalty. His allegiance is no longer that of an indentured servant to his master, but rather, that of a free man freely choosing to bind himself, his honor, and his energy to the cause of Christ. And I say "cause of Christ" deliberately and not the cause of the institutional Church. Unless I am badly mistaken, I believe this is a distinction Father Schallert would want to have made. As he says:

The religious person is one who is, darkly or lightly, seeking to find God somewhere, as the only ultimate source of meaning. . . . He searches for ultimate meaning, not in the sense of "prime mover," or what Thomas Aquinas called the efficient cause, but as someone with whom he can relate or toward whom he can move. You can institutionalize this in any religion, it wouldn't matter. The religious Catholic is one who is trying to understand himself relative to the God of the sacraments and the God of the Church (but not of the bureaucratic Church). I think a lot of avant-garde Catholics, myself included, feel that the bureaucratic Church doesn't really believe in God, anyway. If it did it wouldn't behave the way it does.

Understanding Father Schallert and the growing number of priests like him is of inestimable value if you want the answer to the question *Ramparts* magazine asked in an issue last fall: "What the hell is happening in the Catholic Church?"

Father Schallert (and many laymen who share his sentiments) is a good example of an emancipated postconciliar Catholic—a new phenomenon in the Church. There have always been people with similar sentiments; if they felt that way in the past they used to leave the institution. What is new is that, today, they choose to just hang loose.

Father Schallert, the Fathers Berrigan, Father Riga, Jim Forest, Tom Cornell, Peter Steinfels, John Leo, Sister Corita, Mike Novak, Dan Callahan, Jim Colaianni. And the dozens of other names that could be added from almost every city or state in the nation. They are fed on the same basic social philosophy that inspired many past generations of American Catholic priests and laymen. But there is a new dimension present, for these men and women have become part of the American scene culturally and educationally. They have become Americanized in every best sense of the word, and they are acting now in a political manner in the same mode in which their spiritual predecessors acted in the economic field of unionism.

They are, in other words, responding as committed Christians to the needs of *their* times. They are reacting, I would guess, the same way their forebears would have had they been confronted with the same problems facing Catholics of the 1960's. It is all part of the eternal freshness and application of the personality and meaning of Jesus Christ. And if we can learn anything from history, these men and women of today's Catholic Left will one day probably be regarded as quite proper and acceptable and heroic (it may even be safe to mention them in catechetic texts of the twenty-first century!).

I shall let you, the reader, make your own free and unfettered judgment as to the importance of Mr. Colaianni's book. There is no question, however, of the importance of the subject to which he addresses himself, for unless the institution can adapt itself to encompass the likes of the Catholic Left, it will turn off and tune out some of the most impassioned and creative Christianity available to it today.

Donald J. Thorman
Publisher, National Catholic Reporter

THE CATHOLIC LEFT

I hoped in the most simple and direct way possible to answer the question, "Why have you remained faithful to the religion into which you were born?" This was almost like playing into the hands of the enemy. The risk is proportionate to the simplicity and ingenuousness that have kept me prayerful throughout my life, but that, from childhood . . . have allowed me to feel and touch and possess a love I did not see.

François Mauriac

1

THE LEFT?

The "Catholic Left" is not easy to define, but it exists. As a blanket label it tends to oversimplify and often it is more a source of confusion than of clarification. For example, there are a handful, at most, in the hierarchy whom I would be willing to designate as "Leftist" in our present meaning, yet all through Vatican Council II the popular alignment was progressive and conservative—left and right. But neither the progressive bishops of the Council nor their counterparts on all levels of the institutional Church fit within the category represented by the title of this book.

Brian Wicker had given us a useful synonym for the "progressive," or "left," created by the mass media and the popular exegetes of Vatican II in the term "Modernizer," for one whose point of departure is "the Church as given to him," who sees faith as "something which comes to the individual from the community in which, first of all, it exists," whose "commitment is to the community which offers it . . . from its own profound historical experience," who must either "accept or reject" the preformed belief of the community. Professor Wicker rightly states that the main concern of the modernizer is to tidy up the Church's interior mess:

Do not bother too much about the population explosion; the important thing is to bring St. Augustine up to date by issuing

people thermometers and charts, and so to relieve the immediate
problem of sexual fulfillment in a starving world. Do not bother
too much with a theology of the people of God as community;
what matters is the reorganization of parish and diocesan life
so that the pastoral priest can get on with his job of saving
souls. Do not worry about whether there is any sense in the
notion of a Christian education; let us get on with the job of
improving the standards of institutions we already have, and
which have done good service in the past. (*Toward a Contemporary Christianity*. University of Notre Dame Press, 1967)

Naïvely unconcerned with the real question—Whither are
we going? And why?—the progressive-modernizer-liberal
Catholic marches only by night, claiming victory upon victory, as the liturgical language is increasingly vernacularized,
as laymen are patronizingly appointed to parochial school
boards, as nuns begin to display their calves, as commissioned
safe people update the instructional manuals and catechisms
by means of clever insertions of biblical texts between questions and answers (a method, incidently, which amounts to
little more than an attempt to make the old apologetics more
palatable to the "modern world").

The modernizer will never bedevil canonists with problems
in orthodoxy. The new jargon he enthusiastically endorses
is like a new coat of paint applied directly to the old—there
is no scraping down to the bare wood. Covering up the old
with the "new theology" is like washing a child's face ("before the neighbors see how dirty you are"). The spit-and-
polishers seem to regard the projection of a superficial new
image for the Church as an end in itself, but a parental concern that constantly emphasizes the good, face-saving image
can, by omission, contribute to the eventual destruction of
the child. The problems of a disoriented family will remain
insoluble until the root-penetrating questions are asked: Why
are we a family? What is the concrete meaning of this relationship? Is this community worth preserving? Indeed a
radical examination.

As Anglican Bishop John A. T. Robinson has pointed out, the radical goes to the roots and is not to be equated with "the revolutionary . . . an outsider to the structure he would see collapse." The Catholic radical "weeps over Jerusalem" because he loves her.

In the following testimony of Dorothy Hunt, a Catholic radical, read "Catholic Left" for "New Breed."

The New Breeder is deeply ashamed of his parochialism, and he tries to stifle it when it rears its shrunken head. In the New Breed, there is no place for the man from the provinces, and when the New Breeder finds that man lurking in himself he strives to exorcise that spirit into oblivion. "Catholic ghetto" is not a paradox, but a contradiction. As falsehood it deserves only extinction.

In burying the remains of his parochial outlook the New Breeder digs a companion grave for the interment of traditionalism. The test of the past is sometimes a criterion for the present, but it is not always a sound criterion. What has been done is not necessarily what should have been done, and is often what should not be done now. Tradition allows for little flexibility, and flexibility is basic to the personalist approach. Among those traditions the New Breed discounts are Christian Family Movement, Young Catholic Students, Young Catholic Workers, the Knights of Columbus, the necessity of Catholic higher education, the Catholic Diocesan press (*National Catholic Reporter* excluded), the Catholic Lawyers' Guild, Catholic Action and the Roman Catholic. These traditions erect barricades to the American Catholic; they frustrate the Christian in diaspora. They belong below the Alpha Point.

At the heart of the New Breed's rationale is this idea of diaspora. New Breeders want to assimilate the world with themselves and themselves with the world via osmosis. Through the membrane of being Christian, the New Breeder reconciles himself to the world and the world to himself. In doing this he reveals himself as a strict reactionary. He goes to the Gospel for his direction. He finds there that he must love—no abstract "people," but persons. Most important, he finds there that he must return his talents, including the talent of loving, with

interest attached. He relates this idea directly to the diaspora:
he must be competent in the professions and the trades not
only to live with himself, but also to live with diaspora. He
enters the diaspora alone, free of institutional associations, and
will succeed only on his own. Believing that, he develops a
natural abhorence for the organizational. He hates categories
so much that the label "New Breed" caused him to protest;
he had hoped to escape any monogram. . . .

Fortunately, the New Breeder's love for the Church prescinds
from his distaste for the institutional. He loves the Church precisely *not* as an institution, but as the person Christ striving for
rapprochement with the persons of creation. The New Breeder
wants a healthy Church. Some have attributed his vocalism in
this regard to callow impatience, but the motive for his criticism digs deeper. If New Breeders are too harsh in their evalu-
ation of the past and demands for the future, lay that to concern and not to restlessness. If someone you love is sick, you
may have to yell a little to get the doctor's attention. When,
as in the case of the renewal of the Church, doctor and patient
are the same person, you may find it necessary to sound the
fire alarm. . . . ("A Word from the New Breed," *The New
Breed*. New York: America Press, 1964. Courtesy of Claretian
Publications, Chicago)

This hearty rhetoric is representative, in whole or in part,
of a rebellious wave of Catholic disenchantment with the institutional Roman Catholic Church. Attitudes range between
gross impatience with hierarchic reluctance to "join the
human race" to utter despair over the ability of the Roman
Church to ever provide adequate institutional forms from
which a Gospel-oriented, credible Christian witness can
emerge. Some would shore up the crumbling walls by means
of radical changes in the existing structure; some would
move in with the iron ball, the quicker to begin the task of
erecting an entirely different kind of structure; some would
simply turn their backs, dismissing the phenomenon of a
highly organized bureaucratic Church as anachronistic, religiously impotent, and socially destructive.

The Left does not think in terms of absolutes and therefore does not feel bound, in the traditional sense, to abstract dogmatic formulas. Absolute truth is the mystery of God himself; truth as we know it is always approximate, tentative, speculative. Placed at the service of religion, theology can be of value, but when it becomes identified with religion itself the result is idolatry. Theology is a science dealing in abstractions; religion is an event in a concrete person, a way of life. Standing alone, as a collection of words, the Trinitarian doctrine is devoid of religious meaning, an irrelevancy, as Bishop Pike has rightly said—and, as someone else has said, "will remain so until I catch a glimpse of Father, Son, and Holy Spirit in that rock, in my dog, in you and in me."

With some justification members of the Establishment deplored the "negativism" in the public utterances of their wayward coreligionists. Public criticism of the Establishment has indeed been enormous and perhaps out of balance with constructive proclamations.

This book, therefore, is intended as a positive manifesto of the religious attitudes of the Left, as I perceive them, and more concretely, as I find them meaningful in my own religious experience—a series of reflections, not a sociological study and not a theological tract.

It is not my wish to see the Church destroyed, although I must part company with the modernizers who offer only the relief of catharsis. It is the underlying pathology that is of major concern, requiring, perhaps, a program of radical surgery if the Church is ever to become the healing leaven the world so badly needs.

Father Charles Davis (the celebrated English theologian who stunned the Catholic community with his announcement of withdrawal from the Church in December, 1966) made the following statement at a press conference a few months after his defection: "Since I made my decision [to leave the Church] I find it difficult to argue with Catholics. When I say that the Church is subordinating truth to expediency and defense of authority, that it is an obstacle rather than an assistance to the discovery of truth, that it is crushing thousands of human beings in a system that is impersonal, unfeeling and perpetuated by fear, they agree with me." Then he added, "Why, if they agree, do they remain in?" (reprinted in *The National Catholic Reporter*).

It is the same question put before me by the young modernizer-priest who indignantly reacted to my candid opinion that the popes had erred in making a blanket condemnation of all forms of artificial contraception: "If that's the way you feel, why don't you leave the Church?"

It is not enough to throw the question back at your antagonist. The question deserves an answer. If I *had* done so, my priest-friend probably would have calmly and confidently replied, "Faith." But not long after asking the next question, "Faith in what?" his sense of repose and self-assurance would have vanished. There are no easy answers, neither for Father nor for me. I offer this work, then, as an invitation to the modernizer-priest, to the intransigent bishop, and to my Leftist peers alike: "Let us stutter and stammer together."

2

THE CHURCH?

I believe in the Church of Jesus Christ as a community of persons living in an incarnational world, graced by the presence of God. That is to say, I believe that the Church of Jesus Christ is the whole human race. Christ as Redeemer, Lord and Saviour, as *the* historical event of all time, as the witness par excellence to a God who takes his creation seriously, as the testator of his Father's loving concern for all sinners, is blasphemed by the notion of a privileged group of formal Church members.

The Jewish religion teacher who wrote the Book of Jonah fretted over the "chosen people" mentality of his own people; God's concern extended beyond the faithful descendants of Abraham, even reaching into the great but wicked city of Nineveh. Jonah found it difficult to accept the loss of a private God, and his bitter resistance is not unlike that of the Catholic Establishment, whose updated catechisms still teach little baptized children that God loves them more than their unbaptized neighbors. Vatican Council II merely promulgated a new catch phrase, the "People of God," for the community of baptized Christians. What should have been stressed remains dormant and unheralded, even though it has been implicit Catholic teaching through the ages. For centuries Catholic theologians have opted for the "baptism of desire," open to all men "with at least the implicit intention of doing whatever God wills that men should do for salvation" (*1968 National Catholic Almanac*). St. Paul affirmed the universal salvific will of God: "This is good and acceptable in the sight of God our Saviour, who wishes all men to be saved and to come to the knowledge of truth. For there is one God, and there is one mediator between God and man, Christ Jesus, himself man, who gave himself a ransom for all" (I Tim. 2:3–6). And he worried lest he overstate the infant Church's case: "And how can they hear without a preacher?" (Rom. 10:14–18). The Council of Trent dogmatized the baptism of desire in defining the doctrine of grace, and for centuries thereafter theologians have adopted the problem of infidels (unbaptized persons) of good will as a major pre-occupation. Moreover, in their devotion to duty they have indulged themselves in side bets: Do justified non-Christians live a supernatural life outside the Church, or are they some-how to be called imperfect members? Do they belong to the soul of the Church but not the body? Are they attached, or merely linked? Or related? Do they belong as invisible mem-bers or as spiritual members? Or *in voto?*

One can express admiration for the many theologians whose commitment to a discipline is real and intense, yet the question cannot be evaded: Are these not exercises in fu-tility? How does one relate "linked" versus "attached" versus "related" to the problem of life itself? Is it really much different from the classic exercise in futility which puzzled over the number of angels that could dance on the head of a pin?

If it were merely a matter of "let them have their fun," one could simply ignore these enterprises without consterna-tion. But these theologians are, unfortunately, the public opinion molders in the Church. Their theories are proclaimed from the pulpits and published in religion manuals. Ancient traditions provide them with powerful support in their in-doctrinational systems. I am convinced, *aggiornamento* not-withstanding, that most American bishops and lay pillars of

the parishes are terribly reluctant to dilute the sense of security (however false it might be) instilled in them by their
progenitors' insistence on a privileged relationship with God
by virtue of wet baptism. (During the time of the Vatican II
debate on the schema *The Church in the Modern World,* one
American cardinal, stewing over some fresh ideas being pro-
posed, was heard to say, "This isn't the way I learned it
from my mother's knee." "And he sounded like he really
believed his mother's knee had a mouth on it," said the priest
who recounted the anecdote.)

Stressing and straining to preserve the dichotomy between
Church and world is to offer Christ's plea for human reconciliation on an altar of intellectual snobbery. The function of
theology is to serve religion, which is the seeking after God
in the world, "in that rock, in my dog," and especially "in
you and in me." The strain of Catholic thought on the recapitulation of the entire world in Christ has been profound,
moving, beautiful, and inspiring. And this should be the
emphasis in all Catholic theology—the presumption always in
favor of reconciliation; the thrust always in the direction of
simple open-mindedness; the point of departure always
marked by the one, great common denominator, the agonizing, evolutionary search for fulfillment in truth by all mankind.

Following these lines Catholic theology might well find
itself saying to the "infidel": We are all one in Christ, all
graced by God's presence in us, all bearers of Truth in as
many different ways as there are persons, all of equal dignity
by virtue of that unique Truth which becomes each individual
cell in the human condition, all members of the one true
Church. No howevers, no buts, no distinctions, sharp or
soft, nothing to detract from the inseparableness of truth,
freedom, and the love of reconciliation. Simplemindedness
rather than simple open-mindedness? Perhaps. But I doubt
that it would start any wars.

What I have suggested in no way taints the traditional

Catholic "one true Church" doctrine. Rather, it is a call for
a mere shift in emphasis. It is the mission of the consciously
committed Christian to everywhere proclaim, through his
response to a lifetime of encounter with the world, that the
pursuit for meaning in the world will advance only to the
extent that it is based upon the principle of "oneness," one
world housing *the* one human race without distinction in
membership, enrolled *in toto* in the divinely created school
of learning how to love. Given the proper emphasis in interpretation, there is no difficulty for me with the teaching of
"no salvation outside the Church," for if the "Church" is
indeed all of mankind, it could not be otherwise. Catholics
who have difficulty with this radical reflection might do well
to think on the Gospel's strict admonition.

Judge not, that you be not judged. For with the judgment you
pronounce you will be judged, and the measure you give will
be the measure you get. Why do you see the speck that is in
your brother's eye, but do not notice the log that is in your
own eye? Or how can you say to your brother, "Let me take
the speck out of your eye," when there is the log in your own
eye? You hypocrite, first take the log out of your own eye,
and then you will see clearly to take the speck out of your
brother's eye. (Matt. 7:1–5)

The Church deserves credit for taking this warning seriously.
Concepts of hell and heaven are treated at length in books on
Catholic theology, but it is interesting to note that even
though innumerable souls have been assigned, through formal
canonization, to heaven, the effort to concretize hell by listing
damned souls on a spiritual dishonor role has never been
made. Thus, the Church has always regarded the "judge not"
warning as a conclusive presumption of good will—and all
persons of good will are members of the Church.

   Catholics need not be dissuaded from embracing this up-
lifting notion of the one true Church through fear of heresy
or charges of heresy. The quest for honesty in the Church is
the risky business of all its members; truth is served only to

the extent that the entire community is participating and contributing in the search. Catholics must be willing to break the indoctrinational shackles which have made them passive receivers of the Word—and be willing to say what they think. Laymen should not demand or expect that bishops and professional theologians take all the risks. When the Catholic Church's articulation of self-understanding is left to the very few, moving about in the rarified atmosphere of the hierarchy and the god-scientist, the inevitable result of too few trying to say too much is confusion compounded, often funny, too often tragic.

In September, 1962, I enrolled in a crash course in Catholic theology, six or more classroom hours a day, six days a week, for a year. One day, after listening to a three hour discourse on the "character" of baptism, that "indelible and distinctive mark that is imprinted on the soul and can never be erased," my after-class conversation with the professor, a theologian of the Jesuit major seminary at Woodstock, Maryland, went something like this:

Q.—Father, why all this emphasis on a metaphor?

A.—This is no metaphor; it's an article of faith.

Q.—But what does it mean?

A.—It means precisely what it says. At baptism the soul is imprinted with an indelible mark that stamps you as a member of the Church forever. It cannot be erased.

Q.—But how does this affect me in real life, in my relationship with God, for example?

A.—I think that's obvious, isn't it? You are identified as a member of a divinely constituted Church.

Q.—But didn't you say that this is no guarantee of salvation, that it is conceivable that hell is burgeoning with indelibly marked souls and that it is also conceivable that heaven has been achieved by unimprinted souls?

A.—Yes?

Q.—Then why is it important to stress this distinction between marked and unmarked souls, the permanancy of the imprint, and so forth, when, at the same time, you admit that God is apparently unconcerned about the same distinction? It seems to me that what's good enough for God should be good enough for us.

A.—Oh you just want to argue.

(end of conversation)

I willingly concede that if there is a kernel of truth residing in the ancient Catholic expression of church membership in terms of juridically sealed souls, it completely escapes me. Moreover, I am sure that any hidden beauty residing within this concept escaped the legions of anguished mothers who were instructed at coffinside that the unstamped souls of their late, little unbaptized ones would "never see God."

There is no substitute for honesty in religion; a dishonest conviction is a contradiction in terms. But Catholics find it enormously difficult to develop their religious commitments according to this norm. They are accustomed to squirming out of tight situations by appealing to "faith," a sure-fire guarantor of the last word. The obvious next question, Faith in what? is ordinarily evaded.

More than anything else, perhaps, it is the leftist's drive for honesty that distinguishes him from other progressive Catholics. A case in point is Daniel Callahan, associate editor of *Commonweal,* a liberal, lay-edited journal of Catholic opinion that has been confounding Church beaureaucrats for more than forty years. Author of *The Mind of the Catholic Laymen* (New York: Scribner, 1963), *Honesty in the Church* (New York: Scribner, 1965), and a host of magazine articles on ecclesiastical affairs, all of which has established him as a highly respected spokesman of the *aggiornamentists,* Callahan nevertheless was unable to convince himself that honesty really is the best policy. In an article entitled "The Quest For Honesty," he said:

The Catholic quest for honesty, if I interpret the clues correctly, has now reached a point at which many are discovering that what bothers them is not this or that specific problem, but more: That it is so hard to speak openly in the Church. . . . Honesty, however, can cover a multitude of sins and virtues. Understood one way, it can simply mean the opposite of hypocrisy, which is a concealing of one's true beliefs beneath a veneer of conformity. Understood another way, it can mean a radical willingness to take nothing as too sacred for searching examination, a willingness to pay whatever price is required to get to the bottom of things. . . .

Then, referring to the latter viewpoint, he asks,

Is it in fact possible for Catholics to be wholly honest? I, for one, am not certain. I doubt that the Church is prepared to accept those who would, willy-nilly, undertake the kind of "radical questioning" which Bishop Robinson has urged upon his fellow Anglicans. [The reference is to John A. T. Robinson who, in his best-selling book *Honest to God* (Philadelphia: Westminster Press, 1963) calls for the most radical re-examination of Christianity, "even our most cherished religious categories and moral absolutes."] Even a serious and solemn attempt would run into a barrage of criticism, if not gaining for its author summary excommunication should he refuse to recant. But the incapacity of the Church to stand this kind of "honesty" is not necessarily a mark against it. The Church teaches with authority. This it could hardly do if it was compelled to put its most central truths up for total debate every time someone felt that honesty compelled him to question them.

What a curious stance for the avant-garde Catholic intellectual!

Callahan is properly impressed by Karl Rahner's rough treatment of the "hidden heretics," and he self-consciously admits to "feeling like the emperor when he discovered he was naked" after reading the following passage from Rahner's, *Nature and Grace:*

Although difficult to pin down [there] is an attitude of mistrust and resentment against the Church's magisterium, a widespread feeling of being suspiciously and narrowly controlled by it in research and teaching, the feeling that "one can't say what one thinks" (but one is nevertheless justified in thinking it in

"good" conscience). Doesn't one come across the feeling that
one can say more (at least among friends) than one can write?
Or the attitude that one should be glad that this and that has
been said by Protestant theologians outside the Church, and
one has to go to them to read it because one could not say it
without risk oneself? . . . Isn't there here something like an
esoteric teaching which is spread only by word of mouth? Isn't
there unformulated heresy which avoids clear exposition in
print and works by omissions and one-sided perspectives? . . .
(New York: Sheed & Ward, 1964)

Though Rahner appears much too eager to cry heresy, he
is correct in his assessment of the Catholic in-groups who
seem to value orthodoxy above their honesty. Callahan
merits points for his self-exposure, but whatever it is that
compels him to feel naked is not revealed, and that is a
pity. He has, of course, come full circle since 1964. In a recent letter to this author he stated his present position: "I
would say that the church must continually put its most central truths up for total debate . . . just the opposite of what
I said then. I gave Church authority much more credit and
prestige in 1964 than I would ever do now." What should
be realized is the value of the most honest effort possible
to strip naked an institution which has so clearly demonstrated an uncommon knack for preaching one thing and
doing another. And here a value judgment is in order: Has
the bureaucratic Catholic Church institution been a positive
value in society, say, in the last hundred years, or, on balance, has it caused more harm than good? However ineptly
put here, it is too serious a question to be rejected out of
hand, *especially by Catholics*. For better or for worse, Catholicism's urge to "teach, rule, and sanctify" touches the
lives of billions. It shapes attitudes that last a lifetime among
rich and poor, powerful and weak, intellectual and dolt.

Is the Church's magisterium (teaching authority) in fact
worthy of the reverence demanded for it by Catholicism's
best-known theologian (Rahner) who, by hanging the word

"good" in quotes, cavalierly impugns the good faith of those who "in 'good' conscience" mistrust and resent the Church's magisterium? If by "magisterium" Rahner means the pope and/or the bishops, in other words, real persons, then certainly there is a time for trust and a time for mistrust, a time for resentment and a time for more pleasurable feelings. In all honesty, I, for one, have little confidence in the trustworthiness of the magisterium; I am deeply resentful of its misguided, arrogant, and often forced articulation of truth, with little or no respect for consultation and dialogue with the whole Church (that is, the rest of mankind). I believe I am justifiably suspicious of a teaching authority whose record for yielding to the temptation to overstate is clearly discernible through centuries of its history. I believe I am rightfully wary of a teaching authority whose effort to preserve itself in a certain mold has, for centuries, been a source of inordinate distraction from the central message it purports to bear with unwavering fidelity. In all honesty I feel I must question the credentials of a magisterium that preaches peace but teaches war, preaches fellowship but encourages alienation, preaches humility but fosters pride, preaches freedom but practices coercion, preaches concrete events but refuses to learn from them. In all honesty I am tired of feigning support for the traditional claims on the Divine Mind made by the magisterium whenever it denies, directly or indirectly, expressly or implicitly, every man's right to claim a share in that mind. The magisterium's highly developed style of backing off from previously overstated expressions of "immutable truth" that places heavy emphasis on prestige (that is, reversing itself without admitting error) is scandalously dishonest. Moreover, it frequently appears more important to save face than to be properly sensitive to the alleviation of human misery (for often such reversals in teaching can be directly related to the relief of suffering caused by the erroneous teaching in the first place). Rather than an honest, candid admission of error, the long periods of agonizing re-

appraisal, the farcical search for the magical syllogism that
will put everything right, serves only to tease and torture the
faithful, and there can be no doubt that the resultant confusion is a constant source of misery to those who take the
hierarchy's claims for itself seriously, as well as to those who
are allied in close relationships with such persons.

In the late thirties, as a very young man, I can remember
swelling up with proper Catholic pride as I heard a monsignor deliver the kind of Holy Name Parade sermon re-
vered by Catholics in those days. Among the dozen or so
barbed arrows the monsignor shot in the direction of the
outside world was the standard blanket condemnation of
birth control. I remember the exact words: "As Catholics we
must be united in our contempt for a civil authority which
would permit the use of rubber for such a heinous crime."
Monsignor, in this instance, spoke well for the magisterium.
It had clearly been established for all time that all forms of
artificial contraception were intrinsically evil. Today, the
few remaining proponents of this theory are fighting a rear-
guard action as Pope Paul plays the charade of agonizing
reappraisal, even though the teaching already has been reversed *de facto*. Through it all countless human beings have
suffered—immensely, needlessly. How many hundreds of
thousands of trusting Catholic men and women of "faith"
now look back on years of alienation and frustration in their
marriages, a frustration caused most directly by an ecclesiastical discipline they had been conditioned to regard as the
one true source of easy answers to all questions raised by life
itself. The Church's long experiment with structures imbedded in essentialist philosophy has failed. Freezing the
mysteries of faith into abstract formulas, appealing to divine
intervention to canonize the effort, demanding a pledge of
allegiance to summary slogans, and labeling the whole thing
"orthodoxy" have repressed genuine Christian efforts to lift
up the spirit of the world by preaching the hope of the gospel
of brotherhood, in word and in deed.

It cannot be argued that the Catholic Church has been in

the forefront of man's struggle to attain social justice. She
has not. Her philosophical underpinnings of essences, spelled
out with a once-and-for-all precision, have made her uncom-
monly suspicious and unwilling to identify early enough with
proponents of equitable solutions to human problems through
change. Consequently, it is not surprising that the American
hierarchy is largely absent from civil rights movements or
peace movements. It feels much more at home "defending the
faith," which, when translated, means preserving the historically conditioned hierarchical structure in its present form.

In the not too distant past the Catholic who would argue
against traditional interpretations of doctrinal formulations
would be flirting with charges of heresy and threats of excommunication. The individual Catholic was not regarded
by the bureaucratic Church as a free-thinking agent. Holy
Mother Church (the hierarchy) was the spoon-feeder of
truths that had to be swallowed whole, and regurgitation, or
even an admission of indigestion, was a sign of infidelity.
Those with the weakest stomachs were branded, excommunicated, and left to "the mercy of God." In any case, Catholicism was unwilling to muster up that degree of mercy which
would have allowed for conscientious variations in translating irrelevant concepts into real-life meaning. Now, of course,
the situation has changed.

The plus side of the Vatican II ledger adds up to not so
much what it did but what it didn't do. It did not seek out
new heresies for condemnation; it refrained from decreeing
a new set of anathemas. However lumberingly and cautiously, it nevertheless placed the emphasis on counsel, guidance, and positive values, even though it could have had a
historic field day if it had chosen to move in the opposite
direction. Long before the Council convened, educated
Catholics had stopped swallowing whole. Sparked by the
"new" scriptual exegetes, Catholic products of a secular age
were finding new ways every day to complain about their
sick stomachs.

All the frozen concepts were being called into question:

Interesting though they might have been, what did the old abstractions really mean? Ancient ideas of faith, original sin, mortal sin, infallibility, heaven and hell, angels and devils, transubstantiation, the sacramental system, the Trinitarian formula, the whole economy of salvation, natural law—all seemed very unreal and extremely vulnerable in the face of honest doubts. As a life credenda for a large segment of humanity were they a positive value in society, or were they a retrogressive force in man's search for meaning and fulfillment? As an interpretation of the Gospel did they establish points of contact with the living Christ, or did they stand between Christ and the real world?

Catholicism was coming of age. Radical positions began to find aid and comfort in the development of a "new theology" presided over in the main by West European theologians. Suddenly American radical Catholics discovered they were not alone. Although totally out of touch with their own American hierarchy "who didn't know what was going on and, even when they began to suspect it, wanted no part of it . . ." (Michael Novak, *The Open Church*. New York: Macmillan, 1964), they were able to appeal to the writings of a small group of radical (relatively speaking) theologians who, in a very short time, had managed to build up substantial followings. The Swiss priest-theologian Hans Küng, despite obvious American episcopal discomfort, attracted huge crowds of Catholics as he toured the United States in 1963, preaching his cogent, articulate message of freedom of thought and expression in the Church. He did not hesitate to scandalize intransigent Church bureaucrats by pointing up the striking similarities between totalitarian communism and totalitarian Catholicism:

Like Catholicism, Communism takes as its starting point that the world is "in a bad state" and in need of "redemption." The "revelation" which arrived in the "fullness of time," or at the climax of dialectical evolution, is laid down for the Communist too in four canonical texts (Marx, Engels, Lenin and Stalin or Khrushchev). They are preserved, protected and expounded by the infallible teaching office of the Party, by the Holy Office of the Central Committee, and personally by the supreme infallible Secretary of the Party. The task of the individual philosopher is not to enrich and increase this sum of doctrine, but simply to teach people how it applies to every department of life and to preserve its purity by exposing heresies and deviations. The infallible teaching office of the Party publicly condemns erroneous doctrines. Once it has spoken, the man who has erred by teaching a deviation has to submit and denounce his error. If he fails in this duty he is "excommunicated"— expelled. Thus the Party is seen to be the bulwark of orthodoxy, at once defensive and offensive. What it calls for is strict organization, blind obedience, Party discipline. Everything under the great Leader, who is honored with what almost amounts to a cult, with demonstrations of devotion, great processions and parades, and pilgrimages to his tomb.

Are not these resemblances between the Communist and Catholic systems striking? Are not both absolutist, centralist, totalitarian, in short, enemies of human freedom? Is not this just what is constantly disseminated even today, in pamphlets, by opponents of the Church?

But the accusation goes deeper; it is that the Church has betrayed the very Gospel of Jesus Christ and the freedom that it brought. . . .

Every manifestation in the Church of lack of freedom, however harmless, however much under cover, whatever religious trimmings it may have, contributes toward making the Church less believable in the eyes of the world and of men in general; and that is a disaster." ("The Church and Freedom," *Commonweal*, June 21, 1963)

Hans Küng is no heretic, although one could speculate on what his status in the Church would have been in a slightly earlier age. And his freedom manifesto has been adopted by the radicals who remain "in." It is in fact their very reason for remaining in. They believe in the Gospel as *the* force in the world capable of keeping man's hope alive. They would be Christians and remain Christians whether in or out of the Catholic community. They are reluctant to divorce themselves from a religious tradition which, for most of them, is a natural born heritage. They are as well aware of their own individual imperfection as they are of the "ism" in Catholicism. They see the possibility of a more effective witness from within than from without. And they will remain—as long as they can remain free men.

3

LITURGY AND EMPATHY

Catholics *as Catholics* should gather together to celebrate the liturgy, and for little else. As the Western Church continues to adjust to its new life in the diaspora the parish structure, as it has come to be recognized in America, will fast disintegrate. Stock parish organizations are already anachronisms. The venerable Holy Name Society was founded for the purpose of keeping Irishmen from using cusswords as they drove those big spikes through railway ties. The railroads have been built for a hundred years now, but the society is still around—only Irishmen don't swear anymore. [1]

The parish structure was ill-conceived in the first place. It can't be taken seriously, because you simply cannot geographically organize a city; it has been tried endlessly and has never worked. Cities don't fit into geographical patterns: telephones break them, freeways break them, television sets break them, news media break them. And to try to hold on to them for parishes is unrealistic.

Something that very loosely resembles the parish might emerge, but it will be a functional organization: parishes for doctors or lawyers or other types of functions in society. Doctors talk only to doctors now anyway; lawyers talk only to lawyers. We used to have class ghettos in the United States; now we have functional ghettos. (I don't know why

[1] For a discussion of the disintegration of the Catholic school system, see Chapter 8.

men have to keep themselves separate.) In any case, it is probable that the functionally ghettoized parishes will be the Church's first experiment with a new kind of religious community experience. Hopefully, Catholics will gradually get to recognize that what is important is that we be men to each other, not doctors and lawyers and status-seekers. Perhaps the next real step after that will be the discovery that the person who talked only to doctors is dead anyway, just like the person who talked only to a member of his class is dead. Ghettoism suffocates. It is just another jail man builds for himself to keep from becoming free.

Actually, Catholics are still scoring very high when tested on authoritarian-personality scales.[2] This means that Catholics are people who think they need to have authority figures nearby. In this sense they are immature; they are like kids who need Dad around. But this need for authority is being met by an increasing absence of authority figures. In other words, the bureaucracy is crumbling; it is looking silly to more and more people.

The authoritarian personalities may take up with some other authoritarian structure, although I have a tendency to think that, if liberated for a long enough time, they will grow up. And the institutional neurosis—the authoritarian personalities' compulsive conformity to authority figures—will tend to cure itself by the gradual disappearance of the authority figures. The old people of the Church still bow and scrape to Cardinal McIntyre or Cardinal Krol; the middle-aged people of the Church are still afraid of them; the young people laugh at them. The further removed you get from the present, in terms of the past, the more ridiculous you are going to look. The McIntyres and the Krols are looking as ridiculous as the young lady who appears on the beach in her great-grandmother's bathing suit.

Cleaning out the Church parking lot five or six times a

[2] According to an unpublished continuing study by Father Eugene Schallert, professor of sociology at the University of San Francisco.

Sunday might be considered by some observers as evidence that American Catholics are a liturgically oriented lot. But this is true only insofar as numbers constitute the sole criterion.[3] In terms of comprehension of Christian meaning, the general tone of Catholic liturgical exercises is sub-Christian.

One should enter into the sacramental life in answer to the Gospel call to repentance (metanoia), a reversal of values, a radical change of heart, an opening-up. This new disposition is a necessary precondition for a truly Christian liturgical experience. John the Baptist called for repentance as he preached Christ's coming: "And the multitudes asked him, 'What then shall we do?' And he answered them, 'He who has two coats, let him share with him who has none; and he who has food, let him do likewise'" (Luke 3:10–11). "Repent" is the first word uttered from the mouth of Christ in his public ministry (Matt. 4:17). To the poor in spirit, the meek, the peacemakers (those who had heeded the call to repentance) He then preached his Gospel of love: hate motives degrade human relationships; man's love for God is unreal until it is concretized in real human relationships ("so if you are offering your gift at the altar, and there remember that your brother has something against you, leave your gift there before the altar and go; first be reconciled to your brother, and then come and offer your gift"); not "an eye for an eye," but turn the other cheek; "give to him who begs from you . . . love your enemies . . . sound no trumpet before you, like the hypocrites . . . judge not . . ." (Matthew, Chaps. 5–6). Finally, after the Resurrection story, Luke gives the account of Peter extending his first invitation to his followers to join the Christian community. Having heard Peter's witness to the Resurrection, "they were cut to the heart and said to Peter and the rest of the apostles,

[3] Strictly speaking, the numbers themselves are not terribly impressive when placed in full context: Two-thirds of adult baptized Catholics in the U.S. do not participate as regulars in the sacramental life.

'Brethren, what shall we do?' And Peter said to them, 'Repent.' " Then, opening their hearts and minds as they prepared to embrace their Lord's radical way of life (still radical today), they entered into their first Christian liturgical celebration: they were baptized. Through the symbolic washing —a sign they well understood—they bore witness to a new dedication. They would love one another as He had loved them. And they continued to rededicate themselves in a variety of communal ways as they "devoted themselves to the apostles' teaching and fellowship, to the breaking of the bread and prayers" (Acts 2:37 ff.).

This, then, is the Christian liturgy: the community of the committed, gathering together as such to celebrate their best glimpse of an answer to the "why" of life itself, to express in meaningful signs, to one another and to the community at large, their hope in love as the way toward fulfillment—the difference between meaning and absurdity.

Last year, during the nationally publicized, but soon forgotten, napalm protest in Redwood City, California, I was invited to present my views before a local Catholic parish organization. It was a hostile audience, and I was interrupted frequently. Finally, when the din had subsided, I proceeded to sum up the sense of the meeting: U.S. goals in Vietnam are noble and worthy of pursuit (the "goals" had been defined in terms of the usual, often contradictory clichés and slogans); a policy dedicated to the soonest possible attainment of these goals is quite correct; the liquidation, at the hands of our military, of thousands upon thousands of South Vietnamese civilians, including babies, pregnant women, cripples, and old men, is morally defensible so long as it is calculated as a contribution to the achievement of the noble goals; that many of these defenseless victims are roasted alive by napalm is an irrelevancy—what difference does it make how they die? Yes, we are being called upon here and now to make these fiery human sacrifices, and we do hereby express our willingness to so sacrifice. "Will those who agree that this is a fair statement of the sense of this meeting please raise your hands?" I asked. About twenty-five hands went up; I failed to detect a single dissenter. Then I said, "You have stated that you are willing to sacrifice an indeterminate but substantial number of South Vietnamese babies to napalm and fire bombs in the pursuit of noble U.S. goals. Suppose the circumstances were such that it could be somehow demonstrated that the achievement of these same goals could be enhanced as much or more through the sacrifice of your own babies to fire bombs and napalm. How many of you would be prepared to raise your hands here and now if this were the case?" Not a single hand was raised—of course not! "Then I can assume that it is the sense of this meeting that the lives of U.S. babies count for more than the lives of South Vietnamese babies?" No dissent. "This is genocide." As the meeting was closing, I discovered that this same group was appalled and shocked by the suggestion that a public demonstration of the effects of napalm on a live dog be conducted, on the grounds that it might be helpful to anyone trying to form an opinion on the issue. (I couldn't help wondering if their reaction would have been different had I specified "Vietnamese dog" for the experiment.)

What is most frustrating in such encounters is the realization that the lines of communication are tracking along parallel courses. There is no real encounter here. The Aristotelian, Catholic, American-consensus mind clutches for dear life to the security-blanket world of essences. It hates to be discomforted by the complexities of the real world. Everything must be generalized, categorized, and labeled for easy reference. The process is dehumanizing. "Communist agression" becomes a catch-all phrase, very useful for avoiding any serious study of the historical conditioning and the underlying motives and aspirations of the "enemy." Once the catch-all conscience salve is applied—the answer to why we are fighting *them*—it is no longer important to try to understand why they are fighting *us*. "American boys are dying in

Vietnam" is enough to effect disengagement from the real
question: *Why* are American boys dying in Vietnam?
"Cong" is an abstraction that makes it easy to avoid thinking
concretely about flesh-and-blood young men caught up in the
one human condition. Even "Vietnamese babies roasted alive
with napalm" is an abstraction. Show a picture of a napalmed
baby, and expect a response that suggests the viewer thinks
he is being tricked: "You are just trying to appeal to my
emotions."

Where is that Christlike empathy for people, which is—
or should be—the hallmark of Christianity, and which it is
the business of the liturgy to nourish?

The liturgy is functional, didactic, a means and not an end
in itself. Building oneself up to some sort of spiritual orgasm
by looking at the altar and whispering sweet nothings into
Jesus' ear might satisfy someone looking for a new thrill
every Sunday, but it bears little relation to the true purpose
of the sacramental experience. Modern liturgists, almost to a
man, are agreed that the liturgy is, ideally, the chief instrument for religious education. They are less than unanimous
in their opinions on precisely what it is that the liturgy is
supposed to be teaching. Philip Wylie's aging indictment is
still on target:

This is a Christian Nation, where Sabbath is a holiday, the
property of churches is not assessed, untaxed donations to God
. . . are permitted by the revenue collector, money bears the
name of the Lord, the witness to crime is sworn on the Bible,
most violations of the Ten Commandments are punishable by
law, and statesmen say grace. Yet there are enough different
kinds of Christian churches here to convince any Buddhist or
any worshiper of Baal or any Martian that the Christians themselves have no idea what Christianity means or what it intends
that they should do. (*An Essay on Morals*. New York: Holt,
Rinehart & Winston, 1947)

My opinion is that the entire meaning of the liturgy can be
summed up with precision in one word: empathy. To give

this one-word characterization to the teaching value of Christ's life would be no less precise. And isn't all Christian religion teaching aimed at making people more "Christlike"?

"Worship" is a word religion should try to forget; it is too closely identified with pre-Christian concepts of God which Christians still cling to, the advice of their Master notwithstanding. If we are indeed prodigal sons, we should not be bowing and kneeling before an abstraction. A Christian life is informed not by an idea of God, but by God as *the* Universal Event. God with us. God showing himself to us in everything we touch, hear, smell, taste, see, speak to. "God is everywhere" is as honest a Christian answer as can be found in the children's catechism. The trouble is that Catholics have not been accustomed to giving it much serious thought: "How can God be everywhere, sister? Will I hurt Him if I sit on him?" "That is a mystery, child. We cannot understand it now, but someday we will, in heaven. We must have faith."

In the late forties, when Bishop Fulton J. Sheen was known as American Catholicism's number one convert-maker (of VIP's), he was at the same time a prime exponent of the devil theory in world politics, especially in regard to U.S. relations with Communist China and Soviet Russia. His weekly network program was a showcase for the "God is on our side" mentality; top viewer ratings were concrete evidence of his vast popularity. I remember clearly how emphatically he canonized tales from American Catholic priest-missionaries in China: The very devil himself was discernible to the Christian who looked deep into the eyes of the Red Chinese soldier. God really wasn't everywhere. (In fairness to Bishop Sheen, it should be noted that his attitudes most certainly reflected the general views of the American Catholic hierarchy.) Because they had not sufficiently reflected on the Gospel teaching of the immanence of God, His universal real presence, such Catholics as Sheen and his colleagues (and, under their influence, most other American

Catholics too) could see God here, but not there, without troubling their "Christian" consciences precisely because they did not have Christian consciences. God had chosen to live in a white, capitalist, Western culture; other cultures were either suspect or labeled outright diabolical. And, most tragic of all, the liturgy of the American Church was permeated with the diatribe. The only portion of the Mass in which the laity was permitted to participate was the final prayers for the conversion of Russia, inspired by the Fatima mythology which holds that Russia must be converted—culturally and religiously—or else. How many times have how many Catholics heard the phrases "godless communism," "godless Russia," "godless China" uttered from the pulpits in sermons and homilies—phrases used to convey the notion of a people beyond the pale of God, something quite different from merely saying "atheistic communism." Clearly, Catholic liturgy had become unchristian, even anti-Christian, in emphasis. Instead of teaching Christ's own empathy, it was inspiring war whoops; it was alienating rather than reconciling; it was God is *for* us and *against* them. One might look up at the cross fully expecting to find an American flag draped around Jesus' loins.

And, strangely enough, it was Bishop Sheen himself who became the first American Catholic bishop to make a serious effort to focus Catholic attention on this most dreadful of Christian betrayals. In his Sunday Mass sermon of July 30, 1967, Sheen offered convincing proof of dramatic changes in his own basic religious attitudes. His reversal of values must be interpreted as a sign of true Christian metanoia. Using Matthew as his theme ("so if you are offering your gift at the altar, and there remember that your brother has something against you, leave your gift there before the altar and go; first be reconciled to your brother, and then come and offer your gift" [5:23–25]), Bishop Sheen said:

I speak only as a Christian and humbly ask the President to announce: "In the name of God who bade us love our neighbor

with our whole heart and soul and mind and for the sake of
reconciliation, I shall withdraw all our forces immediately from
Southern Vietnam." . . .

Referring to the President's call for reconciliation between
whites and blacks in the United States, Bishop Sheen further
stated:

. . . is this reconciliation to be limited only to our citizens?
Could we not also be reconciled with our brothers in Vietnam?
May we plead only for a reconciliation between blacks and
whites, and not between blacks and whites and yellows? . . .
To paraphrase the Gospel, "If you are offering your prayers
of reconciliation at the altar of America, and then remember
that your Northern Vietnam brother has something against you,
leave your prayers of reconciliation, go and be reconciled to
your Northern Vietnam brother, then come back and offer your
prayers."

These are difficult times for Catholics. The little streams
of *aggiornamento* seeping through their church from all
directions are hemming them in. Apathy still reigns, but not
nearly so securely as it did before Pope John. There are
gnawing internal pressures on Catholics to become involved
—perhaps for the first time—in a personal decision-making
process, as they begin to recognize the existence of sharp distinctions between their traditional brand of Catholicism and
authentic Christianity. It is becoming less "Why I am a
Catholic," and more "Why I am a Christian."

I can only surmise a high degree of heroism undergirding
Sheen's metamorphosis, especially in view of his earlier,
heavily documented public utterances. However that may be,
it can surely be understood as flowing from a decision to take
the Gospel seriously. And to one who is not ready to say the
final prayers over the corpse of "irrelevant" organized religion, it is a beacon of hope. Most appropriately, I think,
did Bishop Sheen express his new-found Christian radicalism
in a liturgical event, for, as I have said, the chief function
of the liturgy is to generate empathy among human beings.

4

ROOT CATHOLICS, NOW AND THEN

TOWARD A NON-DEFINITION

Almost forty years ago the Rev. Mr. White, an Episcopal clergyman, made a prediction that provoked an angry, *ad hominum* response from the quick-drawing editors of the Catholic journal *Commonweal*. Shortly after the publication of Pius XI's encyclical *Casti Connubii* (1930), which contained that pontiff's famed—or ill-famed—blanket condemnation of all artificial means of birth control, *Commonweal* commented in an editorial:

The Reverend Mr. White . . . goes on to predict a vast revolt of American Catholics, whom he describes as being rebellious in heart against what Mr. White declares to be the tyranny of ecclesiastics over the personal conduct of the men and women committed to their spiritual jurisdiction. We are inclined to believe that Mr. White is as badly informed on this point as was Havelock Ellis. The Catholic laity, of course, know that ecclesiastics have nothing to do with making the moral law. Only God can do that. All members of the Church, from Pope and bishops and priests down to the humblest member of the laity, are precisely on the same footing as concerns the main relation of mankind to the moral law—namely, the duty of obedience. (January 21, 1931)

Moreover, *Commonweal*'s editors dutifully pointed out that Rev. Mr. White was known to have sanctioned the trial marriage of his daughter and, therefore, could be fairly "taken as a completely typical exponent of the practice of companionate marriage, facile divorce and legalized birth control."

That was the year 1931. Now, at this moment in the Church's history, the Rev. Mr. White's attitudes toward trial marriage, divorce, and birth control, and the attitudes of modern Catholic moral theology are fast converging from their opposite ends of the pole: artificial contraception is no longer a moral problem for most Catholics, and a new approach to the meaning of marriage has generated a fresh look at trial marriage and the long-standing Catholic legislation against divorce with the right to remarry. For example, Father Jacques Lazure, who holds degrees in sociology, philosophy, and theology from Ottawa, Harvard, and Notre Dame has suggested a "two-stage" marriage process, "essentially transitory for the purpose of knowing whether the couple fits together—not only sexually but integrally, whether they can integrate their marriage to their professional life and leisure time activities—everything," with "100 percent control on childbirth, without danger of pregnancy during this period of probationary marriage" (*The National Catholic Reporter*, March 1, 1967). A "liberal Protestant" attitude is taking hold in the Catholic marriage debate. Modern Catholic thinkers are re-emphasizing the folly of isolating ambiguous scriptural texts and using them to frame universal, immutable moral principles. No sincere Catholic that I know of would ever question the binding force of Christ's dictum, "What God has joined together let no man put asunder." But, more and more, Catholics are coming to identify the complete arrogance of those who would claim to know the precise meaning of these words of Christ, even to the people of His own time. Such Catholics hold that it is their proper Christian duty to concentrate more fully on the problem, *What* has God joined together?—in other words, what is a Christian marriage, anyway?

These dramatic changes in Catholic attitudes are men-

tioned at the beginning of this non-disciplined reflection on
the development of a Catholic Left over the past half-century
and more in order to emphasize the variety of meanings that
can be attached to the term "Catholic Left." Is there an easy
identification of the anti-Ecclesiastical Establishment Catholic with the anti-Political/Social/Economic Establishment
Catholic? Is the Catholic who is outspoken in his regard of
papal infallibility as an irrelevancy likely to be found in peace
marches and protest demonstrations against racial injustice?
Is the boat-rocking Catholic pacifist, whose wrangling with
civil authority brings him to civil disobedience and jail, just
as openly at odds with Church authority? Although there are
no scientific data to consult for corroboration, my own sense
of things tells me that the answers to these kinds of questions
are always "yes" and "no." The Catholic Left of which we
speak cannot be viewed in terms of a monolithic political
party preparing for a campaign and armed with party line
and platform. There is no structure, no party line, no platform. The term "Catholic Left" in the present meaning is not
intended to include only those persons who have left the Catholic ghetto. Some have left, perhaps never to return, some find
it possible to move in and out quite facilely, while others,
such as those in the Catholic Worker Movement, clearly wish
to bear the Catholic label in their Christian witness efforts.

We find, on the one hand, that a Dorothy Day, foundress
of the Catholic Workers and a radical pacifist, has a total
abhorrence for direct criticism of ecclesiastical authority.
Despite the fact that her strong pacifist convictions are in
direct conflict with her Church's "just war" principles, she
will not bring herself into conflict with the bishops. (This
posture can hardly be interpreted as faintheartedness, since
Miss Day will not hesitate to challenge civil authority with
acts of civil disobedience). On the other hand, a Father
William DuBay will make a frontal attack on his Cardinal's
racial policies [1] by publicly demanding his removal from
office.

_____

[1] James Francis Cardinal McIntyre, Archbishop of Los Angeles.

To further muddle our term of reference, it should be recognized that even though we speak of "internal" Catholic radicals (who address themselves primarily to the ecclesiastical power structure) and radicals "who happen to be Catholics" (who largely ignore the ecclesiastical power structure and generally abhor any activity that will identify them with the Catholic ghetto), there is, nevertheless, an overlapping of motivation and goals that renders these "movements"—organizational and individualistic—inseparable.

At first glance it might not be easy to see how a career liturgical reformer, working strictly within the ghetto, can be relating to the concerns most identifiable with Catholic Leftists: race relations, war and peace, economic reform. A close look, however, has favored me with insights into the lives of at least a few such men, who see their life's work only in those terms. Clearly, the liturgical movement is among the many innovating movements in the Church which have spawned an army of modernizers who cannot see beyond the term "modernization." The Church these days is loaded with progressives who see change itself as the end-all, who, for example, argued for the vernacularized liturgy for reasons no more profound than "making the words more intelligible to the faithful." These we can exclude from consideration as Catholic Leftists. However, there are certain liturgists who are just as socially aware as those normally associated with the firing line, who deplore the apathy of the Establishment world in the face of manifest universal human inequity, who are attuned to the dehumanizing effects of economic totalitarianism and excessive nationalism, and who are not oblivious to their Christian duty to give witness to the need for changes in the dominant Western culture for the sake of the universal common good. As they perceive it, potentially, at least, their influence can reach into the lives of millions, precisely because of their achieved status as professional liturgical reformers, but only so long as they remain in the ghetto, bucking the ecclesiastical power structure from within. And thus they remain to work at the tedious, uncelebrated, often misunderstood, and sometimes seemingly insurmountable task of transforming the declining, irrelevant, divisive liturgy of Catholicism into an influential, relevant, brotherhood-promoting liturgy of Christianity. Perhaps it is foolish for such men to hope that large numbers of Catholics will someday get together regularly—as on Sundays—to give communal witness to the Gospel message of universal love, to shore up and to sharpen one another's social conscience, to renew their commitment to a direction in life which follows the path of reconciliation. Perhaps, but Christians cannot survive as Christians without hope.

There are still more examples of Left-oriented Catholics who find it difficult to kick the ghetto habit: the lone Leftist on the seminary faculty who cannot bring himself to abandon the young seminarians to the exclusive influence of a reactionary faculty; the priest who endures the indignities of a parish feudal system in order to counteract the mischief of his pastor, a practitioner of ecclesiastical tyranny; a lay journalist who knows that his withdrawal from the staff of a diocesan newspaper would mean an increase in the censorious practices of the priest editor-in-chief, whose blue pencil is always poised for a decisive response to the normative question: Will it please the bishop to read this?

This list might be misleading if allowed to run on, since it could create an impression of large numbers of Catholic radicals traveling this most tortuous road to martyrdom. This is not the case.[2] There is no doubt in my mind, however, that among priests and nuns the numbers of such "infiltrators" is on the rise, as reflected in recent sharp increases in defection rates (that is, more defections indicates more at the crossroads).[3]

[2] Obviously there is no scientific evidence to cite in support of this contention. I merely report faithfully a "sense" of things based upon years of close observation and participation.

[3] The sharp increase in defection rates is hardly in need of documentation. The Catholic bureaucracy in the United States closely guards these "secret" figures.

There is no lack of American Catholics, clerical and lay, willing to give lip service to authentic Christian principles governing race relations, war and peace, and economic justice. Most, however, are unwilling, or for some reason impotent, to bring these principles to bear against the existing established orders—civil and ecclesiastical—which refuse to give proper priority, in their expenditure of creative activity, to the enhancement of the dignity of all men.

Catholic Left, then, is meant to embrace those Catholics who are involved wholeheartedly in the process of translating lip service into real service, those Catholics who are speaking for man, as others speak for science, for progress, for country, for business, for profit, for free enterprise, for free trade, for property rights, for flags, for uniforms, for Armageddon.

RECONCILIATION AND RACE

In the year 1967, the U.S. Secretary of State tendered his apology (in the form of his resignation from office) to the American people, through the President, on the occasion of the marriage of his daughter to a Negro. The extent to which American society remains to this day a racist society could not have been more adequately revealed. The mass news media seemed to regard the Secretary's gesture as the sporting thing to do under the circumstances.

The American Catholic Church, as an institution, wedded to this society of racist institutions, remains to this day a racist institution. We have only to compare nineteenth-century notes with twentieth-century notes:

1841—American Catholicism's "leading theologian of the period," Bishop Francis P. Kendrick, reinforces "the Church's decided opposition to the principles of the abolitionists" (and no doubt eased the collective conscience of the Catholic slave-holding gentry, both lay and clerical) with the following moral instruction: "Nevertheless, since such is the state of things [the condition of the slaves], nothing should be attempted against the laws nor anything be done or said that would make them bear their yoke unwillingly." (John Tracy Ellis, *American Catholicism and the Intellectual Life*. Chicago: American Heritage Foundation, 1956)

1858—The American bishops refuse to instruct the laity on the question of slavery on the grounds that it is a political matter wherein they (the bishops) have no competence.

1866—The American bishops entreat the clergy to labor among the Negroes in an effort to improve their lot. "Few responded. [The needs of] The Germans and the Irish and the Italians and the Poles came first. These were the 'children' of the Church; the 'dogs' were not even fed with the crumbs that fell from the children's table." (Theodore Maynard, *The Story of American Catholicism*. New York: Doubleday, 1960)

1947—"In the city where I live—it is not a Southern city— there are several priests in good standing who have made it quite clear that they do not wish Negroes to attend Mass in their churches. . . . In the Catholic institutions of this diocese discrimination against Catholic Negroes is the rule. . . . When a priest preaches 'Love thy neighbor as thyself' do his words come from his heart or merely from his lips? What goes on in his conscience when he tells a Catholic mother whose family has lived in his parish for generations that her child may not enter the parish school because its complexion is just a shade too dark? . . . How does he feel when he distributes Holy Communion, knowing all the while that a Catholic mother has been driven away from the sacraments because she cannot see how a priest can refuse to give her [Negro] child a Catholic burial and still be a true priest? As a Catholic, I am hurt and humiliated by the race snobbery of white Catholics. . . . I know that if race prejudice is strong in a Catholic parish or school, much of the blame falls on the priests and religious who are in charge. Their authority and prestige are such that they could do much to eradicate race prejudice if they wished to do it." (Alice Renard, "A Negro Looks at the Church," *Commonweal,* June 13, 1947)

1953—"*It is not specifically part of the Church's mission to the Negro to try to remove the prejudice against him* [italics added], though of course the Church must preach charity and insist on the essential equality of all men in the sight of God. Whenever prejudice exists in any extreme form, it always leads to injustice, and this militates against the evangelization of the colored. But there is need for prudence, and often we have to be content to wait, in spite of all discouragements and setbacks, for what the Negroes themselves may attain in the way of education and a position that society cannot forever refuse to recognize. . . . it has been shown by experience best to provide, whenever possible, Catholic Negroes with their own church. . . . Even in the North, and to this day, it seems the best solution of the problem." (*The Catholic Church and the American Idea,* by Theodore Maynard, distinguished American Catholic historian)

1965—Racism is "characteristic of a significantly large number" of Catholics. There are others in the Church "who want no part of the heresy of white supremacy, but who recognize no personal obligation to participate in the struggle to eliminate racial discrimination. . . . If we were to total the racists and the inactive nonracists in the Church, we would probably come to a figure that would cover the large majority of clergy and laity in the United States." (Father Louis J. Twomey, director of the Institute of Human Relations at Loyola University, New Orleans)[4]

Catholicism's own historians tend to emphasize one mitigating circumstance surrounding the shameful treatment of the American Negro by the American Catholic Church. The

[4] The line between "racist" and "inactive non-racist" is probably more finely drawn than Father Twomey implies. Those Catholics falling into his latter category would seem to be consciously committed to using the criterion of *race* as the basis of selectivity in performing positive works of Christian charity.

pattern, they say, grew out of the period of vast Catholic immigration from Europe to the United States following the Civil War: "Because of their religious faith these new-comers became the direct responsibility of the Church, a responsibility that taxed every bit of manpower and money in the parishes" (Ellis, *op. cit.*). Although this reality cannot be denied, it does nothing to explain either the American Church's one-sided opposition to the abolitionists or the extended prolongation of its racist attitudes following the curtailment of mass immigration by the restrictive legislation of the early twenties. If Father Twomey is correct in his qualitative assessment, and I have many reasons of my own to believe that he is (for example, the heavy Catholic vote for Proposition 14 in northern California, despite the measure's condemnation by the bishops there, and a sense, developed at close range, of what lay underneath the legal and theological arguments of its Catholic proponents; the opportunity to feel the pulse of the American Catholic grass roots through contacts with lay theologians working in a good cross section of parishes around the country; the reluctance of most bishops, priests, and nuns to cease identifying with the "inactive nonracists"), then it must be admitted that basic attitudes have not changed appreciably over the last hundred years.

It is futile to try to explain away the American Catholic racist phenomenon with protestations of "We were just too busy to be substantially attentive to the needs of 'the least of our brothers.'" The root of the problem extends much deeper. It is imbedded in Catholicism's turn to idolatry, to the abandonment of religion to a system, to the "discovery" of God in an out-of-this-world theology of essences. How else can one explain the fact that in those rare instances, say between 1870 and 1940, when Catholic spokesmen lamented the plight of the American Negro, first priority (with extremely few exceptions, if Catholic historians are to be relied upon) was accorded to the scandal of "souls lost to the

Church," of opportunities missed to "add to our numbers."

Addressing the World's Columbian Catholic Congress, held at the Chicago World's Fair (September, 1893), Rev. John R. Slattery of St. Joseph's Seminary, Baltimore, introduced his analysis of "The Negro Race; Its Condition, Present and Future," in these terms:

The religious condition of our eight million of blacks gives food for anxious thought, and is fraught with lively interest to every citizen of this Republic. American Catholics may be said to have folded their arms for two and a half centuries, especially indeed since the war, and allowed their non-Catholic countrymen full swing in the religious training of the colored race. We did our share for them in other ways; we had more than a proportionate representation in the Union army which emancipated them, while we were in insignificant number on the opposite side. But as far as religion goes our efforts have been trivial. To appreciate how truly so, consider how few of the black race are Catholics—but one in fifty.

As to their religious knowledge, it is no surprise to learn that very many of the Negroes who profess religion are ignorant of the most fundamental truths of revelation. They have some idea of our Lord, a great reverence for His Holy Name, a notion of sin and of the Bible—the latter, however, more in a superstitious than a rational way. . . . Now, as no soul is exempt from the necessity of learning the essential truths of God's revelation, it is a primary question as to whether or not these are acquired by the blacks through their church membership. Behold the drawback in the negro churches. They are taught the fundamental truths of the Christian religion but very imperfectly. Far too often their churches are mere hustings for political candidates, or are like social clubs; and their houses of worship are often used for nearly all kinds of gatherings. (*Progress of the Catholic Church in America and the Great Columbian Catholic Congress of 1893.* Chicago: 1897)

There is no reason to presume any lack of sincerity in this priest's lament. If his sense of values seems not to reflect the

priorities of a Christian, it is precisely because his Catholic
training was so impoverished of Christian teaching—as
though the burden of Jesus' Gospel was not, in fact, a religion
proclaiming brotherhood of the heart, but the institutionalized, juridically structured system he so often condemned.
The Father Slatterys of the nineteenth-century American
Church, like the pioneer missionaries who preceded them,
were no less convinced that pouring water over the heads
of "pagans" was the highest possible form of service to be
rendered to the "uninitiated" than were the countless priests
I have known in my lifetime who *knew* that the Church's
teaching on birth control "would never change." Father
Slattery's "essential truths of God's revelation" gave him
every right to gloss over the notion of social responsibility
toward the Negro as a Christian obligation. What with all
those immigrant Catholic souls to be further impressed with
the "essential truths," there was no time *even to baptize* the
Negroes. Father Slattery's "essential truths" were little more
than a serious distraction from the practice of authentic
Christianity: Obey the rules laid down by the bureaucrats
and you will receive your eternal reward (precisely for your
obedience). As for loving one's enemies, living as a good
Samaritan, leaving the altar to first become reconciled with
one's brother, these were mere "counsels" of the Lord, "not
of obligation, strictly speaking," to be aspired to, perhaps,
but without much hope of real success—and in any case not
worth much fretting over, since the letter of the law is demanding enough for most. Obey and you will be rewarded.
If half the missionary atrocity tales are to be believed, how
many innocent young priests were dispatched to their deaths
in missionary fields on account of those "essential truths"
which kept them constantly informed of the nobility of risk-
ing one's life to pour the water and enforce the rules. Laying
down one's life for an abstraction has no justification in the
Christian Gospel.

A century of wafting incense skyward to an uppercase abstraction by the "Immigrant Church," and then later by the "Americanized Church," has not been at all effective in eradicating the Christian scandal of racism. As I read the monographs touching on the American Catholic Church and the Negro, and as I canvass some of the periodicals, decade by decade, I am reminded of an old cuckoo-type clock I saw occasionally as a small child. In most respects it was very much like an ordinary cuckoo clock. However, when its doors flew open, every hour on the hour, instead of a cuckoo there appeared a pudgy little figure of a high ecclesiastical dignitary (whether bishop, cardinal or pope, I cannot be sure). Its right hand would raise in jerky fashion, as if to impart a blessing, and then lower again as the figure safely tucked itself away for another hour behind the protective doors. The American hierarchy's involvement in the Negroes' struggle against bigotry, in perfect pantomime: popping in and out to make a pious declaration every ten or fifteen years.

No litany of cuckoo-clock platitudes can palliate the Church's prudential deference to the white supremacy power structure. Concrete acts of charity were dechristianized works, since they were invariably tendered under conditions of segregation, as revealed in official Catholic compilations of the Church's Negro benefactions. For example, 1951 official statistics include the following American Catholic segregated institutions (Theodore Maynard, *The Catholic Church and the American Idea.* New York: Appleton, 1953):

428 churches for Negroes
311 elementary schools for Negroes (with an enrollment of 67,738)
1 seminary for Negroes
1 college for Negroes
12 boarding academies and vocational schools for Negroes
30 high schools for Negroes

Three years later, after a quick reading of the United States Supreme Court's decision (*Brown* v. *Board of Education*) which illegalized school segregation, the American

hierarchy once again emerged from the cuckoo clock to lecture one and all with a firmness worthy of a denunciation of
someone else's sin:

Our Christian faith is of its nature universal. It knows not the
distinctions of race, color, or nationhood. . . . Even those who
do not accept our Christian tradition should at least acknowledge that God has implanted in the souls of all men some knowledge of the natural moral law and a respect for its teachings.
. . . *It is a matter of historical fact that segregation in our
country has led to oppressive conditions and the denial of basic
human rights for the Negro* [italics added]. (Statement by the
Catholic Bishops of the United States, November 9, 1954)

In the very first issue of *The Catholic Worker,* Peter
Maurin wrote:

Writing about the Catholic Church a radical writer says: "Rome
will have to do more than play a waiting game; she will have
to use some of the dynamite inherent in her message."
To blow the dynamite of a message is the only way to make
the message dynamic. If the Catholic Church is not today the
dominant social and dynamic force, it is because Catholic scholars
have failed to blow the dynamite of the Church.
It is about time to blow the lid off so the Catholic Church
may again become the dominant social dynamic force. (New
York, May, 1933)

In terms of bringing the "message" to bear on race relations in the United States, the lid is only now beginning to
blow off. And if the Catholic Church has failed to fill even a
modest corner of Peter Maurin's vision of her as "the dominant social dynamic force," it is because she has waited for
others "to blow the dynamite of the message" (the same
message) first. It is a matter of historical record that those
Catholics who are usually identified as the race relations
avant-garde of the first half of the twentieth century put
enormous personal efforts into preserving the American in-

stitution of segregation. The Jesuit John La Farge (1880–1963) and Katherine Drexel (1858–1955) are two of the most prominent examples. Father La Farge devoted much of his time and attention to the plight of the American Negro. Katherine Drexel, daughter of the fabulously wealthy Francis Drexel of Philadelphia, became a nun at thirty-one and subsequently founded her own congregation, the Sisters of the Blessed Sacrament for Indians and Colored People. It has been estimated that she contributed, during her lifetime, some forty million dollars toward the establishment and maintainance of a variety of institutional services for Negroes and Indians. But neither Father La Farge nor Katherine Drexel blew any dynamite. Their sympathy for oppressed minorities and their devotion to their betterment will never be questioned; yet, because they were not radicals, they were incapable of attacking the root problem: segregation. The institutions they created were segregated. Although their good works were performed within the Establishment framework, they have been regarded as avant-garde Catholics of their time in the area of race relations, but only by default. However much good they did for the Negro—and I have no doubt it was considerable—the fact remains that they also made a proportionate contribution toward preserving the institution of segregation in American life.

Special Negro-White tensions attendant on the advent of World War II evoked an analysis by Harry Lorin Binsse, then managing editor of the liberal *Commonweal:*

. . . He [the wartime civilian Negro who was absorbed into the industrial war machine] is still living on a slum standard, and his pants' pockets are stuffed with money. What will he do? Of course it depends on his character, his tastes, his education. In most cases he will try to improve his standard of living. But the first step in effecting any such improvement is to move to new quarters. There are no new quarters. He may try to wedge into a depressed white area. If he succeeds, he angers

the whites, since those who are still living in the area feel that
the value of their property is threatened by the unwelcome "inter-
loper." Remember that these are no white capitalists, but white
working people who often have put their life savings into the
property they now see threatened.

But suppose the young Negro is content with his slum existence, or else cannot succeed in finding a better home of any
sort. He still has money in his jeans. Perhaps he starts a savings
account. But because of war conditions, he can't buy much of
anything with it—except liquor and dissipation and a fancy zoot-
suit. He gets drunk and rowdy and objectionable, and again
he angers the whites who see him thus disporting himself. Of
course exactly the same kind of thing can happen to a white
man, but it is less likely to happen because it is vastly easier
for the white man to move up in status, to improve his standard
of living as long as he has the cash to do it with.

There you have the picture in Detroit, in Pittsburgh, in
Buffalo, in Harlem, in Chicago, in almost any Northern industrial city. And that is how the tension comes to the breaking
point. ("Dawn is a Long Way Off," *Commonweal,* September
3, 1943)

In an editorial preceding Mr. Binsse's article, *Commonweal*'s editors unanimously endorsed a gradualist approach to
race relations which probably represented a consensus of
progressive Catholic thought in the early forties. They said,
in part:

Social equality. It depends what you mean. If you mean that
the Negro should enjoy every right enjoyed by any other American by virtue of his citizenship, well and good. If you mean
the right to make a nuisance of yourself, to walk around with
a great big chip on your shoulder, we are against it. But here
again economic status plays a tremendous role, for low status
can sap that sense of responsibility upon which the enjoyment
of civic rights is, in the end, always based.

These other goals [end of segregation; political and social
equality] . . . we heartily support, but we believe they can be
attained only after long years of effort and after a change in
the Negro's economic status. If quicker methods are urged, the

result will be to inflame passions, to create hatred of the negro where there has been none before, to court bloodshed.

In truth, it might be said that *Commonweal*'s 1943 position is important evidence to anyone attempting to prove that arch-conservative Catholic William F. Buckley, Jr.,[6] patron saint of the Catholic right, is really only twenty-five or thirty years behind the Catholic avant-garde. (*Commonweal,* of course, was soon to be infused with new editorial blood which helped spark an eventual wave of internal criticism of the ecclesiastical bureaucracy's steadfast refusal to get into the front rank of the proponents of social justice for all.)

An early example of the new corps of internal critics is Father George H. Dunne. Writing in 1945, Father Dunne (a Jesuit who later gained a degree of national prominence with the publication of his *A Reply to Paul Blanshard's "American Freedom and Catholic Power"*) freely criticized Catholic mainstream moral theologians whose distinctions between "counsels" and "law" / "justice" and "charity" were keeping the Catholic conscience clear in the face of systematic segregation in Catholic institutions:

. . . Today the Christian conscience instinctively repudiates slavery and without the necessity of recourse to involved casuistry recognized it as incompatible with the dignity of man. Yet less than one hundred years ago the pattern of slavery was so woven into the social fabric that its protagonists found no trouble enlisting in its defense the support of many reputable moralists. The treatises they wrote make interesting reading today. One does not know whether to admire their ingenuity or pity their ingenuousness.

It is probable—at least we must think so if we are not to despair—that one hundred years from now the Christian conscience will repudiate with equal decisiveness the whole pattern of racial segregation. In that happy event the lucubrations of

---

[6] Editor of the *National Review* who, on the lecture circuit, draws belly-laughs from his diehards with, "I look forward to meeting Martin Luther King so that I may have the pleasure of saying 'no' to him."

mid-twentieth century apologists for Jim Crow will make interesting, if sad, reading. . . .

There is no answer to a man who has at his command casuistical techniques which enable him to convince himself that by equal rights one means unequal rights. How is one to argue with a man who can prove that black is white. . . ?

. . . there is the moralist who, in discussing racial segregation, includes in his enumeration of the specific rights in justice which belong to all men whether "white, black, yellow or red," the "right to the pursuit of happiness, that is to say, to such equal opportunities as are required for the pursuit of happiness." And a few pages further on he blandly denies, without giving any supporting argument, that the exclusion of a Catholic Negro boy from a Catholic school is a violation of justice, provided that there is another Catholic school which will admit him. . . .

One of the most naïve sophisms which the unavowed Catholic racist invokes to defend Jim Crow is the assertion that Catholic schools, since they are *institutions,* have the right to admit or exclude whomsoever they choose. . . . In no sense is the Catholic institution a "private institution" *as against the Church,* regardless of what order or congregation or ecclesiastic authority directs it. . . .

A lawyer friend of mine has pointed out that a logical extension of the argument from the "private" character of Catholic schools would be the contention that the prohibition by a state of Jim Crowism in public or private schools was an unconditional invasion of religious liberty. This would give us the bewildering paradox of a Catholic school defending, in the name of religious liberty, the right to defy the doctrines of the Church [*i.e.,* that racial segregation is immoral]. ("The Sin of Segregation," *Commonweal,* September 21, 1945)

In December, 1960, Mathew Ahmann, director of the National Catholic Conference for Interracial Justice, noted that despite symbolic acts of integration by three southern Catholic bishops [7] just prior to and shortly after *Brown* v. *Board of Education,* "Catholic activity in the interracial

[7] Ritter of St. Louis, Waters of North Carolina, and Rummel of New Orleans.

movement in the South has in recent years all but come to a half." Mr. Ahmann saw the possibility of creating an institutionalized *action* program in the area of housing integration. For the forty-five organized Catholic interracial groups scattered around the country, he laid out a plan for utilizing the Catholic parish structure, "among the most powerful community institutions surrounding the racial ghettos in the North, in city after city." Citing the failure of Catholic people and Catholic institutions to face racial problems "frankly" and their reluctance "to work to solve them," Mr. Ahmann made the following proposal:

Catholic people and Catholic parochial institutions in central city areas, and especially in areas which are going to experience racial change, must begin to support and contribute money to strong community organization movements. These movements must be created to maintain good neighborhood qualities while Negroes are allowed to rent apartments and purchase homes. Their ultimate aim must be to create permanently integrated neighborhoods.

To do this the Church will have to cooperate with all the religious and other institutions in a neighborhood. A parish cannot hope to do this task alone. Nor would a healthy neighborhood life for all people grow out of an exclusively Catholic movement. Catholic men, women and pastors beginning such movements must realize that they will have to educate their people on racial justice, as well as wage a difficult fight with the real estate and financial professions of their cities, and in most cases with their city governments, which usually are afraid to face squarely the problem of a changing neighborhood. Such a program, in neighborhood after neighborhood, should have strong backing from the whole Catholic community of a metropolitan area.

Events of the past seven years have shown that the parish as a "powerful community institution" is totally inept in effecting change of a consensus mind-set against fair housing, because the Catholic people who are the parishes (who are the Church) are themselves an important segment of this consensus. I have seen lily-white suburban parishes ("surrounding racial ghettos in the North, in city after city") muster up some fairly impressive campaigns—often winning campaigns—aimed at convincing local governing bodies and agencies thereof, boards of education, publications distributors, merchants, et cetera, to change their attitudes and/or their *modus operandi* in connection with matters of the citizenry's pocketbook or its sex mores, not to mention public school prayers, merchandising on the Catholic Sabbath, and putting Christ back into Xmas. But I have yet to encounter the Catholic parish in the United States wherein any such solidarity of action was achieved in the promotion of open housing. Normally, where they do exist, the little parish interracial committees will be found operating on the parish periphery—no room in the mainstream. Those individual Catholics who are determined to give some kind of meaningful Christian witness in their lives to the cause of racial justice learn very quickly that the parish institution as such is no ally. And the Catholic priests who care enough to actually do something besides pray are still hard news copy for the national media, the more remarkable since, in the sense of organized Catholic effort, they represent none but themselves.

Before the summer of 1964, the name William DuBay meant nothing to either the Catholic community at large or the American public. Until the spring of 1967 the name James Groppi could not have caused a ripple in the mainstream. Now, of course, both are household words identifying two radical Catholic priests. In both instances their sudden rise to fame was triggered by a determination to get out of the cuckoo clock long enough to blow some dynamite.

On June 8, 1964, Father DuBay startled the American public and shocked the ecclesiastical power structure by calling a press conference at which he denounced his bishop, James Francis Cardinal McIntyre of Los Angeles, in a statement noteworthy for its studied avoidance of the euphemism. Said DuBay:

The archbishop has perpetrated inexcusable abuses in two areas: he has failed to exercise moral leadership among the white Catholics of this diocese on racial discrimination; and has conducted a vicious program of intimidation and repression against priests, seminarians and laity who have tried to reach the conscience of white Catholics in his archdiocese.

Then, "his knees shaking with the audacity of it all," the twenty-nine-year-old priest read from the copy of a cablegram he had dispatched to the Pope demanding McIntyre's removal from office on grounds of "gross malfeasance in office."

Thus, Father DuBay had chosen to publicly manifest his passionate concern with the racial issue by zeroing in on the Cardinal, prime symbol of the Catholic Establishment's benighted, ultimately unchristian response to the basic legitimate aspirations of the American Negro. If "intransigency" is strength, then DuBay could not have chosen a more formidable opponent. In this context it would be difficult to draw a caricature of McIntyre, who declared, both before and after the Watts riots, that there were no racial problems in the Archdiocese of Los Angeles.

A Father DuBay is convinced that the success of the social revolution of his time is, in part, dependent upon a vigorous effort from the social ministry of the organized Church. Therefore, he assigns a high priority to the task of rooting out the internal forces that would impede or diminish such an effort. Groppi's and DuBay's styles are vastly different. DuBay's moral indignation is channeled into an intense interest in Church structures as stumbling blocks in the path of a credible witness to the social Gospel; Groppi, on the other hand, tends to regard the Church bureaucracy as an irrelevancy, something to be ignored. For him, preoccupation with the Establishment Church's shortcomings is a temptation to be avoided lest it distract from the really important concerns of his ministry—to identify as closely as possible with those who seek after justice. This same attitude is absent in his regard for the larger Establishment:

He is not interested in what the white community and white press think or say or do. What he does is for the Negro people,[8] not for the TV public. He does not seek out the press; the press seeks him out. Nor is he begging the white community, or even Milwaukee's government, for anything. He is *demanding* the birthright of all citizens. He sees force as more dignified than bowing and begging. (Paul J. Weber, "Groppi's War on Milwaukee," *America,* September 30, 1967)

Groppi's war on Milwaukee—always known as a "Catholic" city, and also distinguished as the nation's most segregated major city—has involved boycotts and demonstrations protesting *de facto* school segregation and the refusal of the municipal governing body to enact fair housing legislation (faithful, obviously, to the will of the people). With thousands of comfortable parish priests blended easily into the secure, sheltered life of comfortable, Catholic, white, middle-class entities, pleasing themselves to shut out the question of racial injustice from their ministries, the impact of one lowly, thirty-six-year-old assistant pastor of a poor, 90 percent Negro parish is monumental by comparison. He is a thorn in the side of racist old Milwaukee, not, first of all, because he is a white man who identifies with the local NAACP and acts as "advisor, spiritual leader, chief strategist and breadwinner" (Warren Hinckle, "Left Wing Catholics," *Ramparts,* November, 1967) for its militant Milwaukee Youth Council; not because he is a white man joining with Negroes in organized expressions of moral outrage; not because he is a white man who will lay his body on the line and go to jail—repeatedly—for the Negro cause; but, rather, because he is a white, *Catholic priest* who does all these things. He is feared by the white racist/inactive non-racist Establishment far more than a black Martin Luther King or even a black Stokely Carmichael, precisely because he is a herald of

[8] Comedian Dick Gregory has observed: "Father Groppi is the only white man I know who thinks like a Negro."

what could happen if substantial numbers of white Catholic priests ever decided to take the Gospel seriously: conditions of racial injustice would change.[9] It is impossible to evaluate the eventual far-reaching effects of Groppi's ministry. The attitude of his bishop [10] could be an important factor. For example, if Groppi is forced someday to resist an attempt by ecclesiastical authority to remove him from the race relations scene, or even to soften his commitment, and if this results in his suspension as a priest-in-good-standing or in his voluntary withdrawal from the sacristy, his potential for effectiveness would be drastically impaired. For whatever reasons, good or bad, it is true that the priest-in-good-standing can be much more a menace to the *status quo* than the priest who has been forced over the line, by fair means or foul.[11]

The backlash signs held high by both American Catholics and non-Catholics in the backlash demonstrations—"God is White," "Father Groppi Rest in Hell" (on the side of a coffin), "We're Right, 'Cause We're White," "This isn't the Church of my First Holy Communion,"—recall Father George Dunne's total expression of moral indignation of several years ago. Here are a few excerpts from his impassioned outburst:

This is one of those days which make me proud to be an American. The Stars and Stripes Forever—DA da-da-DA da-da-DA. "God Bless America, land that I love. . . ." Land of the free and home of the brave! You can see the Statue of Liberty standing

9 This is consistent with an inordinate amount of speculation I have heard that Father Groppi runs a high risk of assassination.

10 Most Rev. William E. Cousins.

11 Archbishop Cousins has stated that pressures brought to bear on him to discipline the controversial priest are "beyond belief. . . . Some Catholics have gone so far as to leave the Church; others have withdrawn or threatened to withdraw financial support from the charity development campaign, from local parishes, indeed from all Church causes." However, Archbishop Cousins believes that he and Groppi, "as Christians, favor the same just cause," and despite differences of opinion on methodology he has indicated that he will follow a policy of non-intervention.

there welcoming to her shore—urging them to come—the poor, the outcast, of every color, land and creed . . . "God Bless America, my home sweet home!" . . . Let the Russians boast of their sputniks and their shots around the moon and their astronauts circling the globe. Cheap publicity stunts! Propaganda flares! When it comes to capturing headlines, Americans can give them hearts and spades and beat them every time. Look at those headlines: RACE RIOTS IN ALABAMA . . . WHITE MOB ASSAULTS BUSLOAD OF NEGRO AND WHITE YOUTHS . . . TWO GIRLS AMONG INJURED TAKEN TO HOSPITAL. Thank God, that vaunted Southern chivalry lives on, come hell, high water or the day of doom!

Look at those great photographs! A young white man, blood streaming down his face, dyeing his white shirt red. Red, white and blue! Oh, it's a grand thing to be an American! He'd been riding around the country in the Freedom Bus with this crowd of young colored people, being a friend. Well, that'll show him. That'll show the world how red, white, and blue-blooded Americans handle that kind of thing. Look at this other picture! A young Negro man knocked to the sidewalk and three big, tough Alabama cops closing in to grab him and give him the works. That should teach those Baluba tribesmen down in the Congo a thing or two. They think they're primitives. It'll take them a few hundred years to catch up with us. . . . Brave, frightened Negroes watching the long wakeful night hours through, besieged in a church by a howling mob of whites outside. A young woman, face contorted by sobs, broken up, broken to pieces by the pounding waves of hatred beating in through the windows, through the doors, through the walls.

I know what she feels, the tearing sickness of feeling yourself hated for nothing that you have done or could undo, but only for what you are. I stood on a debating platform once in Boston and felt waves of hatred coming up at me out of the audience. They came from only part of the audience, a small part, from two or three hundred people who hated me because of what I was—a Catholic and a priest defending the Catholicism they hated. Nothing I could say or do could reach them or touch their hearts or stop those waves of hatred which were tangible, which I could feel and almost taste. When it was over, I went back to New York and into a hotel and was sick. I was sick for three days. So

I know what makes this girl sob her heart out. Mine, however, was an isolated, single experience. She has had to live with hatred all her life, surrounded by it, engulfed by it, and tonight it howls about this church where she is at bay.

Yes, sir, those Communists think they are real good haters. "Imperialists," they call us. "Capitalists." Sticks and stones. We can give anybody lessons in hate. Remember those magnificent pictures a few months back that made the newspapers all over the world? Those New Orleans housewives, good solid American housewives, their faces grotesquely contorted with hate, screaming epithets at a bewildered little Negro child and her quietly courageous father? There was an orgasm of hate that even Hitler might have envied.

We have erected and maintained for a hundred years a segregated social system based upon hatred; hatred and pride, a (literally) God-damned pride in the whiteness of our own skin. A kind of skinolatry. That's what it means to be an American. Always out there in front. Firstest with the bestest. Maybe not in sputniks, shots to the moon, men in orbit, but first in the things that count, the things that *really* make the world sit up and take notice. . . .

Feels great to be a Catholic, too. Associated with those Catholic racists in New Orleans—frequenters of the sacraments, the papers said—who keep the fires of hatred burning bright. "Keep the home fires burning." Great to be a priest, along with those priests who encouraged their racist friends to defy their Archbishop and who quietly sabotaged his efforts to destroy the white-skinned calf in his own diocese. . . .

No doubt Christianity has become quite complicated. But the essence of the Christian way of life remains as simple as Christ said it was: love of God and love of neighbor, summing up all of the law and all of the prophets. And unless we have this, we do nothing more than tinkle the brass and sound the cymbals. Love is a hard saying and, because in two thousand years we have not learned to practice it, the thunder gathers on the left while we sing our pious hymns and walk in pleasant processions.

But enough of these melancholy thoughts. This is a day to exult in. Unfurl the flags! "I pledge allegiance to the flag and to the Republic for which it stands, one nation, indivisible, with [come on now, shout it out] liberty and justice FOR ALL!"

. . . "God Bless America, land that I love. . . . From the mountains, to the ocean. . . ." Hold it! Hold it! Wait a minute! How did that nigger back there get in? Ushers! grab that jigaboo and throw him out on his ear. . . . That's the way to do it. Wait'll *those* pictures hit the papers. That'll make them sit up and take notice. Now—let's hear EVERYBODY join in. "Onward Christian soldiers, da, da, da, da, da. . . ." (Rev. George H. Dunne, "God Bless America," *America,* June 17, 1961)

As of the end of 1967 Father Groppi's name stands near the front of a long list of individual "radical" Catholic civil rights activities, most of which have occurred since the demise of the "separate but equal" doctrine and the emergence of the civil rights movement's patron saint, Martin Luther King—from the nuns and priests who sneaked off to Selma in defiance of ecclesiastical orders to the contrary, to the very real heroism of the Catholic man who sat next to me shaking with fright just hours before he was to execute the dangerous mission of smuggling an important witness in the civil rights worker triple murder case out of Mississippi and into reliable U.S. Government hands.[12]

Over the last dozen years or so, both the secular and the religious press have been recording acts of ecclesiastical tyranny against white priests, nuns, and seminarians for getting "involved" on the civil rights firing line. It is also true that during the same period many white lay Catholics have been subjected to numerous indignities, including economic aggression, by the secular system—and for the same reasons. But, long as this list might extend, it is the honor roll of a gross minority of the Catholic people in the Catholic Church in this country. Whatever the Catholic contribution thus far, it drew its original inspiration and courage, not from some charismatic bishop or monk, not from an abstract reading on the Trinity, not from some Knights of Columbus

---

[12] This was the act of a private citizen, undertaken in the knowledge that if normal processes were invoked, (1) local law enforcement people would suppress the evidence and (2) his life would be in extreme jeopardy.

potentate, not from some Jansenistic anti-sex moralizer on the "mission band," but from a black Baptist minister, who, thank God, is not a prophet without honor in his own time.

The hour is growing late. At an August, 1967, testimonial dinner for Father Groppi, Msgr. John J. Egan, director of the Office of "Urban Affairs" of the Chicago archdiocese, warned: "The long suffering Negro will suffer no more; nor will he be content with the measured equality extended, patronizingly almost, to him over the last few years. The Negro has had his fill; he is ready for revolution." Father Groppi, who "thinks" like a Negro, said not long afterward, "Milwaukee is not only a last testing ground for nonviolence; it is also the last testing ground for the Church. I dream of violence myself and have thought about its effectiveness" (*The National Catholic Reporter,* October 4, 1967).

On the fifth day of the World's Columbian Catholic Congresses, one Charles H. Butler emerged from the segregated "Colored Catholic Congress" (being conducted in "another part of the building," where "questions relating exclusively to the interests of the colored man" were considered, including "Why should not the Negro go back to Africa?") to address the white Congress:

What shall I say of the future of the negro race in the United States? His future depends upon his treatment in a great measure by the white man; whether the proud Anglo-Saxon intends to dispossess himself of mere race prejudice and accord his black brother simple justice. If continual warfare is to be carried on against him because of the accident of color, then all his efforts are in vain. But I am strong to believe that the dust of American prejudice will be cleared from the eyes of our white fellow citizens. . . . (*Progress of The Catholic Church in America* . . .)

That was in September, 1893.

An American from the NCCIJ (National Catholic Conference for Interracial Justice), Stanley P. Hebert, told the World Congress of the Lay Apostolate (in Rome) that "racial discrimination has confronted the world with the spiritual dissolution of society."

That was in October, 1967.

If mainstream American Catholicism's perversity persists much longer, history will note either that it made a major contribution to the dissolution of society or that a spiritual ascendancy was carried out in its absence. In both cases, the American Catholic Church will have been still another name for Judas.

5

"NO MORE WAR, WAR NEVER AGAIN!"

On the night of November 8, 1965, twenty-two-year-old Roger LaPorte helped out on a Catholic Worker soup line serving New York City's Bowery poor—as was his nightly custom. Within hours he was dead, a victim of self-immolation. "I'm against war, all wars. I did this as a religious action," he told police as he lay dying in an ambulance. In a formal statement, the Catholic Worker Movement said:

We are deeply shocked, perplexed and grieved by the immolation of Roger LaPorte . . . before the United Nations. He was trying to say to the American people that we must turn away from violence in Vietnam, and he was trying to say something about the violence that is eroding our own society here in the United States and in our city of New York. And so he made this sacrifice, attempting to absorb this violence and hatred personally, deflecting it from others by taking it voluntarily to himself.

At the same time, we strongly urge people committed to peace to employ other means in expressing their commitment-bearing witness and working nonviolently to build a decent, nonviolent society, a society of conscience. Among these (means) is fasting, which is deeply rooted in our religious tradition—fasting in private or publicly, fasting alone or in groups. Clearly no violence is done against one's own person in fasting, and there is no question as to violating life in this way. . . .

We grieve for Roger LaPorte. We hope that he has commu-

nicated something to the American people. We hope that all
people dedicated to peacemaking will redouble their efforts in a
positive, life-giving way. (*The National Catholic Reporter,* November 17, 1965.)

Catholics of the Vietnam War age who believe in the
urgent need for maximum effort to promote world peace
strongly enough to "put their bodies on the line"—in picket
lines, in fasting exercises, in all-night-prayer vigils, in jail
cells—are not first of the Christian peaceniks:

In the consulship of Tuscus and Anulinus, on the 12th of March,
at Thoveske, Fabius Victor was brought before the court, with
Maximilian. Pomeianus, attorney for the treasury, spoke first:
"Fabius Victor, tax-collector, is before the court with Valerian
Quintian, imperial commissioner, along with the conscript Max-
imilian, Victor's son. As Maximilian is probably liable for mili-
tary service, I request that his height be measured." Dion the
proconsul said to the conscript: "What is your name?"
Maximilian: Why do you want to know my name? I am not al-
lowed to serve. I am a Christian.
Proconsul: Put him under the measure.
   While they were doing this, Maximilian said: "I cannot serve:
I cannot do wrong; I am a Christian."
Proconsul: Measure him.
   Which done, the assistant announced "Five feet, ten inches."
Proconsul: Mark him.
   Maximilian resisted, saying: "I refuse; I cannot serve."
Proconsul: He must either serve or die.
Maximilian: I will not be a soldier. You can cut my head off,
but I refuse to serve in the armies of this world. I am a soldier
of my God.
Proconsul: He must either serve or die.
Maximilian: I will not be a soldier. You can cut my head off,
but I refuse to serve in the armies of this world. I am a soldier
of my God.
Proconsul: Who has put these ideas in your head?
Maximilian: My conscience, and he who has called me.
   The proconsul then said to Victor, the young man's father:
"Give him some good advice!"

Victor: He is old enough to know his duty.

Proconsul (to Maximilian): Be a soldier and accept the leaden seal, the sign of enlistment.

Maximilian: I have nothing to do with your sign. I already bear the sign of Christ, my God.

Proconsul: I am going to send you to join your Christ, here and now.

Maximilian: That is all I ask. That will be glory for me.

Dion the proconsul said to the assistants. "Mark him!" Maximilian answered as he struggled: "I refuse to accept the sign of the world. If you put it on me by force, I will tear it off, for it is worth nothing. I am a Christian. I can never wear this seal, for I wear the sign of salvation I received from my Lord Jesus Christ, the Son of the living God. You do not know him; he suffered for our salvation and God delivered him for our sins. He is the one we serve, all we Christians. He is the one we follow as the guide of our lives and the author of our salvation."

Proconsul: Become a soldier and take the sign: if not, you will die a shameful death.

Maximilian: I shall not die! My name is already written down with my God. I cannot be a soldier.

Proconsul: Think of your youth and become a soldier. It is a fine life for a young man!

Maximilian: My service is under my God. I have already told you. I cannot serve the world. I am a Christian.

Proconsul: In the bodyguard of our lords Diocletian and Maximilian, Constantius and Maximus, there are Christian soldiers, and they serve.

Maximilian: That is their business. I only know I am a Christian and I cannot do wrong.

Proconsul: But those who serve—what wrong do they do?

Maximilian: You know very well what they do.

Proconsul: Strike his name off.

When his name was struck off the proconsul said: "Since you have insubordinately refused to serve in the army, you shall suffer the penalty of the law. Let this be an example to others!" He read out his sentence on the tablet: "Maximilian, out of insubordination, has refused the military oath and is therefore condemned to die by the sword."

Maximilian: Thanks be to God!

He was twenty-one years old, three months and eighteen days.

On the way to execution Maximilian said: "My dear brothers, make haste with all the strength of your desires to win to the sight of the Lord, that you too may deserve the crown!" Then, with radiant face, he said to his father: "Give the executioner my new suit, the one you had made for my army service. My reward will be increased a hundred-fold when I welcome you in heaven. Then we shall sing the praises of the Lord together."

And speedily he consummated his martyrdom. . . .

As for Victor, Maximilian's father, he went home full of joy, thanking God that he had been able to offer such a gift to the Lord, and very soon he was reunited to him.

Thanks be to God! Amen.—Maximilian (near Carthage, A.D. 295) (Jacques Zeiller, *Christian Beginnings*. Copyright © 1960 by Hawthorn Books, Inc. Published by Hawthorn Books, Inc., 70 Fifth Avenue, New York, New York)

In 1260, when the cities of Italy were torn by dissensions, "the devotion of the flagellants," says an historian of that time, "prevailed in Lombardy. Then hermits came forth from their caves, and entering cities, preached the Gospel. The citizens of Asti, with the bishop and clergy, went in procession, and kneeling down in the public places, cried aloud: "Grant us, O Lord, mercy and peace." In those days many discords were appeased, and elsewhere we read that "men began to lash themselves at Perugia. . . . Peace was then made between many at Bologna; and twenty thousand men came from thence to Modena and lashed themselves," with the result that "all discords and wars ceased there and in many other cities."

In 1261, another chronicler tells us that, "by means of the devotion of the flagellants, who went about crying, Peace! Peace! many enmities and wars both new and old, in the city of Genoa and throughout Italy, were exchanged for peace." (Marian Nesbitt, "Some Old Time Devotions in Time of War," *The Catholic World*, Vol. C. November, 1914)

Such liturgies are hardly indicative, however, of any long-standing, mainstream Catholic unconditional rejection of war. The Catholic Church has not yet been able to extricate itself from the Constantinian tradition of identifying the practiced violence of the Fatherland State with its own institutional Church aspirations. In this context, St. Augustine took the position that war was a valid instrument of peace—that wars could be justifiable, even wars of aggression. Even in pre-Augustinian primitive Christianity there can be found no formal ratification of conscientious objection on absolute pacifist grounds.

When Urban II began in 1099 to mobilize the Western Church for the first Crusade, he recognized that:

> Gradually, in the course of the eleventh century, pacific institutions had taken shape and spread. Since . . . efficacy depended on mounted warriors, the Church concentrated on transforming the mentality of this class. It was able to stress the religious value of the oath of knighthood, which created moral obligations in whose observance or neglect the Church had an interest. It introduced its ministers and its spirit into the initiation ceremonies accompanying the presentation of arms to the young knight: the sword was blessed and placed in the hands of the candidate by a priest who exhorted him to protect the weak and fight the heathen; the ceremony, which was preferably held at Easter or Whitsuntide, included a vigil or a Mass. The investiture came to resemble the receiving of a sacrament; it was the introduction to a new manner of life . . . death in a battle hallowed by the Church opened the gates of heaven. (Bernard Guillemain, *The Early Middle Ages*. New York: Hawthorn, 1960)

The canonization of war as an institution by the institutional Church is undeniable. Dorothy Dohen recalls the Civil War-time words of Archbishop John Ireland:

> It is good for a people that supreme emergencies arise to test its patriotism to the highest pitch. If patriotism remains dormant for a long period it loses its strength, whereas the reflection and self-consciousness which resolute action awakens result in a fuller appreciation of the value of the country and the institutions which it is the duty of patriotism to defend. (*Nationalism and American Catholicism*. New York: Sheed & Ward, 1967)

And the World War II words of Cardinal Spellman:

> The oppressed, suffering, deluded and eventually rebellious, defeated people of the nations ranged against us know nothing of

the attitude of the United States except that they must know in their hearts that America is on the level and on the square. Their leaders cannot squelch that thought nor can they suppress the knowledge that America has been invariably victorious. And she will be victorious again, cost what it may. (*Ibid.*)

The belligerency of Christendom has been scandalizing the Gospel for centuries. Catholic theologian James W. Douglass points out:

. . . the twin habits of fear and aggression remain deeply rooted among Christians. One is not surprised to read the findings of a peace research institute: that in a recent survey taken, Christians were decidedly more war-like in their attitudes than non-Christians, and among the Christians, Catholics stood out as the most belligerent of all. Thus, on the question of nuclear weapons, Protestants wanted them more than agnostics, and Catholics more than Protestants. ("Christians in a Century of Fear," *The Catholic Worker*, April, 1966)

Augustine's "just war" principles have been consistently ratified by the American Church through every major U.S. military adventure. In the Civil War, Catholics, like their fellow Americans, aligned themselves brother against brother, each side blessing its own effort as "just," their consciences sheltered by the tenets of a theological system which totally distracted them from any earnest consideration of the morality of war itself. Since then, Catholic ingenuity has never failed to bring "our side's" cause within the bounds of these "just war" conditions:

1. Unjust aggression must be clearly imminent.
2. Violent self-defense is the only remaining course of action open to the beseiged.
3. That which is threatened must be life itself, bodily integrity, or substantial property or territorial rights.
4. All avenues toward peaceful solution must be closed.
5. The impending evil must be proportionate to the means exercised to ward it off.

6. Duly constituted civil authority must be morally convinced of the rightness of its cause.

7. Unjust means of prosecuting the conflict must be avoided; for example, there must be respect for the bodily integrity of non-combatants.

Until recently, Catholic moralists, although admitting in theory the possibility of a time for conscientious objection, nevertheless saw to it that the time never came. In effect, they established a presumption in favor of the State; the burden of proof was placed on the citizens, who, in any case, "rarely know enough of the facts to assess their rulers' decision competently. So complicated are political and diplomatic affairs in the modern world that it can happen that even the warring governments themselves very sincerely believe that their own cause is just." And, by way of reassurance: "God . . . hears the prayers of each of us and in His infinite wisdom and mercy decides what form His answer will assume and what is best for us. In other words, the people who pray are always the victors" (Rev. John V. Sheridan, *Questions and Answers on the Catholic Faith.* New York: Hawthorn, 1963).

Contemporary Catholic participation in the anti-war movement embraces three classes of dissenters: (1) the hard-core, absolute pacifists, who see the total deterrent policy as a confirmation of their commitment to the absurdity of all war; (2) converts to pacifism, who have been nudged into their position by modern nuclear capacity to kill on an unprecedented scale; and (3) those who condemn U.S. military presence and/or U.S. military tactics in Vietnam—as tested in the laboratory of "just war" principles.

American Catholics in the peace movement are accustomed to expect little in the way of encouragement and inspiration—leadership—from their own hierarchy. At this moment American hierarchical opinion on Vietnam is most notable for its absence, for its silence. *The Official Catholic Directory* (New York: Kenedy, 1966) lists a total of 252 American bishops. So far only six or seven have raised any moral questions with respect to United States policy. Institutional pacifist support, therefore, is largely limited to recent voices issuing from Rome: John XXIII, Paul VI, Vatican II.

In *Pacem in Terris,* Pope John addressed an urgent appeal for disarmament to the international community:

The production of arms is allegedly justified on the grounds that in present-day conditions peace cannot be preserved without an equal balance of armaments. And so, if one country increases its armaments, others feel the need to do the same; and if one country is equipped with nuclear weapons, other countries must produce their own, equally destructive.

Consequently, people live in constant fear lest the storm that every moment threatens should break upon them with dreadful violence. And with good reason, for the arms of war are ready at hand. Even though it is difficult to believe that anyone would deliberately take the responsibility for the appalling destruction and sorrow that war would bring in its train, it cannot be denied that the conflagration may be set off by some unexpected and obscure event. And one must bear in mind that, even though the monstrous power of modern weapons acts as a deterrent, it is to be feared that the mere continuance of nuclear tests, undertaken with war in mind, will prove a serious hazard for life on earth.

Justice, then, right reason and humanity urgently demand that the arms race should cease; that the stockpiles which exist in various countries should be reduced equally and simultaneously by the parties concerned; that nuclear weapons should be banned; and that a general agreement should eventually be reached about progressive disarmament and an effective method of control.

Among demonstrators and pickets, the words of Pope Paul to the United Nations—"No more war, war never again!"—are a popular choice for signs and placards.

And, though not endorsing the extreme pacifist position, Vatican II was forceful in its condemnation of much that constitutes modern warfare:

In spite of the fact that recent wars have wrought physical and moral havoc on our world, war produces its devastation day by day in some part of the world. Indeed, now that every kind of weapon produced by modern science is used in war, the fierce character of warfare threatens to lead the combatants to a savagery far surpassing that of the past. Furthermore, the complexity of the modern world and the intricacy of international relations allow guerrilla warfare to be carried on by new methods of deceit and subversion. In many cases the use of terrorism is regarded as a new way to wage war.

Contemplating this melancholy state of humanity, the Council wishes, above all things else, to recall the permanent binding force of universal natural law and its all-embracing principles. Man's conscience itself gives ever more emphatic voice to these principles. Therefore, actions which deliberately conflict with these same principles, as well as orders commanding such actions are criminal, and blind obedience cannot excuse those who yield to them. The most infamous among these are actions designed for the methodical extermination of an entire people, nation or ethnic minority. Such actions must be vehemently condemned as horrendous crimes. The courage of those who fearlessly and openly resist those who issue such commands merits the highest commendation.

. . . it seems right that laws make humane provisions for the case of those who for reasons of conscience refuse to bear arms, provided, however, that they agree to serve the human community in some other way.

. . . this most holy synod makes its own the condemnations of total war already pronounced by recent popes, and issues the following declaration: Any act of war aimed indiscriminately at the destruction of entire cities or extensive areas along with their population is a crime against God and man himself. It merits unequivocal and unhesitating condemnation.

The unique hazard of modern warfare consists in this: it provides those who possess modern scientific weapons with a kind of occasion for perpetrating just such abominations; moreover, through a certain inexorable chain of events, it can catapult men into the most atrocious decisions. That such may never happen in the future, the bishops of the whole world gathered together beg all men, especially government officials and military leaders, to give unremitting thought to their tremendous responsibility before God and the entire human race. (Vatican II, *Pastoral Constitution on the Church in the Modern World*)

It is certainly true that "the great mass of Christians have given scandalously little thought to the moral implications of nuclear weapons" ("Peace, Justice and the Christian Commitment," the editors, *Commonweal,* May 18, 1962). It is also true that some Christians are urgently concerned, including Catholic Christians:

There is no need to insist that in a world where another Hitler is very possible the mere existence of nuclear weapons constitutes the most tragic and serious problem that the human race has ever had to contend with. Indeed, the atmosphere of hatred, suspicion and tension in which we all live is precisely what is needed to produce Hitlers. . . .

In atomic war, there is no longer a question of simply permitting an evil, the destruction of a few civilian dwellings, in order to attain a legitimate end: the destruction of a military target. It is well understood on both sides that atomic war is purely and simply massive and indiscriminate destruction of targets chosen not for their military significance alone, but for their importance in a calculated project of terror and annihilation. Often the selection of the target is determined by some quite secondary and accidental circumstance that has not the remotest reference to morality. Hiroshima was selected for atomic attack, among other reasons, because it had never undergone any noticeable air bombing and was suitable, as an intact target, to give a good idea of the effectiveness of the bomb.

It must be frankly admitted that some of the military commanders of both sides in World War II simply disregarded all traditional standards that were still effective. The Germans threw those standards overboard with the bombs they unloaded on Warsaw, Rotterdam, Coventry and London. The allies replied in kind with the saturation bombing of Hamburg, Cologne, Dresden and Berlin. Spokesmen were not wanting on either side, to justify these crimes against humanity. And today, while "experts" calmly discuss the possibility of the United States being able to survive a war if *"only fifty millions* (*!*) of the population are killed; when the Chinese speak of being able to *"spare"* three hundred million and "still get along," it is obvious that we are no longer in the realm where moral truth is conceivable.

The only sane course that remains is to work frankly and without compromise for the total abolition of war. . . . The first duty of the Christian is to help clarify thought on this point by taking the stand that all-out nuclear, bacterial or chemical warfare is unacceptable as a practical solution to international problems because it would mean the destruction of the world. There is simply no "good end" that renders such a risk permissible or even thinkable on the level of ordinary common sense. . . .

. . . Are the masses of the world, including you and me, to resign themselves to their fate and march on to global suicide without resistance, simply bowing their heads and obeying their leaders as showing them the "will of God"? I think it should be evident to everyone that this can no longer, in the present situation, be accepted unequivocally as Christian obedience and civil duty. . . .

. . . The actual destruction of the human race is an enormous evil, but it is still, in itself, only a physical evil. Yet the free choice of global suicide, made in desperation by the world's leaders and ratified by the consent and cooperation of all their citizens, would be a moral evil second only to the crucifixion. . . .

It must be possible for every free man to refuse his consent and deny his cooperation to this greatest of crimes. . . .

. . . It is no longer reasonable or right to leave all decisions to a largely anonymous power elite that is driving us all, in our passivity, towards ruin. We have to make ourselves heard. . . . War must be abolished. A world government must be established. We have still time to do something about it, but the time is rapidly running out. (Thomas Merton, "Nuclear War and Christian Responsibility," *Commonweal,* February 9, 1962)

It remains for every American Catholic with even a spark of Christian hope still residing in his deepest heart to put on the yoke of world citizenship; to throw himself to the lions; to declare in every conceivable manner at his disposal the death of the institution of War; to identify his national patriotism with peacemaking; to be among those peacemakers who will insist that the tremendous resources of this nation be marshaled to support a peace effort which, *at the very least,* will be as gross as our latest war effort.

6

NEW LEFT PROPHET

Christian values simply do not coincide with certain American values. The Christian who happens to be an American who lives by the Gospel must face this problem squarely.

Peter Riga

Let each one examine his conscience, a conscience that conveys a new message for our times. Is he prepared to support out of his own pocket works and undertakings organized in favor of the most destitute? Is he ready to pay higher taxes so that the public authorities can intensify their efforts in favor of development? Is he ready to pay a higher price for imported goods so that the producer may be more justly rewarded? Or to leave his country, if necessary and if he is young, in order to assist in this development of the young nations?

Paul VI, Populorum Progressio

Woe to you scribes and Pharisees, hypocrites! for you tithe mint and dill and cummin, and have neglected the weightier matters of the law, justice and mercy and faith; these you ought to have done without neglecting the others. You blind guides, straining out a gnat and swallowing a camel! Woe to you, scribes and pharisees, hypocrites! for you cleanse the outside of the cup and of the plate, but inside they are full of extortion and rapacity. You blind pharisees! first cleanse the inside of the cup and of the plate, that the outside also may be clean.

Jesus Christ

The following appeared in the letters page of the Jesuit weekly, *America* (June 17, 1967):

Some time ago I wrote off *America* because of its stand on birth control and Vietnam. It was a foolish and stupid thing to do, unworthy of a man who supposedly lives by the mind, and I confess my sin. Your article "The Story of Charles Davis" brought me to my senses; and while I disagree vehemently with you on both above-named subjects, this article expressed so vividly and lovingly the exact nature of my own *malaise* as a theologian, that I must offer you my apologies for the bad feelings I have had with regard to your journal.

The last paragraph of the article struck home with an accuracy that I have found nowhere else. So many times have I been strongly tempted to leave the priesthood when so many within the Church—including bishops—have been so painful to me in their denunciations of my "dangerous" and "leftist" ideas. So little love and understanding accompany the work of the theologian that I can understand—if not approve—of what Fr. Charles Davis did.

It is not that we don't weep—we do. When you get home from a chancery office after being told that you may not speak on Vietnam when your conscience tells you to speak, or that your sermons "disturb" people because you tell them of their sins of racism and heartlessness with regard to the poor—then you go to your lonely room and you cry because there is no one to say to you: "I disagree with you completely, but I love you and will stand with you." Then your thoughts naturally turn to the woman who would have understood in other circumstances and in another vocation.

All the words of "suffering with Christ" become somehow hollow when you cannot existentially experience a love from your brother priests or your father, the bishop. When that happens, there arise an anger and frustration and a loneliness that can break a man in a thousand pieces, even if he continues to love physically. How many times have I thought that what we need is just a little understanding and love which could have saved so many of these desperately lonely men—myself included! So when one of them falls away, I beg you not to judge him too

severely; I beg you to judge yourself in asking where we—
priests, laity and bishops—have failed to love this man.

I am sorry if I seem so melodramatic, but it is a reality that I
live daily and that I know a lot of other very good priest-theolo-
gians live daily. *Vices a tergo.* We—along with the rest of the
Church—are undergoing a severe crisis.

And yet, if we cannot experience evangelical love as the distinguishing mark of the Christian community, I, for one, do not
know if I shall have had the strength to continue in it.

Once again, thank you.

Rev. Peter J. Riga, St. Mary's College, Calif.

Since his ordination in 1958, Father Peter Riga has been
parish priest, hospital chaplain, seminary professor, professor
of theology at Notre Dame, peace and civil rights activist (he
received the Man of the Year Award of the American Civil
Liberties Union, 1965), and prolific writer. His writings
(twelve books and numerous contributions to theological and
other journals) have consisted mostly of interpretation and
exegesis of that body of Vatican documents commonly known
as the "social teachings" of the Church. His works reveal
definite socialist leanings, not in defiance of official Catholic
positions (Vatican positions), but rather, in Riga's eyes, in
strict conformity thereto. I shall deal at great length here
with Riga's work, (1) because I believe it is representative
of the socioeconomic sense of radical Catholics on the Left
who, like Riga, received the social teachings of the "modern"
popes with the kind of respect that provokes serious study
and analysis—contrasted with, for example, "the bureaucrats
who, certainly don't take the social teachings very seriously
at all," [1] and (2) because Peter Riga is one of the very few
American Catholic theologians who is willing to publicly
endorse the anti-capitalist/pro-socialist thought of John
XXIII and Paul VI—contrasted with the Establishment-
oriented theologians who gloss over the gut passages with

[1] See Chapter 8.

arched eyebrows and patronizing platitudes. For this honesty Riga has been disowned by his bishop, shunted from the Notre Dame campus, and generally badgered and harassed by the ecclesiastical bureaucracy during most of his productive career. Riga is now functioning on the campus of St. Mary's College, California, where thus far the administration (Christian Brothers) seem not to have regretted its decision to engage him as a faculty member. (In 1967, a major campus crisis—with Riga as the key issue—was narrowly averted: Floyd Begin, Bishop of Oakland, instructed St. Mary's officials to get rid of Riga, but backed off when some eight hundred students prepared to strike against the college.)

During most of his priestly ministry, Peter Riga has been in the front rank of a variety of civil rights movement and peace movement skirmishes. He administers his income much like a trust fund for the poor. In 1966 he gave away, in the form of direct aid to needy cases, nearly all of his $22,000 earnings as author, lecturer, and teacher, keeping for himself only bare survival money.

Does the system have for its end "the promotion of the dignity of men"? This, the only authentic Christian basis for an examination of the social order in a moral context, is the cornerstone of Riga's social philosophy. It is also the foundation of modern papal teaching on the social order:

National wealth, inasmuch as it is produced by the common efforts of the citizenry, has no other purpose than to secure without interruption those material conditions in which individuals are enabled to lead a full and perfect life. Where this is consistently the case, then such a people is to be judged truly rich. For the system whereby both the common prosperity is achieved and individuals exercise their right to the material goods, conforms fully to norms laid down by God the Creator. (Pius XII)

. . . the economic prosperity of any people is to be assessed not so much from the sum total of goods and wealth possessed as from the distribution of goods according to norms of justice, so that everyone in the community can develop and perfect himself.

For this, after all, is the end toward which all economic activity of a community is by nature ordered. (John XXIII, *Mater et Magistra*)

Any human society, if it is to be well-ordered and productive, must lay down as a foundation this principle, namely, that every human being is a person, that is, his nature is endowed with intelligence and free will. By virtue of this, he has rights and duties of his own, flowing directly and simultaneously from his very nature. These rights are therefore universal, inviolable and inalienable. . . .

Like the common good of individual political communities, so too the universal common good cannot be determined except by having regard to the human person. Therefore, the public authority of the world community, too, must have as its fundamental objective the recognition, respect, safeguarding and promotion of the rights of the human person; this can be done by direct action when required, or by creating on a world scale an environment in which the public authorities of the individual political communities can more easily carry out their specific functions. (John XXIII, *Pacem in Terris*)

Development cannot be limited to mere economic growth. In order to be authentic, it must be complete: integral, that is, it has to promote the good of every man and of the whole man. As an eminent specialist has very rightly and emphatically declared: "We do not believe in separating the economic from the human, nor development from the civilizations in which it exists. What we hold important is man, each man and each group of men, and we even include the whole of humanity." (Paul VI, *Populorum Progressio*)

The capitalist system is therefore to be scrutinized in this light: to what extent does it enhance or degrade the human dignity? The temptation of Christians in the West to canonize capitalism, at least by implication, as the other end of the pole of good and evil—communism being the evil end—is, as Riga puts it,

. . . disastrous, for the capitalist system being vitiated at its very root, must also be condemned by the Christian as inhuman and demoralizing, as any history of nineteenth-century industrialism or its effects on the twentieth will clearly show.

Thus it is the structure of capitalism itself which we must investigate to see if it does in fact meet the unique criterion for morality, namely, that of the promotion of the human person. This is doubly important today in a period of a highly developed social system, where . . . the socialization of modern life has become the vital milieu in which men live and which, for better or for worse, has immense influence on the individual who lives and works with such a socialized structure. The distress in the economic and social sphere on both a national and, above all, an international scale is not dependent on any particular individual or individuals, but on a whole system of capital which runs its own course with its own laws and which can be cured only at its root cause: personalizing what has been brutally and inhumanly depersonalized in this system. The distress proceeds from a profoundly dislocated social and economic structure in the East (communism) and in the West (capitalism). It is for that reason that both systems have had inhuman effects on the human person; the individual is caught up in the system on both sides of the iron-dollar curtain. Both systems reduce the human person to a means for economic progress—communism, by putting him at the complete service of the state and progress of the community, and capitalism, by using the human person in its all engulfing profit motive. Therefore, both of them must be condemned by Christian morality. The popes have not been remiss in this task, even if it seems that their condemnation of the communist system has been enunciated more often. The difference is only an apparent one.

The profit motive as an end in itself, carried over into contemporary U.S. neocapitalism from nineteenth-century capitalism, is the very crux of the problem: work is a means to the end (profit), completely divorcing the worker from the fruits of his labor through the device of "wage" or "salary." The result of this depersonalizing process is the dehumanization and degrading of people. For this reason Riga asserts:

Profit here is dislocated and has perverted these modern enterprises in a way clearly seen by Marx (and, of course, many before and after him). It is one thing to speak abstractly of profit-

capitalism in one's theological chair, and there to work out all
sorts of ways which would bring it in conformity with human
dignity; it is quite another to examine the historical and factual
brutalizing effects, say, on the nineteenth-century proletariat,
dominated as it was by economic *laissez faire* capitalism which,
to a very great degree, still infects neocapitalism in the West,
since it suffers from the same congenital disease as its immediate
predecessor: work used as a commodity and sold at a price, in
order to make profit for the owners of capital-productive goods.
In such a system, profit takes over as the essential determinant in
the whole process of production, with the human factor—work—
being nothing more than something to be paid for in the process
of making a profit. This was the essential vice of the capitalist
system of the nineteenth century as well as that of the present
day, in spite of the fact that the major abuses of the latter have
been curtailed by welfare legislation to insure some sort of more
human distribution of benefits. Thus we have a system in Western societies in which the capitalists have made no real human
contribution to the productive process. Both labor and capital
produce goods, but in this system, only the capitalists retain
profit, while labor simply is given "pay" while having its human
effort torn to pieces.

In making this argument Riga can appeal to now deep-
rooted papal instruction on the point. In his encyclical
Quadragesimo Anno (1931), Pope Pius XI made the following observations:

. . . For what else is work but the use or exercise of the powers
of mind and body on or by means of these gifts of nature? Now,
the natural law, or rather, God's will manifested by it, demands
that right order be observed in the application of natural resources to human needs; and this order consists in everything
having its proper owner. Hence it follows that unless a man applies his labor to his own property, an alliance must be formed
between his toil and his neighbor's property; for each is helpless
without the other. This is what Leo XIII had in mind when he
wrote: "Capital cannot do without labor, nor labor without capital." It is therefore entirely false to ascribe the results of their
combined efforts to either capital or labor alone; and it is fla-

grantly unjust that either should deny the efficacy of the other and claim all the profit.

Capital, however, was long able to appropriate too much for itself; it claimed all the products and profits, and left to the worker the barest minimum necessary to repair his strength and ensure the continuance of his class. For by an inexorable economic law, it was held, all accumulation of capital falls to the wealthy, while by the same law the workers are doomed to perpetual want or to a very low standard of life. It is indeed true that the course of things did not always and everywhere correspond with this thesis of the so-called Manchester School; but it cannot be denied that the steady pressure of economic and social tendencies was in this direction. That these erroneous opinions and deceitful axioms should have been vehemently assailed, and not merely by those whom they deprived of their innate right to better their condition, will assuredly surprise no one.

The "moderate" (the word is Riga's) socialism which Catholic social doctrine has espoused as redemptive is the result of a three-quarter-century evolutionary development, beginning with Pope Leo XIII's encyclical *Rerum Novarum* (1891), on the condition of labor. Leo was opposed to socialism—radical or moderate—his own effort being largely confined to a call for certain reforms in the capitalistic system: "profits" and "wages" according to what was "just." He did not bring the capitalist wage system itself under attack. Several decades later, Pius XI became receptive to the Marxist indictment of capitalistic inequities and injustices, and even though he still rejected even moderate socialism, he did not specifically exclude an interpretation of Marxism which, as Riga puts it, "would exclude the principles of dialectical and historical materialism. It is on this basis that dialogue with communists can hope to proceed." Moreover, Pius XI appeared to anticipate the coming convergence of Catholic social teaching and moderate socialism in these words: "Socialism seems as if it were drifting toward the truth which Christian tradition has always held in respect, for it cannot be denied that its programs often strikingly ap-

proach the just demands of Christian social reformers"
(*Quadragesimo Anno*).

With John XXIII, Riga contends, Catholic social doctrine began to be enunciated

. . . in the tradition of socialists seeking after justice. The encyclical *Mater et Magistra* is more an attack on capitalism than
a critique of traditional socialism. Thus, socialization is a good
and at the service of man (pars. 59–62), inequalities must be
eliminated (par. 71), a correspondence must be maintained between economic and social progress (par. 73), workers must
share in the profits of the industry that accrue from capital investment (pars. 75–77), workers should take part in economic
decisions at the highest levels (pars. 97–100), large corporations
and monopolies are criticized (par. 104).

Finally, we have the testimony of Paul VI, whose United
States address in 1964 to Italian businessmen left Peter Riga
wide-eyed: ". . . one of the most powerful indictments of
capitalism I have ever seen." Said Pope Paul:

The business enterprise, which by its nature demands collabora-
tion, concord, harmony, is it now still today a clash of minds and
of interests: And sometimes, is it not considered an indictment
of the one who puts it together, directs it and administers it?

Is it not said of you that you are the capitalists and the only
guilty ones? Are you not often the target of social dialectic?
There must be something profoundly mistaken, something radically lacking in the system itself, if it gives rise to such social
reactions. It is true that whoever speaks of capitalism today, as
many do, with the concepts that defined it in the past century,
gives proof of being out of touch with reality. But it remains a
fact that the socio-economic system generated from Manchester-
ian Liberalism still persists. It persists in the connection of the
one-sidedness of possession of the means of production and of the
economy directed toward private profit. . . . Such an outlook
(materialism) is attributable not only to those who make the
fundamental dogma of their unhappy sociology out of an antique
dialectic materialism (communism), but also to the many who
erect a golden calf in the place belonging to the God of Heaven
and Earth. (*Catholic Messenger,* June 18, 1964)

Pope Paul is clear about this: the capitalist West is no less materialistic than the communist East, "and being so," says Riga, "it represents a serious temptation to the Church, since the West tries to cloak its political ambitions and basic materialistic intentions in moral terms."

Moreover, Pope Paul continues to press the arguments of Pius XI and John XXIII for a fuller participation of the worker in the fruits of his labor. Pope John had called for more than a mere work contract embracing wages, insurance, health, holidays, and the like; the ultimate would be found in partnership contracts—co-operatives, profit-sharing, share-holdings, and so forth. Paul recalls that Pius XI had deplored as unjust a system wherein either capital or labor should seize all the profits; Paul goes on to say:

Experience suggests that this demand of justice can be met in many ways. One of these, and among the most desirable, is to see to it that the workers, in the manner that seems most suitable, are able to participate in the ownership of the enterprise itself. For today, more than in times of our predecessor, "every effort . . . must be made that at least in the future a just share only of the fruits of production be permitted to accumulate in the hands of the wealthy, and that a sufficiently ample share be supplied to the workingmen. (*Populorum Progressio*)

There can be no doubt of the validity of Father Riga's assessment:

. . . what is evident from Leo XIII to Paul VI is an evolution of the attitude of the Church towards moderate socialism: starting with a program to reform capitalism (Leo XIII), followed by a positive program for replacing capitalism (Pius XI, XII), to *de facto* acceptance by the Church of the non-ideological, non-philosophical basis of moderate socialism (John XXIII, Paul VI) as a critique and *point de repère* against neocapitalism.

I believe his thesis to be quite correct and self-evident, and there is a certain irony here: Precisely because of his fidelity to the established modern tradition in Catholic social teaching, he is regarded by the American Church bureaucrats with suspicion—a fringe man, a troublemaker. The bishops who would harass and silence him because of his papal-oriented social philosophy—concerned primarily with the elimination of the gross exploitation of men by other men—can establish easy relationships with others who not only lack Riga's concern for equity in the social order, but who, in fact, are part of the system of exploitation deplored by the popes. The American bishops have given practically no evidence, beyond occasional lip service, that they are as concerned with the real problems as much as with the non-problems.

In his application of the papal norms for a decently ordered social system, Riga does not flinch from his duty to see the world around him as it really is. Money and gain dominate the Western capitalist system; the system is caught up in a vicious circle of capital generating profits and profits in turn producing still more capital.

Money is for man, not man for money, and it is precisely this vice which infects modern capitalism to its very core, no matter how many laws are passed to curb its abuses. These latter are only palliatives covering its terminal human cancer.

Today this fundamental abuse is contained in the exclusive attribution to the owner of capital goods the surplus benefit of production, and to him alone. It is not that he always keeps it for personal fortune (even if this is also a fact), but rather, that in and of itself, the continuous and progressive investment of these riches into new establishments of production, from which the human concept of work is rejected, ends by an automatic multiplication of power which cannot be stopped by itself. Technology, unavoidably concentrated economic credit, for example (which are neither good nor bad in themselves but, rather, simply technical procedures), have now become the instruments of this appropriation of great riches with its above-mentioned vice. This process, then, is truly "unnatural" in its most basic meaning, that is, a dehumanization of man as well as of his extension in space and time: his work.

The great vice of neocapitalism is the refusal to see enterprises as communities of labor (proprietor, director, and worker) all producing in communal effort. The system "pays" the worker for his work and calls it "just," leaving all the profits for the others. Riga condemns this neocapitalist vice both philosophically and theologically:

Neither a man nor his work is a thing one can pay for and leave aside like other types of property in nature; they are generically different from all other types of property. A man cannot be "bought" with money or anything else—precisely because he and his work are of infinite value. We therefore do great violence to man by separating him from his work by payment only of a salary or wage. By this act, one has robbed him of his most precious possession: his human dignity.

While it is true that the practice of "passive" profit-sharing is becoming more common in the United States, it is not enough to satisfy the demands of a "community of work":

For a worker to receive more money is not, strictly speaking, more human; to add a greater human dimension to his role in industry, the worker must accept responsibility, and this can come through an active participation in industrial ownership and management. The reflection of the worker's personality in his work cannot be achieved except through responsibility, which in turn cannot be realized without an effective voice in the enterprise in which he works. In his work, a man's actions must be those of a free and responsible human being; and for most men, this is almost impossible without an effective sharing in what they do. A man's humanity is expressed in his economic activity, and if this is not free and responsible, his work lacks human dignity. When a man has the opportunity, which is rightfully his, to perfect his human dignity by and through his daily work, his work then represents, in a true sense, a reflection of his person, which is made in the image of God.[2]

The humanity gap between American political democracy (whatever its imperfections) and American economic de-

---

[2] As Riga points out, this notion is more easily grasped in the case of the professional man, whose work expresses his personality in a very special way.

mocracy is apparent. In *Pacem in Terris* Pope John emphasized that political participation according to one's ability and one's need corresponds with man's dignity as a human person and is therefore a demand of human nature. The American citizen can approximate full responsibility politically because his country's political institutions are ultimately directed by him through his representatives. However, such is not the case in American economic society, which is not democratic. It takes no responsibility for the promotion of human dignity. Man's sense of duty and responsibility (which promotes his human dignity) is promoted in the political order by the system of political democracy. On the economic level he is treated as "a perpetual minor, a number that can be dismissed or hired according to the 'need,' determined solely by market demand. His muscles and professional skills are needed, but his opinion and consent are never requested. He is an automaton who is turned on or off . . . [and] an automaton cannot be or develop as a human being."

It is incorrect to assume that more wages, more gadgets, more goods, more material benefits, are in themselves capable of enhancing the human dignity. Because this is so, "both communism and capitalism fall under the same censure when their goals áre solely concerned with the material advancement of man." Rather, man's dignity is enhanced "by the intellectual, psychological and moral fulfillment of his personality through the work which he does."

Riga's social philosophy is by no means destructive of the right of the individual to "own and administer private property" (he remains at all times within the bounds of Catholic social doctrine). But this right is a "relative" and not an "absolute" right:

God has created man as a body and soul, an incarnate being, and as such, man has a natural right to use the world's goods for the conservation of life, the fruition of his talents, and the protection of his health. This right precedes the right of property, and in traditional Catholic social thought, the right to property is a derivative, or a concretization, of the right of usage. In other words, the right to use material goods is fundamental and primary, while the right to own material goods is secondary and derived. The right to property exists so that an order may be established by which the right of usage is assured and guaranteed.

The right of property, then, must be ordered toward the enhancement of man's human dignity. It is, therefore, a means to an end, not an end in itself—relative, not absolute. Pope John has endorsed this concept of social responsibility concurrent with the right of private property:

" . . . it is opportune to point out that there is a social duty essentially inherent in the right of private property" (*Pacem in Terris*). This principle of social philosophy allows for such necessities in modern social life as agrarian reform, the nationalization of basic industries in case of true public need, the right of eminent domain, and civil rights legislation, which demands equal public accommodation for all citizens.

(California Catholics engaged in heated debate among themselves over this point during the famous Proposition 14 election issue in 1964. Those who favored passage of the Initiative, which was aimed at wiping out existing and future California fair-housing legislation, were not at a loss to supply papal quotes in full page newspaper ads to "prove" that the Catholic Church regarded the right of private property as an absolute—an end, not a means. Not only did they take short texts out of context from hoary papal statements, but, worse still, they failed to see the social thought of the Church as a developing, evolutionary whole. They felt free to seize upon something a nineteenth-century pope had said and to present it as Catholic teaching—as if nothing further had been thought or said since. The real aim of the Proposition 14 proponents was, of course, the continued exclusion of Negroes from white neighborhoods.)

Actually, some Catholics of extreme liberal bent have taken the preceding words of Pope John to be tantamount to a

denial of the "natural right" to own property. Riga, however, does not accede to this interpretation. But this natural
right is to be understood in the context of man in his present
stage of development. Most men no longer live and work on
farms; almost three-fourths of people in Western society
today live in metropolitan areas, where they depend upon
their professional skills for their livelihood. Consequently,
there has been a shift from the farmer's reliance on capital
goods for security to the urbanite's and suburbanite's de-
pendence on professional skills. Riga sees this as:

. . . an important effect of socialization and, as such, is to be
considered a step forward. By its very nature, socialization has
been both the cause and the effect of the complexity and the
enrichment of our modern civilization; and since the process of
socialization has been intensified through the increasing interrelationships of professional and technical skills, these skills
must now be an integral part of any consideration of modern
civilization. Through these complex interrelationships, the objective culture of mankind has been enriched—that is, the objective elements such as art, architecture, painting, writing, technology, and so on, which are realized by human labor and which
transform the world. In its turn, the objective culture has enriched the subjective culture of humanity; each person in a
society perfects himself scientifically, intellectually, culturally,
morally, and in every way possible, limited only by his will and
by his abilities. This enrichment has been brought about through
the specialization in professional and technical skills by an ever-
increasing number of people in modern society. Their dependency
is no longer on a patrimony of capital goods, but on these acquired professional abilities—a better expression of the human
personality—and these abilities and the social security which
comes out of them must now rank in equal importance with
the traditional patrimony of private property.

In the interest of human dignity, the task to be undertaken in our time is to attempt the best possible evolvement
from the profit motive salary-wage system to a more humanizing enterprise—that of "the consortium and human com-

munity of work." We must recognize that capitalism has caused a progressive division between man and his work. So long as profit for its own sake remains the prime motivation, the very heart of the system is corrupt because it is inhuman.

Vast powers rest in the hands of a *de facto* economic ruling class. For example, Riga points to a 1962 statistic which shows that the hundred largest manufacturing corporations in the United States controlled almost 60 percent of the net capital assets (financial, land, buildings, and equipment) of *all* manufacturing corporations. The combined assets of the top ten add up to nearly sixty billion dollars. Their power and influence is enormous; money talks. Antitrust laws are anachronisms insofar as they are intended to keep economic power reasonably diffused. Riga explains:

Today, the capitalist system merges not just potential competitors, but subsidiaries in alien fields, producing "conglomerate enterprise." General Motors doesn't just manufacture Chevrolets, but makes refrigerators and diesel locomotives as well. The Columbia Broadcasting System buys the New York Yankees. Martin-Marietta makes concrete pipe and sophisticated spacecraft equipment. Olin-Mathieson can give you farm chemicals, sporting goods, or a very fine brand of toothpaste; General Dynamics runs from sand and gravel to Atlas missiles. Textron is an amalgam of twenty-seven separate divisions and 113 separate plants: it has a line of helicopters, chicken feed, chain saws, and work shoes, along with lawn mowers and bathroom accessories. These are not monopolies (in the traditional sense), but "conglomerates," and conglomerate giantism is growing.

The conglomerate system can hardly be defined on grounds of creating an economic good to fill social needs. Economic director Willard Mueller of the Federal Trade Commission reports 1,956 acquisitions by two hundred of the largest of the giants during the period 1951–1963. And this represents the swallowing-up of profitable ventures—not sick companies. The only discernible motive is profit and more profit. The bottom line is the end-all. Social needs be damned; is

Detroit's record one of concern for the production of safer cars? Does big industry seem to care at all about its barbaric pollution of air and water? Does big advertising ever tire of exploiting America's youth with commercial extravaganzas in every medium, glamorizing high-speed pleasure cars, longer and still longer cigarettes, and the like? The cigarette industry has already spent tens of millions of advertising dollars on programs calculated to give birth to a new generation of smokers—a brave response to overwhelming medical evidence pointing to the harmful effects of tobacco. Clearly, the system is corrupt at its core. So deep-rooted is the regime of profit that hardly a ripple of moral indignation has manifested itself in this crime against the young. So deep-rooted is the regime of profit that it might never occur to the cigarette manufacturing or advertising executives (who might still be human enough to worry about their own kids' smoking habits) that they have allowed the system to dull their moral sense to the extent that it no longer has any meaning.

Riga aptly describes our economic environment:

This is the age of Wall Street speculators, of share trading, of the up-and-down points of Dow-Jones averages, of panic buying and selling—totally inhuman activity separated from all care of consortium or human product of labor, whose sole function is to make money; of entrepreneurs and speculators who are really parasites on the work of other men, where we have an absolute disassociation of direction, capital, and workers of any one enterprise, or of many. We have here the vast trusts and monopolies of vast power for evil on an international scale, which, since their sole object is pure profit, couldn't care less for the human problems posed in each country, in each particular sector where one or another enterprise is located. Money in this system no longer goes to workers nor to stockholders, but is continuously redirected within a closed circle of capital ruled only by its own law of profit. All ties with man are broken and thereby capitalism has attained its proper end and moral corruption. When a crop will not bring in correct profits it is liable to be burned (as happened in Colombia with its coffee, leaving thousands to beg or starve, all because the Colombian-American coffee interests and trusts so dictated it). One telephone call from United Fruit headquarters in New York to practically anywhere in Latin America means either profit or indigence for many within that country. The extent of the system's economic powers on an international scale is simply unknown, but one thing we do know: its own interest becomes its own end, before which everything must give way, including the national or even international common good. Such power can destroy a whole political order (as has happened many times in Latin America), engenders insecurity for prices and markets, reduces millions of men to the whim and wish of a tiny few, while all the time preparing a materialistic culture of profit and gain as the first and only law of life. Antitrust laws are palliatives to curb such a system's more blatant abuses, but the source of its aberration remains within it. Even in the area of palliatives, how very difficult is it to get these enterprises to do something to correct the terrible injustices they inflict on an unsuspecting public—such as water, air, and cultural pollution!

Riga's perspicacity embraces a clear view of the inoffensiveness of war itself to the bottom-line devotees, who never cease to clamor, compete, and connive for shares in the undeniably immense profits flowing from U.S. commitments to institutionalized gross carnage. Why, after all, should a system which for the sake of profit will indiscriminately and unconscionably contaminate the very air we breathe, the water we drink, the lungs and arteries of adolescents, be less willing to be party to any and all war movements proposed by "legitimate authority." And in the system, science for science's sake is not nearly so powerful a motive as profit for profit's sake. Is the manufacturer of the napalm bomb or the local politician who provides him with factory facilities any less amoral than Wernher Von Braun? Is the Christian Establishment Church that dismisses Riga and his sort as "impractical," "naïve," "unrealistic," even "dangerous," any less amoral than the fire-bomb maker?

Riga extracts from his world view a number of truisms

which, as a Christian, he cannot accept with pious resignation. For example:

—Seventeen per cent of the world's people consume somewhat less than 80% of its goods, while the rest must subsist on what little remains.

—The U.S. consumes 50% of the world's wealth and controls, directly or indirectly, 80%.

—American investments abroad add up to about $25 billion. The return on this capital investment is extraordinarily high: 23% in Africa, 36% in Asia, 13% in Latin America.

—Over the last six years, American transfers of investment capital abroad were $2 billion less than American income on these investments.

—in whole continents countless men and women are ravished by hunger, countless numbers of children are undernourished, so that many of them die in infancy, while the physical growth and mental development of many others are retarded and as a result whole regions are condemned to the most depressing despondency. (*Populorum Progressio*)

He condemns the rich power structures' dehumanizing value system, which not only refuses to give first priority to a determined effort to use its excessive wealth for relief of the suffering have-nots, but also feeds on their misery and destitution through exploitation for profit. Riga also endorses with enthusiasm certain suggestions made by Paul VI, who has departed somewhat from the tradition of his predecessors by making specific proposals in the area of international socioeconomic reform. Among these proposals is an urgent plea for the world-wide redistribution of wealth through the establishment of a world fund to be administered by an international agency. The Pope asks the rich countries for increased taxes to support foreign aid (luxury taxes are mentioned specifically), long-term interest-free and low-interest loans, technical aid, and price stabilization of the developing nations' basic commodities.

We must, says Riga, "cut right through the *laissez faire*

talk of 'free enterprise' and 'free market' if we are to manifest a proper concern for equity in trade relations between the haves and the have-nots." In a system where the value of the manufactured goods of industrialized nations keeps going up and up, and where the value of the raw materials of less developed countries is always subject to sudden and wide fluctuation, there will always remain the case of the rich nations getting richer and the poor nations getting poorer. Or, in the words of Paul VI, "The rule of free trade, taken by itself, is no longer able to govern international relations." The inequalities of economic power are too excessive. A cross-county race between a 1968 Cadillac and a horse and buggy could hardly be called fair competition.

The mass media-formed American mind usually is able to conjure up an attractive image of the United States as a benevolent, friendly power generously pouring out aid to its poor neighbors. This is not necessarily the case, as Riga indicates in the following example of Alliance for Progress operations:

Alliance for Progress aid is not a gift—except for a small part in technical aid and Food for Peace—but a loan. The $140 million scheduled as "aid" for Chile this year, for instance, breaks down into a $100 million loan, a $20 million sale of agricultural commodities (why this is called "aid" is not clear), and $3.5 million in technical-assistance grants. The loans have low interest rates—often only one percent the first ten years and 2.5 percent thereafter—but they are not donations; they are to be repaid. Moreover, the recipient countries must meet certain conditions. All materials and equipment required for the various projects must be bought in the United States, even if they can be purchased for much less in Japan or England or elsewhere. Half of what is bought must be shipped in U.S. ships, at much higher rates than could be obtained on ships of other countries. If these additional costs, plus the relatively higher fees of U.S. construction firms, are included, the "low" interest rates are no longer low.

There are other conditions. If any recipient government should expropriate an American corporation without what the United States considers "fair" payment, all loans are cancelled. . . .

To put American aid in proper perspective it must be considered in conjunction with two other phenomena: terms of trade and repatriation of profits. The United States gives Latin America in loans and grants about $500 million a year. Another $500 million or so comes in loans from such agencies as the Export-Import Bank or the Inter-American Development Bank. But both together—$1 billion—are only half of that which private American entrepreneurs *take out* of Latin America each year. Adverse terms of trade, according to an estimate by one U.S. Embassy official, cost the nineteen republics $1 billion a year, and the repatriation of profits drains away a like sum ($11 billion for the decade 1950–1960). Thus, the U.S. public puts in $1 billion, mostly in loans, and private U.S. business takes out $2 billion.

United States policy toward the developing nations of the world has been one of systematic exploitation. It has supported international trade and tariff and monetary agreements giving rise to a world economic order that guarantees a continued widening of the gap between developed and developing nations. It has consistently failed to support (and therefore, in effect, has consistently thwarted) United Nations efforts to narrow the gap between haves and have-nots through revisions in existing tariff and other trade standards. Clearly, it is United States capitalist profit-regime thinking which is dominant in the argument defending this policy of inequity: "We cannot be expected to act against our own best economic interests, can we?" Riga's answer is simple, serious, and very direct:

If capitalism as a system is accepted as having as its direct and final object the regime of profit, then the only way out for the Christian would be to eliminate such a system. Where market values above all else determine the livelihood of millions of men and women, we are surely in the realm of the pure perversion of man by man. . . . It is a crime against humanity which cries to heaven for vengeance and from whose ultimate logic we in the West have, unfortunately, not graduated, since the essential evil remains.

Paul VI has given us a neat little summary of his own understanding of Catholic social doctrine tradition:

"If someone who has the riches of this world sees his brother in need and closes his heart to him, how does the love of God abide in him?" It is well known how strong were the words used by the fathers of the church to describe the proper attitude of persons in need. To quote St. Ambrose: "You are not making a gift of your possessions to the poor person. You are handing over to him what is his. For what has been given in common for the use of all, you have arrogated to yourself. The world is given to all, and not only to the rich." That is, private property does not constitute for anyone an absolute and unconditional right. No one is justified in keeping for his exclusive use what he does not need, when others lack necessities. In a word, "According to the traditional doctrine as found in the Fathers of the Church and the great theologians, the right to property must never be exercised to the detriment of the common good." If there should arise a conflict "between acquired private rights and primary community exigencies," it is the responsibility of public authorities "to look for a solution, with the active participation of individuals and social groups." (*Populorum Progressio*)

Most Catholics do not take such Gospel-oriented, authentically Christian words seriously. Consequently, the distinguishing mark of a Catholic such as Riga is his "radicalism." Anyone, in fact, who takes the Gospel seriously will bear the stamp of "radical" in his own time.

Peter Riga, on more than a few occasions, has addressed this counsel to fellow American Catholic priests:

There can be no living, authentic Christian faith in God without "works of faith," and among these there is first of all that of caring for others "without distinction of persons." To love one's neighbor as oneself is not confined to satisfying, by means of Catholic charities, the most urgent necessities of our neighbor. It means also and above all to effectively desire for him what we desire for ourselves: civil rights, health, education, development, civilization and culture; to do our best to eliminate the great economic and social inequalities and all human oppressions. Unless priests get across this social message to their people as part and parcel of the Christian message, then we can forget about any *aggiornamento* in the Church.

Peter would agree, I am sure, that if the words "priests" and "people" in the last sentence were to be transposed, the admonition would retain its original validity. In either case, however, it is not a very radical statement—until it is made by a radical.

7

MARXIST-CHRISTIAN DIALOGUE

For myself, Birchism and its multiple variants are more destructive of human freedom than the crudest form of Marxism. If ever we sought dramatic evidence to validate George Bernard Shaw's cynical assertion that a Catholic university is an impossibility, we would have to look no further than the ranks of those who once attended Santa Clara. Not all, of course, nor even most, but it is undeniable that a goodly cross-section of our alumni and friends think and demand that the University be a controlled experiment utterly divorced from the world of reality.

Thus, each time that the University proposes a program which involves ideas or positions different from or hostile to other ideas and positions, the vocal minority raises an elephantine hue. Antiseptically pure of ideas themselves, they cannot distinguish between dialogue and espousal.

The University is not a planet spun off from the world. The Catholic university has to grow up. So do Catholic alumni and friends of the University. The formal work of the institution is not to prepare monks and nuns, but citizens of the world—and the world is made up of a vast spectrum of ideas ranging from Mao to Robert Welch (founder of the John Birch Society).

Have they so little confidence in the world of American academe that they really think that a talk by an accomplished Marxist can convert to communism an American sophomore or senior? If this were so, the American proposition must indeed be vulnerable. I am quite certain it is not.

This statement (taken from the *San Francisco Chronicle*) by Very Rev. Patrick Donohoe, president of Santa Clara University, was made in the wake of a barrage of criticism— by telephone, letter, and personal visit—from "alumni and friends" of the university who were outraged because a Christian-Marxist dialogue [1] was allowed to be held on Santa Clara's sacred ground.

To the university's critics, it was one thing—and bad enough at that—to enter into conversation with the dreaded enemy, but it was quite another to *sponsor* the heinous deed. (Some still haven't forgiven Pope John for receiving Khrushchev's son-in-law at the Vatican.) But, while they regarded the appearance of Communist Herbert Aptheker as a desecration, the sponsoring Center's director, Father Eugene C. Bianchi, saw it as a sign that "a university had come of age."

The Santa Clara dialogue was a pioneering attempt to join the somewhat more advanced Marxist-Christian dialogical movement in Western Europe. Largely (on the Christian side) the result of the work of the Paulus Society, this movement was organized by a group of West German Catholics and now claims a membership of over six hundred intellectuals from around the world.

The dialogists pursued the theme, "Could an open dialogue between Christian and Marxist scholars illumine past obstacles and clear new avenues toward a more humane society?"

American Marxist Robert L. Cohen, chairman of the physics department at Boston University, called on both sides to put aside some of their standard rhetorical paraphernalia which inevitably stirs up prejudice and fosters ignorance. He told his fellow-Marxists to look for signs of a positive Christian humanism and to back off from idolatrous party worship. To Christians he posed the question: Would Christ indulge in Red-baiting and smear campaigns? He also commented:

---

[1] On "New Humanism," sponsored by the university's Center for the Study of Contemporary Values, October 16–18, 1967.

I believe that the socialist ideal is correct for Christian doctrine. . . . Those Communist words, "brother" and "comrade" are Christian words. . . . That there should be no human exploitation, that the world's material produce should be shared . . . the attitude of Jesus towards the rich and the poor—these seem to be not merely Christian but socialist. If this be the case, then those Christians who don't know it and those Marxists who don't know it should get to know one another. (*Jubilee,*[2] December, 1966)

Mr. Cohen felt, optimistically, that past inhumanities on both sides should force Marxists and Christians, both, to be open to critical exchanges, and he pointed to the distressing picture of the great world powers, with their awesome nuclear capabilities, hurling epithets back and forth over a largely destitute sea of humanity, as a compelling answer to the "Why?" of the Marxist-Christian Dialogue.

Louis Dupre of Georgetown University lucidly explained the origin of Karl Marx's opposition to religion. Dupre praised the existentialist and creative factors of Marxist "praxis," but he concluded that this theory of action was basically incompatible with religion on the theoretical plane. Practical co-existence and cooperation was urged by Dupre, but he found the Marxist theory of action too narrow to encompass the religious dimensions of human experience. The Georgetown philosopher-theologian expressed the hope, however, that the Marxist notion of "praxis" might be widened by the actual experience of history to comprehend deeper, spiritual dimension of the human situation. (*Ibid.*)

John Somerville, Marxist philosopher at California Western University, reviewed the deplorable condition of labor and the exploitative economic system of the world which spawned Marx and Engels as prophetic voices calling for a new social order. "If these men had not existed," he said, "we would have had to invent them."

Father Bianchi describes the cordial atmosphere in the give and take:

2 Published by Herder and Herder, New York.

The accomplishments of Marxist nations, especially the Soviet Union, were elaborated by both Somerville and Aptheker. But an especially interesting aspect of the conference was the willingness of all the Marxists to criticize weaknesses in their own systems. They recognized failures in Marxist countries to provide for the rights of individuals in matters of personal ethics, artistic and literary freedoms. Catholic abuses of power were accurately criticized by Berkeley Marxist Hall Draper of the University of California, while Catholic scholar Michael Novak of Stanford laid bare Catholic failures in moral and social matters with a scalpel sharper than that of any Marxist. (*Ibid.*)

Other excerpts from the dialogue:

I would say that at least half of our grave problems, tensions and fears arise out of the fact that each side has a great many . . . misimpressions about what the other side stands for. And out of this, lack of understanding, proliferate fears, anxieties and the spirit of having one's finger always on the trigger. The assumption is always present that the other party is not only a competitor, but an enemy. He is not only inconvenient, he's immoral. He is not only disagreeable, he's criminal. *John Somerville*

. . . has the time not come to incorporate into its (Marxist) theory the changes which are taking place in its own living *praxis?* Such an attitude would ultimately be more consistent with Marx's philosophy than the rigid preservation of a theory which is rapidly proving too narrow to interpret the fullness of human action. *Louis Dupre*

Thus, a Marxism that becomes fully conscious of the religious element in its hope will be in a better position to use the energy of its utopian aspirations as a creative force for its scientific *praxis,* just as a Christianity that has become aware of the worldly dimension of its concern will be better able to bring its great eschatological image into vital connection with the concrete facts of existence. *W. Richard Comstock,* Protestant Theologian, University of California, Santa Barbara

If it has been possible to move from systems based on the private ownership of the means of production to socialism in one-third of the world and the elimination therefrom of the private appropriation of profit, it will be possible to move institutionalized Christianity from its present commitment to capitalism. That commitment ties Christianity to a corpse and not to a living God; it certainly is not in accord with Christianity's own reading of its original concepts and practices. *Herbert Aptheker* (*Ibid.*)

Father Bianchi was satisfied that the dialogue's "counter-theme"—could a private church-related college become an open forum for intellectual inquiry, and could it make a distinctive educational contribution by staging a conference which in Reagan's California would prove too embarrassing for state-funded schools?—received an affirmative answer:

On the level of rethinking past ideas and of forming new attitudes, the dialogue was generally successful. Some of the participants were so enthusiastic about the outcome of the meeting that they wanted to organize a sequel in an Eastern university. The ferment on campus, caused by the controversial gathering, also helped to educate students about the purposes of a church-related university. Such an institution could place special emphasis on the study and development of a great world tradition like the Christian heritage. But in doing this, it cannot be closed or defensive. A Christian university exists for the welfare of the *whole* community. It must, therefore, cultivate honest and critical confrontation with other traditions in its quest to deepen values and serve human development.

It was in this spirit that Santa Clara's President, Patrick A. Donohoe, S.J., answered the outspoken critics of the conference. His statement will long be quoted by those who cherish academic freedom.

The Christian-Marxist conference at Santa Clara made both a contribution to the worldwide dialogue and to the self-understanding of a university. (Eugene C. Bianchi, S.J.)

8

EUGENE SCHALLERT, S. J.

The charge of "anti-clericalism" has been a familiar response to the Catholic Left by the Church bureaucracy, and one which the author feels is largely unjustified. The interview which follows is intended to demonstrate that Catholic Left positions are not restricted to non-clerics. The interviewee, Father Eugene Schallert, is professor of sociology at the Jesuit-owned University of San Francisco. This interview was taped on the University campus in June, 1967.

J. Colaianni

Interview with Eugene Schallert, S. J., priest-sociology professor at the University of San Francisco.

Q. As you know, Gene, the gross polarity that exists between the Catholic Left and the rest of Catholicism has raised this question in many places : Has this wide divergence in religious orientation and response resulted in Catholicism's having drifted into a de facto two-Church situation ? Do you think the radical departure from the medieval Roman tradition is de facto schismatic?

A. I don't think so, really. I think we have now a Church with two bases, or two levels of existence. I suppose, in a healthy situation wherein the Church was less debilitated and sick than it is today, the same person could move back and forth between these two levels without any problems. But in our present system there is the very real fact of a major division between the bureaucratic Church and the holy people of God. I must add that this is not a terribly critical problem for the masses of Catholics who are largely unconcerned with the holy people of God facing the Church. Many of the intellectuals in the Church are concerned; the left wing of the Church is; so is the avant-garde. But, by and large, the on-the-street Catholic is not.

In a sense the bureaucracy has devised what I would call a rather neat gimmick that would sell cars on Van Ness Avenue by the thousands. The gimmick is, for minimum service you get maximum reward. If you are a Catholic, all you have to do is make sure you get to Mass on Sunday, and, until recently, be sure not to eat meat on Friday. If you commit any sins against the Jewish Law —the Ten Commandments—then you go to the priest to get absolved. You give propositional assent to ten or twelve doctrines or dogmas of the Church. For this service, which is certainly minimal, you get an eternity of happiness in heaven. I can't think of a better deal than that. First of all, it's not hard for people who live this kind of life to go to church on Sunday. Anyway, they tend to go because the law of the Church says so. Theirs is a gimmick sort of religion—and they look forward to this tremendous reward. You invest a nickel and look what you get in God's return. I think that is the general Catholic populace. I'm making a value judgment here, a historical value judgment. Then there is the other face of the Church—rather small. Those in this minority group generally end up talking to themselves in their little in-groups. They have very little influence on the general Catholic populace—that is, the everyday, Sunday-Mass Catholic. There is very little communication.

Q. Doesn't the avant-garde go to church on Sunday?

A. Certainly not for the same reasons. There is a difference in intention, in direction, which pays no attention to the legalisms.

Q. That is to say, if they didn't go on a given Sunday it
wouldn't drive them straight into the confession box?

A. No, they'd probably go on Monday. From my point of
view they look more religious. I don't think one is religious when one relates to a law; one is religious when one
relates to God. It seems to me that they are trying to find
a God to relate to. The rest of the Catholics relate to a
concept of God who becomes a mere theological definition
or explanation. I think they find this more satisfying.

Q. Two different Gods?

A. No, it's a concept of God, and the reality of God. Not
really two different Gods. Although the separation here
is real, I don't think it's significant, precisely because the
avant-garde is such a small minority. And we cannot
overlook the fact that among the bulk of the Catholic
people you do find a lot of very devout souls, the little old
ladies who go to church all the time, who say their rosaries
every day and go to all the novenas and participate in all
the religious activities of the parish. These are relatively
pious souls. I think their security comes from the rigidity
of the Church rather than their concept of God. They have
a need for the rigidity of the Church. It's their security
blanket. On the other hand, the avant-garde people don't
place value on security. They are not looking for security
in the Church in the sense of security within a structured
framework. They find their place in the dynamics of
things. There is no doubt that there really are two rather
clearly differentiated faces of the Church. Ideally, there
is no problem about this. But realistically there is today,
because they are pulling apart, farther and farther all the
time.

Q. As a Catholic on the Left, how do you carry the burden
of giving both internal and external assent to the doctrines
and the dogmas? Are you a Catholic in spite of, or because of, the Church's doctrinal position?

A. This is not bothersome, really. If you were to ask me, "Is there a Trinity?" as a doctrinal formula I would say "Yes." But this doesn't bother me in the least. It is the question "What does that mean?" that bothers me. I think the avant-garde is not terribly concerned about how doctrines are formulated, but, rather, "What does it mean?" For example, if you ask an avant-garde Catholic who is intrigued by this new insight we call "transignification" how it is possible to square the term with the Church's doctrine of transubstantiation, he probably won't take any time to deny or affirm transubstantiation. He'll say, "O.K., fine. So there really is transubstantiation; so what else is new?" He is not going to, unless he gets mad at something, care much what you call it. But he does want to search for real meaning in the "Real Presence," even though his pursuit of meaning may, in the eyes of some, mollify the ideal because he's trying to understand this comprehensive meaning for himself. He is concerning himself with something much deeper than the formula. Whereas the other Catholics, the bureaucratic Catholics, since they have never been much concerned about meaning, get very upset because somebody makes up a new word. If you asked them to explain transubstantiation in the scholastic meaning, they would never do it, because most of them have not studied "substance" and "accidents" in any profound way. So the word "transubstantiation" really doesn't mean anything to them because the word "substance," from which it is derived, doesn't mean anything to them.

I have interesting encounters in my classes all the time because I won't allow the students to become preoccupied with formulas or verbalization. What does it mean? What does it mean? What does it mean? I had one student (this is typical) who was very upset all semester because I was saying there are limitations in scholastic philosophy: It's not the last word. Aristotle didn't have the last important thought; there is movement, evolution,

and we have got to move out from under Aristotle just
as Galileo and Copernicus moved out from under Ptol-
emy, just as existentialism moved out from under Plato
and Aristotle. So, religiously, we move out from under
these things. These students were very upset about that,
and they defended St. Thomas to the last ditch. I would
ask, "How much of Aristotle have you read? How much
of Plato have you read? How much of St. Thomas have
you read?" In reply I would get, "Well, I really haven't
read much of it but I know it's good." It is their security
formula and it is not unlike this among the clergy, most
of whom have not studied their own philosophy in any
sophisticated way. But the formula is there, the security
formula. It helps them to feel that one doesn't have to
question; one doesn't have to bother his mind because the
Church has all the answers. "That's the way things are,
so why bother?" It's hard to describe: a kind of non-
intellectualism or anti-intellectualism which is so rampant
in the Catholic Church.

I don't think that you can say that the avant-garde
people do not assent to the propositional structures. I
think you *might* say that they are people who simply don't
care much about them. If someone accused me of heresy
I would say, "But what have I denied?" They would say,
"X, Y, or Z." And I would reply, "But what does that
mean to you?" And there it would end. In the age of
rationalism, heresy was a very important item, because
rational logic persistently was a key value. But in the age
of existentialism, logic is not that important a value.
People who think in the existentialist way recognize that
human living isn't really all that consistent. Why do we
have to have such a consistent rational profile? I am sure
that there are a lot of Catholic people around who would
deny some of the propositions of the Church. I've done it
myself. I said one time in public that I agreed with Bishop
Pike, who said that the doctrine of the Trinity is irrele-

vant to modern man. I added that this was also a tragedy
for Christianity. Various people were horribly upset—
bureaucrats who understand everything in absolute terms.
When I said that the Trinity is irrelevant to modern man,
they thought I meant *absolutely* irrelevant. And I don't
think in terms of absolutes; nor do I *try* to think in terms
of absolutes. I don't have that kind of mind. So I wouldn't
take the trouble to investigate if the Trinity was *absolutely*
real or unreal. I myself believe it's real. But I also know
that it is irrelevant, that modern man doesn't think much
about the Trinity. It is simply not a factor in his life. It
is not a factor that helps him make sense out of his life.
It's not a source of meaning or a source of vitality to
him—to the normal Catholic cardinal or bishop or working priest or sister or layman.

Q. What happens when you have an eyeball-to-eyeball confrontation with the typical ecclesiastical bureaucrat which
ends up with your asking him to attach his own meaning
to, say, the doctrine of the Trinity?

A. The experience is very unreal. He doesn't have any meaning to attach. All the questions come back blank: "The
Trinity means there are three persons in God." They have
the definition, but the word "meaning" has nothing to do
with definitions. The Trinity is defined as three persons
in God, but the next question, "What does that mean?"
is never answered. They all look at you as if to say, "Is it
supposed to mean something?" It doesn't matter much
whether you talk about the Trinity or bring up some of
the crucial non-problems in the modern Catholic Church
in America, for example, birth control. I try to engage in
this kind of discussion: "Would you say the same thing
if you could realistically fantasy yourself in bed with the
woman you love and with whom you had found this to be
a very beautiful way of expressing your love, a loving,
generous, and joyful act, not just biological, but simply
human? Would you say the same thing if, in your human

joy's reflection, you see how much your wife loves you as a function in this experience? Would you then maintain the same position on birth control?" Well, you see, you can't pursue that discussion because you can't get these people to discuss things on that level. You can't say "Let's sit down and let's not talk about this theory of birth control as it is derived from natural law. Let's see if we can't work out a philosophy or theology of human love from which we may or may not be able to derive a conclusion condemning artificial contraception." You simply can't discuss things this way with the bureaucrats: The Church says so, natural law says so, end of discussion.

Q. Church says so in this case meaning two Popes, is that correct?

A. Yes, meaning two Popes. The statement of one is in an encyclical, the other in an allocution. These are the only two statements that have ever been seriously quoted from papal literature by the bureaucrats. On the other hand, perhaps paradoxically, the avant-garde tends to take much of the encyclical literature of the Popes quite seriously. In many respects I think the Holy Father has been the spokesman for the Catholic Left, particularly in the social encyclicals. I think the Left takes the social teachings of the Church much more seriously than they take the doctrinal teachings, because it defines "Church" as being in and of this world. Therefore, it finds these social statements meaningful to this world, whereas it finds law and doctrine to be relatively meaningless to the concrete order. This is not to say that the Left takes the Church's social teaching as dogma. Leftists take it as something that will stimulate thought as they partake of the adventure of "the Church in the modern world." This is in contrast to the bureaucrats who certainly don't take the social teachings very seriously at all. For instance, Cardinal McIntyre of Los Angeles has no sympathy for encyclical literature, particularly social encyclical literature.

Q. Isn't this a case of picking and choosing by both sides?
After all, I doubt if either of us could name a single
Catholic even remotely identifiable with the Left who
doesn't reject out of hand the papal blanket condemnations of all forms of artificial contraception.

A. Yes, but I don't think one can be a member of an organization like the Catholic Church, which is two thousand
years old and which probably has the richest cultural
heritage of any human organization, and not pick and
choose. There is too much variety. The whole spectrum
of Catholic culture is incomprehensible. It is too rich and
divergent for any one person to consent to the whole thing.
All of these things are dramatically contrary, not contradictory. I cannot grasp and solve all these dilemmas
which oversensitive, thinking Catholics create for themselves. So I must pick and choose. I think this is quite
appropriate. You look at the Church, which is kind of
spread out across time and space, and you see that it has
been part of many different cultures. I would find it
strange or odd—I don't think I'd feel guilty—to participate, say, in ecclesiastical dances of African natives. I
wouldn't understand them. It's quite proper to pick and
choose from African native music and other music. Sim-
ilarly, when I listen to some of the music that I hear in
Mexico or Central America or South America, I feel
strange, and I'm not much at home there. So I choose
from that cultural formula and my own cultural formula.
I'm free to choose either. The world of music is so varied,
so diverse, and actually so contrary, one *has* to pick and
choose.

Q. You said earlier that the poles between the ecclesiastical
bureaucrats and the new existentialist Catholics were
progressively moving further apart. Can you elaborate
on this point?

A. Well, I think that one of the most dramatic processes in
the Catholic Church, in America at least, is this dividing

of itself into four or five, or six, different-looking camps—
different orientations, different directions, different preoccupations, different value systems, different complexus
of meanings. I think what Vatican II did was to make us
more aware of the fact that the Catholic Church is an intensely divergent organization which incorporates into
itself, over time and space, many different cultures. I
think this is now being seen in the United States, where
people are choosing those forms of Catholicism which
allow one to be more oneself and still be a Catholic. One
doesn't have to be an automaton to be a Catholic. He can
just be himself, think his own thoughts, feel his own
feelings, make his own judgments, follow his own conscience, and still be a Catholic.

Q. Therefore, you would hold that this increasing polariza-
tion is a good sign?

A. Yes. I personally feel that it's healthy when sisters in a
convent can stand toe to toe and shout at each other on
some controversial issue. It's much healthier for them than
always to be saying "Yes, sister, no, sister" and simply
burying all the differences. I think husbands and wives
do this rather well, and I think we Christians, who pur-
port to love one another should have enough belief in one
another to be able to disagree, however violently. I think
this is healthy. I think that a wife who doesn't bug her
husband has already capitulated to his death. When a
husband doesn't bug his wife, he has already capitulated
to her death. When they bug each other, disagree with
each other, on important, gut-level issues, I think this is
much more vital.

Q. I would like to talk a bit more about the bureaucracy. To
what extent would you say the existing structures are
essential to the Church as Church?

A. See now, I don't like to think that way. You try to get me
to think on a level which deals in the essences of things.
I don't know what the essence of the Catholic Church is,

so I can't tell you what is essential to it and what is not
essential to it. Historically, we have had a Church which
initially was democratic; which, through the medieval experience, became quite monarchistic. It modeled itself
after militaristic monarchism and has more or less held
on to these points until now. The present structures of the
Catholic Church are modeled not so much on the feudal
monarchies, as they were in earlier times, as on the American corporation. This is a cold, efficient, and effective
organization within its own framework. General Motors
is concerned with keeping General Motors alive. And the
Catholic Church is like General Motors. It is concerned
with keeping itself alive. That's what bureaucracies do:
they keep themselves alive. And I think this is the picture
model the Catholic Church is following. You used the
term "Church as Church" in your question. When I think
of Church as Church, which I don't do too often, I tend to
be more phenomenological and existential; that is, when I
use the word "Church" I think of that event across time
and space which I refer to with the words "Catholic
Church." I use the word "event" purposely here, because
event is an ongoing, dynamic sort of reality. So the Catholic Church is that event which has grown and developed
in the family of man, under the direction of God, and
which still grows and develops from within itself out
toward the world around it. In the history of this event,
or this presence, there have been many organizational
forms, some of which have been democratic. We didn't
have hierarchies in the early Church at all. Hierarchies
came much later, in the seventh or eighth century. So, to
say that the Catholic Church, which we know as a historical phenomenon, is a hierarchically constructed Church is
to make a big mistake. Only a piece of it has been that
way.

Q. But didn't we have bishop's meeting in councils and
synods in the early Christian centuries?

A. Of course, but that is one thing, and it is another thing to have a highly structured bureaucratic hierarchy in the highly organized Church of today. The present Church, organizationally, doesn't in any way resemble the organization of the Church in early Christian times. It was much more democratic, and this was true even in the days when the king—who I suppose was thought of as the representative of the people (though not an elected representative)—nominated bishops. This is unheard of in today's Church. We've become much more rigid. The bishops are appointed much like the President of General Motors is appointed—by a board of directors. We've become much *less* democratic, actually.

Q. Is the great wealth of the organizational Church a debilitating influence?

A. Perhaps I would call it a necessary evil. Evil in the sense that it *is* debilitating. I don't know what we can do with it; it's there; it's a fact of life; it's like having a club foot.

Q. Why couldn't it just be given away? Recently, in an open letter to the Pope, Donald McDonald—who is on the staff of the Center for the Study of Democratic Institutions—made the following suggestion: that the Roman Catholic Church "contribute one-half of its wealth to a World Fund to be administered for the benefit of the poor and underdeveloped peoples of the world, on the condition that each nation in the world agree to contribute 2 percent of its Gross National Product to the same World Fund for the same purpose for a period of the next ten years", so that "By this act, the Church would demonstrate concretely and generously to the world that its concern for the poor and the destitute peoples is sincere, that it is real and that it is deep." What is your opinion on this?

A. I doubt if it could be given away that easily; there would be all sorts of legal problems. The Church's wealth is distributed over the whole Church. It is not the private property of one man. I don't see how bishops could, for example, give away the assets of individual parishes, which belong to the people, really. But suppose the Church had, by some stretch of the imagination, some $20 billion in cash and securities, and suppose it decided to redistribute this wealth for the benefit of poor people. I doubt if it would make much of an impact, practically. The federal government of the United States spends enormous sums each year in foreign programs aimed at helping underdeveloped countries—about $6 billion a year right now—and these countries are still poor. What I am saying is that even if the Church could give away everything it owns in one magnanimous stroke, it wouldn't do much to solve the world's poverty problems. But token value, yes. Witness value, yes. A pledge of serious-mindedness about helping the poor, yes. But I don't think that the value of the Church's redistribution of wealth is very great in itself. If the Church could generate enough inner energy to give birth to a charismatic figure like Pope John XXIII again, it wouldn't have to fuss with things like finance; it would be able to exert intellectual and moral leadership in the world with or without giving away its assets. In other words, I think that the Church that could produce a leader who would even consider the question of liquidating its wealth for distribution to the poor, would have produced a leader who could do much better work elsewhere in ecclesiastical affairs. Our problem is we're so rigid and stiff in our investment programs and with our stock portfolios that we spend all our energy on those things. And we generate, from within ourselves, leaders who can take care of our wealth for us—like Cardinal McIntyre, who is an excellent financier but who exercises no leadership in the world at all. I just don't think that the witness value of redistribution of wealth is that great in the absence of charismatic leadership. And if we have that charismatic leadership, then we don't need this other witness value. I must say, however, that we would have a better chance of developing real, charismatic leadership if we gave our money away. That would certainly be a tremendous value for ourselves. It wouldn't help the world much, except maybe eventually because of our new-found value system.

Another factor I think is crucial to look at is that we in this country, for example, live in a very affluent society. I don't think that the witness value of poverty in American society—where there are perhaps six million deprived people out of 185 million—is as great as other kinds of activities. I don't think the normal American citizen would take a poor-looking priest seriously. There are a lot of factors involved in that, too. I don't think the average American takes any-looking priest seriously. Those priests who are serious about the kinds of problems that confront America, like the problem of meaning, the problem of morality, the problem of becoming, the problem of discovery of who I am, the problem of the identity crises—these kinds of problems—find that the average American citizen is not concerned with bothering to listen to somebody. The intellectuals will, yes, but the average American citizen would much rather watch cowboys and indians on television.

Q. Are you optimistic toward the possibility of the production of the kind of charismatic leadership you have described?

A. No, but I have a lot of hope, which is a lot different to me, a much deeper feeling than optimism. This is largely a terminological problem. I am optimistic, too, as I see the bureaucratic walls crumbling, as I see what is happening among some of the young people in the Church. The young seminarians, almost to a man, are making inroads that are beginning to be effective. They have learned how to play the ecclesiastical game, but interior to themselves they are, by far, much more forward-looking people. I had occasion to attend a meeting with some theologians down at St. John's Seminary in Los Angeles, the hotbed of yesterday's Church, and I found the seminarians there far more avant-garde than any seminarians I had met in a long time. I listened to them and talked to them for several hours, surreptitiously, of course. . . .

Q. Why surreptitiously? Can't a priest from San Francisco talk to seminarians in Los Angeles?

A. Not this type of priest. I'm sure if Cardinal McIntyre knew I was down there he would not have let them talk to me. I said to these young seminarians, "How is it that you fellows are so up on the progressive thinking in the Church today, down here in this bastion of conservatism?" They replied, "Well, you know, Father, we have candles and we have closets," which meant that even though the progressive literature is banned they read it under cover. And I personally think that this literature makes a much deeper impression on them because they have to read it this way, much deeper than if they just read it in the library. The bureaucratic structure is crumbling because people don't take it seriously anymore. Who is going to take McIntyre's place when he dies or retires? We're running out of bodies like McIntyre. So I'm very hopeful in that respect.

Q. Very well, so you are hopeful, and the bureaucratic walls are crumbling and therefore, in your view, will collapse. What's going to replace them when they do?

A. I don't know; I'm not a bureaucrat. I don't think in terms of this kind of reform. I suppose there are people who do. I would feel very naïve if you asked me to write a plan for the Church. It would certainly be a naïve plan. I think what we need in the Church are administrators who understand the value of order and maintain it, understand the value of freedom and maintain that, too. We need administrators who understand the thing man needs most in his life: the opportunity to grow, from within. You know, when you grow (in the way you think, in the way you feel about things) you don't know where it's going to

take you. You fuss with this and that and you just don't
know. But you develop, within yourself, a direction in
your life. And that's where man has to grow from—from
within. We need administrators who understand that man
is a growing, developing, evolving sort of being and
that you must respect that and let him make his mistakes.
I think one of the things we need is authority figures who
have no tolerance for authoritarian personalities. I would
go for bureaucrats who were non-bureaucratic, bureaucrats who were charismatic.

Q. Would we still call them bishops?

A. They certainly wouldn't have to be bishops. I think we
could maintain the present episcopal staff as geniuses at
maintaining order and say, "O.K., now you go over in
that corner and maintain order. Meanwhile, the Church
has to be alive; the rest of us will keep it alive." If there
is anything we are going to have to do, it is to develop in
the Church two legitimate kinds of authority: charismatic authority and administrative authority. Right now
charismatic authority in the Church is not legitimate.
Pope John had it.

Q. Ideally, would the charismatic authorities be episcopal?

A. I don't see why. They haven't been, historically. Some
bishops have been charismatic, but, by and large, religious
leaders of history have not been bishops. Francis of Assisi
was not a bishop; St. Dominic was not a bishop; St.
Ignatius of Loyola was not a bishop; St. Thomas More
was not a bishop. Idealistically it won't be episcopal anyway. What the bishops have to learn to do is to make
room for the charismatic figures to grow—and to follow
their leadership. They don't have to be priests, either.
Thomas More was a great charismatic figure, and he
wasn't a priest.

Q. Would you say that Catholic Leftists tend to come up on
the same side of social and political issues, and if so, is this
because of their basic religious orientation? Do Catholic
Left and Political Left go together?

A. Generally, Catholic Leftists tend to be political liberals. I don't think there is any doubt of that. I can't think of a single person whom I would identify with the religious avant-garde who is not left of center in the political and social arena. There is an interesting thing going on, however. Just as nineteenth-century liberalism was rethought through and repudiated by twentieth-century liberals, so, too, I think twentieth-century liberalism is being rethought through and being repudiated by later twentieth-century liberals. I think the true liberal is one who will not allow himself to be caught up in the rigid, organizational structures; that's what being liberal means. So that, say, when the vision of a Roosevelt—who certainly was a very liberal man—becomes part of the institutional structure of a country like the United States, the liberals attempt to pull away from that. And I think this is true of the Catholic Leftist as well, who, I suppose, is alive enough to want to be free. As soon as you start thinking "freedom" you start thinking "shackles," the real shackles which are part of any institutionalized structure—like the shackles of the American institutions which the liberals themselves fashioned. As soon as you start feeling the pressure of shackles, then you start breaking them to move on. I think that the Catholic Left is like that. It is questioning the policies of a liberal administration like Johnson's, for example, the Johnson policy in Vietnam. At the same time, the liberal Catholic will break away from the liberal Establishment in the Church, as the liberal or progressive movement in the Church becomes more and more part of the institutional structure.

Q. What about the tremendous resources that the Church pours into the parochial educational systems on all levels? This is a major preoccupation of the Left, which seems to be eagerly anticipating the destruction of the whole thing.

A. The Catholic liberals, who are by far the most highly educated people in the Church, having had a meaningful educational experience of their own, are naturally quite critical of other educational experiences. They are quite critical (justifiably so, I think) of the expenditure of $7½ million dollars a day for Catholic elementary and high school education alone. They can't seem to detect any measurable effects from this whole operation.

Q. Did you say $7½ million a day for grammar and high school education alone?

A. Yes. Not counting higher education; not counting the university or college or seminary education. And those figures are about seven years old; now it is much more, I'm sure.

Q. Do you think it should be phased out? I mean the whole system.

A. Well, it is being phased out, and I'm happy it is. I always have felt that it is a source of shame that the Catholic Church which defines itself as a leaven in the mass of men would segregate itself into an impenetrable shell from whence it could never exert this leavening influence. I think it is a scandal that we would take the people that we ourselves, rightly or wrongly, regard as our best Catholics and segregate them from any meaningful confrontation with the real world in order to protect them—and protect means only to get them to assent to certain ecclesiastical propositions. We're not protecting them from anything but that, so that they will be able to debate (in the strict sense of the word) debatable (in the strict sense of the word) issues. I think this is a shame. We would be a better Church if we did what the rest of the Church has always done; just send our people to a regular school. This parochial school emphasis is an American experiment. In other words, in a two-thousand year history we are looking at a fifty-year-old phenomenon.

Q. The ecclesiastical bureaucrats defined the system by saying it is the basis for keeping the faith alive.

A. Yet it stayed alive for 95 percent of its history without this kind of school system and, I suppose, in a much more vital way. When you have an educational system that's closed, as ours is, to meaningful encounters with other kinds of thinkers—like atheists and agnostics, and other kinds of religious thinkers like Hindus or Buddhists— your students' ability is diminished. To effect influence I don't see how you can have a narrow Catholic, when the very word means universal. Our teaching priests and sisters have had a dramatically narrowing influence on the students. And so I'll be happy to see it phased out. I don't think our small women's colleges, for example, will last another fifteen years. They are that close to collapse.

Q. And the larger institutions of higher learning?

A. Twenty-five years, unless some dramatic event takes place, unless they are supported by the State or something like that. I don't see how this university [University of San Francisco] can survive—fifty years, maybe. As the drama of education continues and develops—a very costly development—we are just going to be left out in the boondocks.

Q. So whether we like it or not, the sheer economics of the situation will control?

A. I think we should have some people sitting down now and seriously thinking about this thing, so that we'll know what we are going to do when we are finished with this particular project.

Q. Are there such people?

A. Not that I know of.

Q. We keep on building and expanding?

A. We're expending all our energy in just trying to keep the thing alive for the next few years, instead of facing the fact that it's going to die and starting to think about what we are going to do next. In the congregations of religious orders more seriously concerned with renewal, these questions are being asked continually. But the questions never get down to the implementation level. For example, in the Jesuit General Congregation last year it was very seriously questioned: should we be in the education business at all? And it was decided that we should be where the action is. But on the level, say, of this university, this question is never asked at all. We are in education; that's a fact of life. So we can't do anything about it. These people become impervious to facts. But you just can't go on ignoring the facts.

Q. You really believe, then, that the Catholic educational system as we know it now will become more or less extinct in the next twenty-five years?

A. Certainly. In spite of the fact that our schools tend to be full all the time—our grammar schools especially—and in spite of the fact that we just go on building, the whole experiment will be defined as a failure. Or maybe not as a failure. Maybe it did what it was designed to do. But I think that a lot of people tend to make the mistake of regarding our school system as a permanent part of the ecclesiastical structure.

Q. Catholic people in this country no longer need it as a kind of self-defense mechanism?

A. That's true. It was orginally designed to accommodate the peasantry coming in from foreign countries.

Q. Didn't you make a study of California Catholics which tended to show that there was no discernible difference in religiosity between those who attended and those who did not attend Catholic schools?

A. There were some minor differences, just insignificant things.

Q. What sort of criteria did you employ?

A. I used behavior criteria first of all. Does the Catholic who goes to a Catholic school receive Communion more than the person who goes to the public school? He doesn't. Does he go to confession more often? He doesn't. Is there a greater tendency to go to church on Sunday? No. Does he obey the laws of the Church any more completely? No. Does he marry in the Church more frequently? No. Out-

of-the-Church marriage records are the same for both
groups.

Q. However, none of these criteria have much to do with
whether or not a person is truly religious.

A. I don't think it reveals whether they are truly religious
or not. Some people do. I don't. I picked out of one study
a random sample of weekly communicants and inter-
viewed them personally, trying to find out why they went
to Communion weekly. Ninety-five per cent responded,
"Because we're supposed to," which is an informal type
of legalism. And this was true of both groups, the religiously educated group and the secular-educated group.

Q. A purely utilitarian approach to Communion?

A. Yes, in terms of the way I asked the question it's utilitarian. Maybe there is something else going on which I
couldn't tap. There may be some very profound religious
reasons why people have been going to Communion on
Sunday, but I haven't been able to find them. That doesn't
mean there aren't any; it simply means I haven't been
able to find them. When you are doing a study within a
framework of trying to confirm or disconfirm a specified
hypothesis, there is a kind of rigid methodology you have
to follow. So in terms of my hypothesis and my methodology, I wasn't able to detect anything but legal reasons
for receiving Communion. But there may be others. I
don't know. I certainly hope so.

Q. Weren't your criteria largely the criteria the ecclesiastical
bureaucrats would use to identify good Catholics?

A. Of course. They promote priests who have a lot of people
in their churches going to Holy Communion. These are
the going criteria. On other things, as in attitudinal
structure studies which ask, "What is your attitude on
the Church's stand on birth control?" I again found no
differentiation.

Q. What about attitudes on race relations?

A. You see, here you are tapping a kind of a ghettoism, and

so you are tapping a negative attitude, a hands-off attitude. Here the Catholic school product came off much more poorly. The Catholic student tends to be conservative. He doesn't associate himself with those kinds of problems. Catholic students are much less aware of social problems, much less concerned with social problems. We don't find any students here at the university who are parading in marches to protest something. They are quite happy with things just as they are. It takes a tremendous amount of force to move the student body to take a stand on social questions. The Catholic, in terms of such questions—take race relations—doesn't look any different when he finishes than when he entered college. He doesn't look any different in terms of values, morality structures, attitudes toward the world around him.

Q. As a good Catholic Leftist, can you tell me, what is a religious person?

A. I would suppose that he is a person who is concerned enough with the problem of who he is and who he is becoming to bother looking, and who is reflective enough to look beneath the surface of things and to chase down the who he is and the who he is becoming to something that is more ultimate than peripheral. The religous person is one who is, darkly or lightly, seeking to find God somewhere, as the only ultimate source of meaning. Being human, he wants to understand himself, and being reflective, he wants to understand as deeply as he can. And the more he pursues the problem of understanding, the more he comes up against this ultimate reality, and it kind of makes sense out of the whole thing. He searches for ultimate meaning, not in the sense of "prime mover," or what Thomas Aquinas called the efficient cause, but as someone with whom he can relate or toward whom he can move. You can institutionalize this in any religion, it wouldn't matter. The religious Catholic is one who is trying to understand himself relative to the God of the sacraments and the God of the Church (but not of the bureaucratic Church). I think a lot of avant-garde Catholics, myself included, feel that the bureaucratic Church doesn't really believe in God, anyway. If it did it wouldn't behave the way it does. The bureaucrats are not agnostics. They just don't take a stand. They just don't bother.

Q. Is the bureaucracy in schism?

A. Cardinal McIntyre, certainly—in informal schism. He doesn't agree with the Catholic Church. He agrees with what lots of Irish-Catholic mothers of priests thought was the Catholic Church. If we are going to say that Vatican Council II represented the modern-day thinking of the Catholic Church, then those who do not agree with the *de facto* Church are in schism. It's one thing to associate yourself with the thirteenth century, but that isn't anymore; that's not a reality. It's a struggle or an event that is over. If one is to identify with the Catholic Church, then it is *this* Church, *this* now.

Q. Would you bring yourself to say the same of the American hierarchy majority?

A. Certainly a lot of them sound like McIntyre. The direction of the American hierarchical Church is toward McIntyre. I think there is more energy expended to preserve what McIntyre stands for than is expended to do the opposite. But I just don't take them seriously. You know, if you were selling Model-T Fords on Van Ness Avenue, people would laugh at you. They'd probably call the paddywagon. Catholics eventually will recognize that fact: that the Church can no longer depend on people like that, even cardinals. The Church once existed independently of the Pope.

Q. You said a religious person is one who is in search of God. Where do you look for God?

A. Oh, in my cigarette, in my friends, in the work I do. The man who says that he has found God is a fool; the man who is in search of Him is a religious person. Primarily, as a religious person myself, I try to find God by union with the physical universe of the world of man. I don't look up to heaven to find God except in the sense of a oneness I can develop with the stars out there. But I don't look for God "out there." I recognize in the God I see that there is an unmistakable transcendence, that the same God who is present to that cigarette is present to that star out there, but I am concerned with finding Him here in this real world rather than out in space someplace. And therefore I feel that the religious man is much more united to his real world than is the irreligious man. He knows that this fuller being is much closer to the world in which he lives: this dirt, these trees, that building, this freeway, this person who is living, that person who has died. He learns, after a while, to sense the reality of that which is beyond each of these things and yet which is present in all. Because I am a Catholic I happen to phrase this in terms of the sacramental presence of God. That is the viewpoint I am taking to look at the world. There are other viewpoints which are equally as religious, like the Hindu viewpoint and the Buddhist viewpoint.

Q. But as a Catholic, where do you look for direction in your search for God?

A. Well, I personally look for direction in the history of the Church. As an individual, I don't disassociate myself from its history. It is a real history. It is a real event. I find comfort in the fact that I can feel united with the Church in the search for God. But I don't rigidify it. It brings me to the Gospel and to the religious tradition of the Church—both. I think people will be exploring the meaning of the Gospel forever, because in terms of the search for a meaningful God it is a living document. It is alive, or can be made to be alive, by men who think about it. Men keep the Gospel alive by thinking about it from different cultural perspectives.

Q. What does the Gospel mean for you?

A. It means that there is a real presence of God in the world, a living, vital, evolving developing presence of God in the world.

Q. What does that mean?

A. That means that the God of whom I speak and for whom I search takes the world seriously, and affectionately, lovingly, and all that—but seriously. What I see is the seriousness of God which encases the world. So then the Gospels are revealing to me a fact of God which I may not otherwise detect, because men who live in the world don't always take their world too seriously. They blow each other up in wars, and that's not a very serious kind of confrontation. They are not taking each other too seriously as human beings. But undergirding this and transcending all these human events, there is a God who continually takes both Arabs and Israelites seriously. I suppose that the God I know from the Gospel is one who is very seriously concerned with the vindication of me and you. He wants me to be sure, unmistakably sure, that I'm worthwhile. And so He seriously affirms or vindicates my worthwhileness, in His death on the cross or in His sacramental presence over time and space. (Which is what He says in my cigarette too.) Then he is also the God I am continually forced to doubt when I see wars and conflicts and contempt and hate and death all around me.

Q. Well then, if the Christian God takes not only you, a Christian, seriously, but the Israeli and the Arab too, and everybody else, then wouldn't your God's definition of the Church be the whole human race?

A. Yes, and mine too. Everyone is potentially a Catholic. You know, potency was a very crucial word in scholastic philosophy. Potency is a reality. So everyone is potentially Catholic and some are actually members of the Catholic Church. But actualization is a juridical thing which the Church has made into too much of a problem for itself.

Q. Well then, if this is the most profound and the one real

definition of the Church of Christ, why do we need the juridical institution at all?

A. You might say that the primary insight of the American people is that it is good for men to be free. And you can ask the same question: "Since we have *already* accepted this, that it is clearly good for all men to be free, why do we have to have this juridical structure in Washington to protect freedom?" The struggle for freedom in America was a heroic and creative moment in world history. But how often in a man's life can he be a hero? How long could you or I, in real life, reel off creative and heroic moments? How many times, out of all the times you have had relations with your wife, have you been able to say, "This was really creative; now I *know* who my wife is." This is rare, isn't it? So you institutionalize, you develop habits, and you put the burden of your commitment on a routine sort of life. We just don't have the energy, I guess, to be creative at each moment of our lives. And so we have to develop institutions to carry us through from creative moment to creative moment. Looking at this in terms of a people rather than in terms of an individual man, as part of a total community our creative moments don't have to be that frequent in order to preserve the value we want to hold onto. John XXIII was the first creative moment we've had in the institutional Church since Leo XIII. But see, we have the institution to carry us over until the next creative moment comes along. We have institutions and they are a fact of life, and I think they can be helpful for us. But when they get overstructured or overinstitutionalized, they suffocate whatever it is they are structured to preserve. The institution, after all, is designed to preserve the charismatic moments. You know, you kiss your wife when you first meet her, and it's a gratifying thing to do. And you repeat this because in repeating it you gratify the person. So then after twenty years you walk in the door ready to plant the same old kiss on her. Only now she is holding up the broom, and you kiss the broom without knowing the difference. Now you need a sweeping, you see; something has to happen to break that routine (perhaps a smack on the head with the broom). And that's what we're trying to do in the Church now, which is terribly in need of a sweeping to bring her back to life again.

Q. Not long after he left the Church, Charles Davis said that he found it difficult to understand Catholics who agreed with his critique of the Church and yet remained in. Why do you remain in?

A. Why does a man stay married to an alcoholic wife? Why does a woman stay married to an alcoholic husband? Why do mothers visit murderers on death row? I guess it is an unfathomable kind of love relationship we're talking about. I think that Charles Davis was right in leaving the Church, because what he saw in the Church was not Church. It was always the ugly bureaucratic face that was Church for him. And the only other thing he saw was the theology of the Church. He never saw the other people around. I think though that now, as he continues to talk to Catholics, he will hear them say, "That's only the ugly bureaucratic face, the red-tape face, that we, too, consider unworthy because it shackles." I think he will find, as he talks to Catholics, that many of them are increasingly coming to understand that this is wrong. Then he'll find that there is a lot of compassion and a lot of human value that we seek, and that these are, in a sense, vitalized by the continuing encounter between the persons who are actual members of the Church. I don't think Davis ever saw those people in the Church who are sincerely searching for the loving vitalizers to come alive. He saw the garbage can of the Church, and I don't blame him for leaving; perhaps that's what I would do, too, if that's all I saw.

Q. Do you see as much of God in your cigarette as you do in a fellow human being? Is there a hierarchy of values here

for you? Isn't the Gospel telling us that our clearest per-
ception of God is in brother human beings?

A. Why do you think hierarchically? It's an interesting way
of thinking, but it's archaic. St. Paul says that at one
time God spoke to men through nature; later on He spoke
to them through his Son. And that's fine; that's the trace
through history. Then along came the Middle Ages, and
they made out nature as the lowest way of God speaking
to man, the prophecy testaments the second-highest way,
and through the Son the highest way. They made it
hierarchical. I don't think this is legitimate. I think St.
Paul is just recounting a historical event. To me, sometimes God is brilliantly present in a garbage can and
completely absent from the Eucharist. At other times He
will bounce out at me in the Eucharist and I don't see
Him at all in the garbage can. The great things don't have
to always be seen in some magnificent sunset. It can be
in the clouds in the sky, or it can be in some fog or in a
state of depression. Why do we have to be obsessed with
this hierarchy?

Q. But my relationship with my wife is different from my
relationship with my cigarette.

A. In both cases the relationships are a oneness, though.
This is your world. You belong here as much as any tree
belongs here. I think that the problem in trying to di-
chotomize men over against nature is that you do just
that, and you make men unnatural. It is much more appropriate for a man to understand that there are continual
meetings between himself and his world, which is non-
human and human. I don't think he can disassociate meaning with his wife from meaning with his cigarette or with
the food he had that day. It's all one meaning. True, the
heightening of what is consciousness of oneself and of
the other is greater if there is a dialogic life going on. The
I-thou can be between a cigarette and a person, but the
dialogic part is heightened when it is between persons.

My problem is that I don't understand this language that the trees are speaking. And sometimes I would rather they spoke to me in human terms—preferably English, which is my language. But trees speak to me in *their* language, and I have to tune in and pay more attention to a tree than I do to a man because I can understand a man more readily—but probably more superficially because, as we speak the same language, I don't have to think about it so much. I think I understand your writing, because I understand what the words are, but I am not sure I understand the rustling of the leaves of a tree. I have to think about that more, cause myself to focus my attention on it. Otherwise I take it for granted and don't see it at all. So I do believe that an I-thou relationship is enhanced when it is dialogic, when it is facilitated by an exchange in a common language. But that's one thing. It's another thing to say that there is this hierarchy of values, that there is more of a "thou" there than there is here.

Q. You can't have compassion for a cigarette, can you?

A. No, but cigarettes don't want compassion; they want to be burned. Compassion is a human value that structures a relationship between a man and a man. You are asking the cigarette to provoke the same kind of response from me as you do, and that's not fair to the cigarette. Some people do not provoke compassion very readily. Others don't need it. And I think in many instances in my life I have had more empathy with a tree or a rock than with some other person. I think we all experience that. It's hard to get inside a rock to see what it's really like to *be* rock. But it's also very difficult to do this with some people— especially if they are foreigners, out there in time and space somewhere. How does one understand what Aristotle really felt about his students? You don't know from reading his words; his words are very abstract. I think that I have a better feeling for what it's like to be a tree than what it's like to be Aristotle. My imagination tells

me what it's like to be Aristotle, but it's all fantasy. I
don't know. But that tree is living, breathing. It's shooting
forth its leaves. I can see that it is fructifying; it is expending energy in order to be seen. And that's rather easy
for me. Aristotle I can't really see.

Q. How do you translate the word "grace" into the concrete
order of things?

A. All those words are interesting words, and I assent to
those propositional words as propositional words. But I
don't have to use the word "grace" in order to convey a
modality, or to try to converse with you about a modality
in my relationship with God. But if you insist, I would
try to think about grace as being brought to bear on me.
I have an experience with grace, or I call grace, a piece of
experience that I have when I am alive. It's that piece
which I refer to as vitality or life. When I am most alive
or most vitalized or most stimulated relative to a face or
a dimension of you that I had maybe not seen before, or
a face or a dimension of God that I had not seen before, I
call that source of vitality grace. But I don't use the word.
It's when someone comes in, someone I just don't like,
and I sit there and try to perceive in that person whatever
it is that God perceived (and turned him on), and try to
understand "Now how come God loves this person?"
and suddenly I see something. Now, *I* did the seeing, and
I attribute that to myself. But I have the experience of
someone kicking me in the fanny, if you will, but not to *do*
what I do for myself; I take the responsibility for what I
do or don't do. Making me to be so that I can do this, I'll
call that grace. I'm sitting in my room, worn out, and
somebody comes to the parlor for me and wants some
help, and I think about it and I don't really want to go.
Then I have to ask myself, "Isn't there something in that
person that I am not seeing?" And then I have to think
about it so I personally will see it. The energy that I need
to think about it I can refer to as grace.

Q. Is it extrinsic to you?

A. The *source* of the vitality as I experience it is extrinsic to
me.

Q. But doesn't this do something to your freedom? Isn't this
a coercive thing?

A. Yes, it does do something to my freedom. It enhances it.
It frees me from fatigue and boredom. You see, if *you*
think about freedom in that neat, little scholastic way, *I*
think about freedom in another way. I tend to think of
freedom as the power I have of transcending myself, the
de facto energy that is going to energize my power to
transcend myself. And if I do transcend myself, commit
myself to something over space and time, then I am being
most free. That's what "truth shall make you free" means
to me. You are the Truth; it is You who liberates me,
You who makes me to be so that You can liberate me—
and this person who makes me to be, we call God. Freedom, then, is not a question of choosing between alterna-
tives. That's the superficial, rationalistic freedom. Freedom is the power a man has to make a commitment that
transcends time and space. When you said "I do" to your
wife and bound yourself to this particular jail for life,
that was your most free moment.

Q. At the risk of sounding like a crabbed old scholastic again,
how would you translate the Catholic teaching on the
afterlife, in terms of heaven and hell?

A. Actually I don't spend twenty minutes a year thinking
about hell. If you want me to, I'll force myself and say
that hell is a phenomenon that witnesses to the dramatic
freedom of man to say "no" to God. So that if I am going
to say that I am free, I am going to have to ask, "how
free?" If I want to say that I am totally free, then I have
the power of total negation, and I'll call that the actualization and power of hell.

Q. Do you believe that you are that totally free?

A. Yes, I do. I demand it because I want to be that free. I

want to be free enough to explore anything. If the opportunity isn't there, then I'm not free. The moment I deny hell to myself then I've blown it, I'm not free. I like to keep it there because it reminds me of how free I really am.

As for heaven, first of all, as a becoming kind of being it is difficult to think about oneself as ever getting finished. As soon as I start thinking about myself as getting finished, I get bored. For example, if my mind were suddenly to say to itself, "You have thought your last good thought, you don't think anymore," I'd be bored to death. (Dull people are people who have stopped thinking.) Since that is who I am now, I cannot conceive of a state of life in which I have become perfect, so I don't think about heaven as that state of perfection which the scholastics constructed: "The actualization of all potentialities." If I am no longer potent I am finished.

Q. Let me stop you there for a second. If you can't achieve this perfection, then how can you achieve that which is the total antithesis of this?

A. I think that negation is as unfinished as affirmation.

Q. And therefore, you don't go along with the hell of the scholastics either.

A. No, because it was built on a false cosmology. But I think there is a hell in the sense that I can get caught up in a process of negation which will be irreversible. That's how much freedom I have to have. And I can get caught up in a process of becoming that will be irreversible and eternal. I think heaven and hell are only ways of talking about ultimate outcomes for man. I am a person who will not have any ultimate outcome; I will be becoming forever. When I die, the adventure of my life will be only beginning. All the people I wanted to know I will begin to meet without a lot of barriers, like the simple time barrier that separates me now from Alexander the Great. I have to die to see him. And in this affirmative world that I choose to live in I will see him; that's a belief.

Q. Where will you see him?

A. I don't know. Certainly there is no other universe for me, so it will have to be in this world. Why would I want to disassociate myself? Why would I have to? What good would it do? You might say heaven is the permanency of man, the permanency of his power to affirm, to commit, to be free. The scholastics talk about states of being; that means nothing. I can conceive of God, I can use the term "God is perfect," and in the negative sense I can understand what I'm saying; but I don't see how man can be perfected or completed. We'll be growing forever. Our eschatology has been so stupid and so superficial and so static and so juridical.

9

THE CRISES OF CHANGE

The American Catholic Church has been in major crises ever since it began to feel the impact of what might have been the universal Church's most significant charismatic moment since Jesus Christ: Roncalli's papacy. To some they are good crises—positive, liberating. It is the way to a more personally experienced faith, hope, and charity. It is a sincere quest for honesty, a time of purgation and repentance. It is a descendancy into the soul's deepest regions for re-examination and discovery; it is the desire for rebirth. It is the beginning of a renewed proclamation of an Incarnational Gospel which bridges the gap between the sacred and profane. It is a challenge to the world to reflect on the real basis of the Christian movement itself: God's universal salvific will, man's universal brotherhood, the challenge of Love:

Every Francis-like saint has a great message for his age. Pope John's, it seems to me was this: it is good to be a man. For a tired, pessimistic, unhappy world he served as a living illustration that the Lord he believed in came not to deny life but to make it more abundant. . . .

He was a quiet, gentle revolutionary, this Pope, whose dynamite—as might have been expected of another Saint Francis—was faith, hope, and charity. In an age of despair, he boldly suggested happy endings, whether he was talking about a divided Christianity or a war-threatened world. Half the world

called him Holy Father; to the other half, he made it clear that
whether or not they would have him for a spiritual father, he
would take them for brothers. "I am Joseph, your brother,"
Angelo Giuseppe Roncalli told a group of Jewish visitors. "They
tell me you are an atheist," he told Mr. Khrushchev's son-in-law,
"but surely you will accept an old man's blessing for your children."

Always the Pope saw beyond the theological, ideological, or
political barrier and struck directly at the person. I never heard
of a single man or woman whose ideology was invulnerable to
this sweet wound. This much at least, then, he taught the world,
that behind all the trappings of the "systems," truths and errors
that make modern history, with its cruelties and its wars, are
human beings. He was not the first Catholic theologian to distinguish between error and the person who accepts error nor
was he the first to insist that no man is as good or as bad as his
principles. But he was the first I can remember who made that
simple, almost obvious proposition credible as Catholic teaching. Pope John from the beginning, stepped out of the shadows
of the Inquisition that has darkened the view of the Catholic
Church for, oh so long, for so many modern men. (John Cogley,
"Another Saint Francis?" *Commonweal,* June 28, 1963)

For others it is not a good crisis—perhaps because it is
too humanizing. The notion that the priest has not really
been endowed with the power of easy insight into every
human problem, nor the wisdom to provide swift, sure
"Catholic" solutions thereto (the express claim of popular
moralist writings until the Johannine era), is unsettling. The
idea of a God who will tirelessly and benevolently respond to
regimental offerings of gifts of extrinsic glory is too deeply
imbedded in the "rock" to be rooted out in a generation. The
parochialism of a private salvation system is not at once
ready to make room for all those others. The transition from
the rarefied air of triumphalism into the denser atmosphere
of a pilgrim church appears breathtakingly risky—too ad-
venturous. The tight hold on "absolute truth" is jealously
guarded.

We know only too well that the "opening of the windows," as
Pope John expressed it, has had some weird results. What concerns us especially is the danger of injuring the traditional,
sturdy confidence of our people in their faith. Extreme ecumenical writers ask us to soften the concept of heresy. Extreme
modern theologians ask us to soften the concept of sin. Extreme
liturgists ask us to minimize devotion to Mary and the saints.
What aggravates the situation is that the extremist always has
a good press coverage. Unfortunately, too, some of the articles
appearing in so many magazines, supposedly Catholic, remind
us of the words of Hamlet: "The time is out of joint;—O cursed
spite/That ever I was born to set it right!" (James E. Kearney,
as Bishop of Rochester, 1965)

Do not permit your faith to be weakened by writers, be they
priests, religious or lay, who in their enthusiasm for the new,
the modern, lose sight of the teaching of Christ and His Church.
Their enthusiasm is not founded on humility and God's help,
but rather on personal ambition and desire to be the first to
adopt all that is new and destroy all that is old. These authors
of confusion are Christian believers as well as unbelievers. They
are Catholic as well as non-Catholic . . . they seek publicity
and headlines and are tyrannical in their condemnation of those
who might disagree. They speak of freedom but admit none
unless it conforms with their terms; they preach charity but
fail to practice it when confronted with opposition; they wish
everyone to accept their terms of peace and justice but acknowledge no authority except their personal opinions; they attempt
to destroy all that is ancient and sacred and replace it with
what is modern and secular. They even anticipate the mind and
thoughts of the Holy Father, the Bishops and the Council, and
rebel in their license which destroys. They have found their
loud and influential way into the Catholic press as well as the
general press. (Albert R. Zuroweste, Bishop of Belleville, Ill.,
in a 1967 "Year of Faith" sermon, *Belleville Messenger*)

Central to the tensions is the entire concept of authority
in the Church, both teaching and disciplinary. Issues surrounding the former cut the deepest. The traditional understanding holds that the Church teaches authoritatively on

two levels: infallibly, or extra ordinarily, and non-infallibly, or ordinarily. In the present crisis most of the internal turmoil and anxiety is concentrated in areas embraced by the lower level of authority—the ordinary magisterium. It is here, rather than on the formal, doctrinal level, that the real-life problems of man are sifted, interpreted, legislated, and "solved." Modern Catholics who worry every day over what it means to be a Catholic are far less preoccupied with the vagaries of the infallibly pronounced doctrine of the Assumption [1] than with the ordinary magisterium's body of intrusions, legislations, precepts, and sanctions on questions of day-to-day morality. The dogmatic formulation lies somewhere "out there," unrelated to real life, remote—"whatever that means!" But only the apathetic can feel untouched by ecclesiastical attitudes toward marriage, birth control, race relations, nuclear weaponry, just or unjust war, abortion, divorce, priestly celibacy, economic and social justice, and so on. Before the age of renewal and reform, the institutional moralists did their utmost to blur the distinction between the infallible and the ordinary, an effort most vividly apparent in the birth control controversy.

In this instance, the stress was not on "What does this mean? Why have two Popes categorically denounced artificial contraception as immoral?" but rather, "Into which category of teaching authority does the condemnation fall?" Any interested Catholic married couple who felt a need for consulting the authorities could find their very real problems discussed in such terms as found in the following exchange between American Catholic moral theologians:

There were some who considered this solemn declaration an *ex cathedra* definition: but this is not clear. Others see here a truth infallibly proposed, inasmuch as it is authentically stated that there is question of a *doctrina in Ecclesia semper tradita.*

---

[1] Promulgated in 1950 by Pius XII: "The Immaculate Mother of God, Mary ever Virgin, after her life on earth, was assumed, body and soul, to the glory of heaven."

But this interpretation is not convincing either. Let us say rather: we have here such a solemn authentic declaration, renewing previous decisions, and thereafter confirmed again and again, that one who is unwilling to admit it sins against the virtue of faith, although he does not lose the faith. (Joseph Fuchs, S.J., quoted in John C. Ford, S.J., and Gerald Kelly, S.J., *Contemporary Moral Theology*. Westminster, Md.: Newman Press, 1963, Vol. II)

To which comes the reply:

One might reasonably ask whether Fr. Fuchs merely wishes to assert that the Church's repudiation of contraception is not clearly *"de fide credenda"* or whether he wishes to deny it all infallibility, even as a truth *"de fide tenenda."* To be certain about his meaning one would have to know whether he accepts or rejects the theological note, *"de fide ecclesiastica."* At any rate, those authors who give that note could say just what Fr. Fuchs says, namely, that one who refuses to accept the Church's teaching sins against the faith but is not a heretic. (*Ibid.* [The reply is that of authors Ford and Kelly])

Obviously these exercises had little relevance to the real live couple trying to formulate a conscientious position on contraception. Nor was it, in the view of the authorities, important that they did:

The Catholic, therefore, must internally accept this doctrine as true and must externally conform to it, even to the extent of heroism—as is actually the case in many difficult marital circumstances. And for Catholic living, this internal conviction and external conformity is enough; *it is not necessary to know why the Church teaches that contraception is intrinsically immoral* [italics added]. (*Ibid.*)

Recently, a venerable, but confused, priest—who had just come around, however reluctantly, to solving the confessional contraception problems of his penitents with the advice, "Follow your own best instincts"—asked me in unfeigned anguish: "What is the ordinary magisterium of the Church, anyway?" My answer was that he should abandon his flirtation with a question that was becoming more and more irrelevant and not allow himself to be tortured further by a nonproblem. He should come to understand that the term itself is in the process of abandonment. He should see the capacity of a hierarchy to make authoritative pronouncements on contemporary moral problems as limited by the extent to which it is willing to participate with the larger community (upper case Church) in the arduous, evolutionary process of developing new insights and fresh wisdom into the problem of life and the destiny of man.

I suggest that this answer is more or less representative of the attitudes of the American radical Catholicism within the meaning of this book.

On August 29, 1966, Donald J. Thorman, publisher of the *National Catholic Reporter,* spoke well for the layman's "new wave" in an address before the National Newman Congress in Dallas. The American bishops, enmeshed in their web of authoritarianism, were incapable of communicating with Catholic people who no longer are

. . . willing to accept their religious values and beliefs unthinkingly and uncritically. . . . [Vatican II] created the conditions which have encouraged men to re-examine many of their beliefs and—most important—their fundamental attitudes. As a result, for the first time American Catholics are seriously questioning their most basic and most cherished beliefs. And because their religious education in the past taught them primarily rote answers to rote questions, they are face-to-face with the possibility of unbelief in their lives. . . . [Yet,] most people in authority have no real face-to-face, "I-thou" relationship with the members of their flock who are undergoing the throes of unbelief. It underscores again the scandal of lack of communication within the Church. Even before they faced unbelief, these Catholics often had no real means of genuinely communicating with those in authority, the guardians of the faith, and now that they are in a state of personal crisis they often are looking outside the official Church for answers. As one person told me: "I simply couldn't stand another form answer right out of the apologetics or theology text. These people don't even know what my problem is and so they look wildly around trying pre-packaged answers to questions I'm not asking."

With admirable perspicacity Thorman contends that "no single class of people, as a group, understand less of what is going on in the Church today than the bishops." Catholics, traditionally, "desire to play it safe. . . . We have avoided taking stands and instead have been comfortable Christians, busying ourselves with all the minor details, but unwilling to confront the major issues." In an age well prepared to ignore (or laugh at) any religion which cannot relate itself to humanity in crisis, is it any wonder that a Catholicism "willing to let 'authority' substitute for our own religious commitment" is particularly vulnerable to the crisis of unbelief? Moreover:

This has led to a major crisis in the American Catholic Church —the magnitude of which is hardly even recognized. Namely, the increasing loss of young adults who have measured the Church and found us wanting. They have found us to be phonies. The prelate who mouths official pious platitudes about poverty, but who lives in glorious aristocratic splendor. The pastor who is too busy with fund-raising to relate to the financially and spiritually poor of his parish. The religious who bray about poverty while living in lifetime economic security. The mother and father who are daily or weekly communicants but who throw rocks (verbally and literally) at civil rights marching nuns or priests. We have failed to give more than lip service to the message of the Gospel. The fact is that most of us today don't even know what the message of the Word is, since we have obfuscated it with legalisms and highly rationalistic apologetics.
    Young people today (and here I would even include chronologically older persons who are looking for the first time at the Church with young eyes), have a ring-side seat of all the exciting and vital movements within our society. And they see that the Church of Christ—apart from the official documents which are always quoted at them—stands virtually speechless in the face of the modern world. The People of God stand actionless before

the escalating events of our times. They see that Christianity often seems to have no more and sometimes even less to say of relevance concerning the world than the secular humanist. (*The National Catholic Reporter*)

Within a week of Donald Thorman's address, Father Daniel Berrigan, S.J., spoke equally well for the "new wave" of clerics (present and to come) at the annual Northeast Seminarians' Conference held in Albany, New York:

We would like to be allowed to be men. We do not want our lives suffocated by methods of control, methods which are horrifyingly reminiscent of what Paul calls the dominations and powers of this world. We do not wish to become parts of systems of power and privilege and exemption. We do not wish to be silenced in the name of ecclesiastical safety, or to be forbidden the love which is the first instinct of our heart. We wish simply that the Church would simply bless our determination to be human beings and leave us alone. (*The National Catholic Reporter*)

"Leave us alone." If you do not wish to prophesy, to heal, to offer yourselves as leaven, to bind up wounds, to understand, to seek empathy with others, to speak as men and to speak for man, to reconcile, to identify with a world Incarnate, then in the name of Jesus Christ, leave us alone to do His work.

Better still, join us. Let the age of transition be as short-lived as possible. Let us cease now our endless quibbling, our exercises in semantics over the "nature" of ecclesiastical authority—pope alone, pope and bishops, bishops alone, bishop alone. Millions of dollars and millions of man-hours were expended in organizing and carrying out the Vatican II debates. Decrees were formulated and promulgated. But to what avail, if the apparent spirit of the words continues to run far ahead of the spirit of the framers? New levels of educational and communications standards have altered irrevocably the American Catholic's approach to faith. No longer possible is a faith that is sustained by the kind of reverence

for the man of Orders which gives him unlimited credit for
"knowing more than we do" (the notion of his access via a
mysterious pipeline to some sort of "final proof"—never sat-
isfactorily articulated, but nevertheless real, "or why would
he ever remain what he is?"). The God so painstakingly
constructed by the scholastics has fallen apart. He is quite
dead and buried, along with His standard paraphernalia.

The Church is facing the task of working out a harmoni-
ous relationship with what John Cogley has described as a
"post-Christendom era":

I don't think it will be a post-Christian era. It may in fact be
the greatest of all Christian eras. Maybe we will finally come
into the full Christian realization of what it means to render
unto Caesar what is Caesar's. "Christendom" as a concept is
dying. . . . In one way or another the bishops (at Vatican II)
are saying "Christendom is dead. Fellows, what are we going
to do about it?" . . . How is the Church to relate itself to the
"post-Christendom" era? What structural changes are necessary? What reforms are necessary? What changes in attitudes
are necessary? What changes in discipline are necessary?
("Looking Back, Looking Ahead," *Commonweal*, November 20,
1964)

Vatican II held out the promise, at least, that the Catholic
Church was poised and ready to contribute mightily to the
work of constructing what "may in fact be the greatest of all
Christian eras." But with at least one foot firmly imbedded
in the old era, the question is still open: Will the Catholic
Church once again be dragged through time kicking and
screaming, or will she have repented sufficiently to pick up
the momentum of her brightest moment in centuries and
move ahead of the times, out of the mainstream, putting on
the yoke, daring to be different, according to the "hard
sayings" of her own Gospel?

Will the tightly held institutional rein of a Patrick
Cardinal O'Boyle (Washington, D.C.) be the pace setter?
In a sermon given at St. Matthew's Cathedral, July 9, 1967,
O'Boyle says:

Religion has always had its enemies. Mostly they were easy to recognize, and most of them came from without. Today the enemies of the Catholic Church, in particular, are more likely to come from within. Driven at times by intellectual pride, unable to adjust to an age that is impatient of all virtues save its own concept of freedom, they are victims of the cancer of doubt which is the forerunner of complete loss of faith.

Or a Bishop Dwyer (Reno, Nevada), who scolds the avant-garde for:

. . . an insistence upon an immediate purification, a thorough housecleaning. . . . So we are to achieve overnight that reconciliation of the sacred and the secular which has eluded every age up to now (and may, actually, be the Forbidden Fruit); we are to reassess the whole tradition of the Church in the light of the most rigid (even Jansenistic) standards of contemporary relevance; we are to leap headlong into the New Age (the 21st Century?) long before anybody else, so as to be there before-hand with our "I told you so!" (Quoted in "Issues that divide the Church, Final Position Papers, *The National Catholic Reporter,* March 22, 1967)

Or a Brent Bozell, editor of the "archtraditionalist, conservative" Catholic magazine *Triumph:*

The Christian who urges the Church to come to terms with *this* world, with *this* age (and that is what most of the nervous chatter about "relevance" comes down to), is either a victim of despair, or has ceased to be a Christian at all. (*The National Catholic Reporter*)

(These words are reminiscent of a phrase Bozell's brother-in-law, William F. Buckley, Jr., keeps at hand in his bag of debater's tricks: "Who knows, some day God may simply clear his throat.")

Is the eminent Paulist priest-psychologist, Father Arthur F. LeBlanc, an "enemy from within"?

Mental unhealth will increase among the clergy "in proportion to unmeaningful behavior," he predicted. In an era of change in the Church—and with an older generation of superiors re-

quiring obedience "to the will of God"—there is widespread
clergy restiveness, according to Father LeBlanc. Young priests
are questioning the "meaningfulness" not only of "putting oil
on someone who's dead" but they are asking, "What is the will
of God? Who know the will of God?" At this point, "obedience
is finished," he continued.

Father LeBlanc also spoke of widespread confusion among
laymen on birth control. If Pope Paul doesn't change the traditional Church teaching against artificial birth prevention, he
said: "There will be a great exit of priests who are intellectually
convinced that the natural law argument is crazy." The high
degree of concern among American Catholics with the issue,
he said, stems from a "compulsive Irish concern" with, and
opposition to, sexuality. Father LeBlanc hoped the papal commission's report to the Pontiff did not specifically stress the
birth control "pill" and its usage. It should have been concerned
with the "goodness of sensuality," he said. (Quoted in Jo-ann
Price, "A Psychologist Looks at the Church," *The National
Catholic Reporter,* August 31, 1966)

Is Rosemary Ruether [2] guilty of "intellectual pride, unable
to adjust to an age that is impatient of all virtues save its
own concept of freedom"?

. . . if I happen, as I do, to consider Luther's understanding
of grace to be considerably more profound than that of Trent,
I see no reason to think this a forbidden position. In the actual
give and take of theological discussion, I simply discover that
the "guidance" of the Church on what to think is no very tenable
guide, and in the last analysis one is thrown on one's own wits,
uncertain lights as these may be. A good Benedictine friend is
constantly choking with astonishment at this fact, and asking
me how I can possibly assume that my own "poor reason" is
better than the infallible guidance of the Church. This is one
of those assertions which is at one and the same time unanswer-
able, and utterly useless. What do you do with the "infallible
guidance of the Church" when, in fact, your "poor reason" leads
you to disagree with some position or other? Do you practice
double-think? Pretend you really don't disagree? Obviously

---

[2] Catholic writer, holder of a doctorate in religion from Claremont Graduate School (Calif.) and member of the faculty of Howard University.

there can be no honest course but to pursue this disagreement to the deepest understanding possible, and what guide does one have for this but one's "poor reason"? Poor it may be, but I have come to believe that it is, in the last analysis, the best we have, and we had better begin to use it.

When these "Catholic ready answers" prove to provide no answers at all, then there is really no alternative but to go beyond them and to cease to be bound by them.

We have felt the intimations of a new Pentecost and have rejoiced, but I feel that the Spirit must come with might and power to resurrect our spirits and, in the words of Paul to the Hebrews, "purge our hearts of dead works to serve the living God." (Quoted in "Catholicism and Catholicity," in *Generation of the Third Eye,* ed. Daniel Callahan. New York: Sheed & Ward, 1965)

The present church discipline on divorce is intolerable. . . . The traditional ecclesiastical discipline on marriage has become untenable because it no longer has anything to do with the present social reality of marriage. Stemming from a period when marriage was really a public institution, it views the marital bond in legal terms and not in interpersonal terms. . . . When, in the process of counseling, the possibility for authentic relationship appears so lacking that no viable future for the couple is in sight, then the guidance should be directed, not to forcing the couple to remain together, but rather toward breaking the bonds of egoism and mutual accusation with which the partners seek to clothe themselves and making them face truthfully the personal responsibility for the failure. If serious church discipline really operated in these two areas, it would be possible, with no loss of seriousness toward the marriage relationship, to drop altogether the present casuistry of remarriage, and allow anyone to remarry within the church who, having really come to terms with their previous failure and their potential for a good relationship with the new partner, seems capable of starting afresh in an authentic way. (Rosemary Ruether, "Divorce: No Longer Unthinkable," *Commonweal,* April 14, 1967)

Is Sister M. Charles Borromeo's [3] concern for "relevance" merely part of a chorus of "nervous chatter," a sign of one

[3] Professor of theology at St. Xavier College, Chicago.

who is either a "victim of despair" or who "has ceased to be
a Christian"?

The man who has genuinely surrendered to Christ turns to the
loving service of the persons he contacts. He can no longer
be satisfied with mere financial support for an organized Church
which supposedly does his charity for him. Once he knows that
the apostolate is not merely impersonal membership in a large
project, he cannot but evaluate and criticize the organizations
to which he previously belonged. . . . The Christian must love
and serve, and he must serve genuine human needs. Therefore
he must allow to die any of the forms of previous service which
are now outmoded and escapist. . . . The final quality of the
postconciliar Christian is his healing the old dualism between
body and soul, matter and spirit, Church and world. He knows
that man is a bodied spirit, that he makes his world by coopera-
tive effort with others, that the Church is that part of the world
that has found its meaning. This attitude is the opposite of the
old stress on baptizing the world, consecrating it in the sense
of lifting things and persons out of their natural setting and
bringing them somehow "into the Church." Rather today's Christian is . . . conscious not only of Christ and of his love, but
of Christ's love for each thing and person in their uniqueness.
. . . As Christians live more fully out of personal love and
service of Christ in man, they will surely affect the economic,
cultural and political societies and institutions in which they
operate. The great movements of our times are pointed toward
human betterment whether through civil rights, the establishment of new nations, work for aid to underdeveloped nations, or
the alleviation of world poverty and overpopulation. The Council,
as well as the encyclicals of Pope John, have made clear the
obligations of the Christian to take part in some way in these
human efforts at growth and progress. Far from standing aside
and criticizing projects done by non-Christians, such efforts
should be viewed today as the signs of the Spirit at work in
the human race. The building of ever more just and human
cities is man's basic task in Christ in our times. The tragedy
of the Churches would be to avoid this task in favor of mere
preservation of religious practices or religiously owned insti-

tutions. ("A World Come of Age in Christ," *Worship in the City of Man,* Proceedings of the Twenty-seventh North American Liturgical Week Conference. Washington, D.C.: The Liturgical Conference, 1966)

I may be counted among those Catholics who believe that what is at stake here is inextricably bound up with the kind of future mankind plots for itself, perhaps for centuries to come. The true believer *knows* that he is constantly choosing, not between the world and Christ, but, as Thomas Merton has put it, "choosing the world as it really is in Him, that is to say created and redeemed by Him, and encountered in the ground of our own personal freedom and of our love." It is the discovery of the real world (of Christ) from the depths of our own being, the discovery, as Merton says,

. . . of our own inner ground. This "ground, this world" where I am mysteriously present at once to my own self and to the freedoms of all other men, is not a visible objective and determined structure with fixed laws and demands. *It is a living and self-creating mystery of which I am myself a part, to which I am myself my own unique doer.* . . . the habitual and mechanical compulsions of a certain limited type of Christian thought have falsified the true value-perspective in which the world can be discovered and chosen as it is. To treat the world merely as an agglomeration of material goods and objects outside ourselves, and to reject these goods and objects in order to seek others which are "interior" and "spiritual" is in fact to miss the whole point of the challenging confrontation of the world and Christ. . . .

Do we really renounce ourselves and the world in order to find Christ, or do we renounce our alienated and false selves in order to choose our own deepest truth in choosing both the world and Christ at the same time? If the deepest ground of my being is love, then in that very love itself and nowhere else will I find myself, *and* the world, *and* my brother *and* Christ. It is not a question of either/or but of all-in-one. It is not a matter of exclusivism and "purity" but of wholeness, wholeheartedness, unity. . . .

Such root-Christian notions are understandably scary to an institutional authoritarian figure mentality even yet conditioned by the Church's historical position in the Holy Roman Empire, committed to a world view admirably sketched by Merton:

. . . We are living in the last age of salvation history. A world radically evil and doomed to hell has been ransomed from the devil by the Cross of Christ and is now simply marking time until the message of salvation can be preached to everyone. . . . Meanwhile, men being evil and prone to sin . . . must be prevented by authority from following their base instincts and getting lost.

They cannot be left to their own freedom or even to God's loving grace. . . . They have to be told at every step what to do, and it is better if what they are told to do is displeasing to their corrupt natures, for this will keep them out of further subtle forms of mischief. [How often have I heard a moral theologian, defending this or that moral dictum, say—with his back to the wall—"But if we allow them to do *this* then before long they will want to do *that*."] Meanwhile the Empire has become, provisionally at least, holy. As figure of the eschatological kingdom, worldly power consecrated to Christ becomes Christ's reign on earth . . . the Christian prince is a guarantee against complete chaos and disorder and must be submitted to—to resist established authority is equivalent to resisting Christ. ("Is the World a Problem?" *Commonweal*, June 3, 1966)

On October 12, 1965, Father John L. McKenzie, S.J., one of the American Church's best-known scripture scholars, made it painfully clear in a meeting of the Canon Law Society of America (held in Chicago) that, in his scriptual view, to imagine that the Christian way of life can be codified in law is a denial of the teachings of Jesus. He spoke out against a system of ecclesiastical law which attempts to regulate life itself and stifle individual freedom: "The obligation which does not involve love is not a Christian moral obligation. Love is ultimately the only imperative in the Gospel." And he warned the Church's legal experts to be mindful of the dangers of producing harmful effects with overlegislation that inhibits the pursuit of personal good and places road-blocks in the path of personal fulfillment. Church law, he said, should be limited to the area of Church business.

These samplings have been chosen as illustrative of the root-problem cause of most of the internal tensions currently bedeviling the American Catholic Church and the resultant unfortunate image of a Church divided into opposing camps. However unfortunate the image, the root Catholic cannot dismiss what he *knows:* that the world *needs,* desperately, to experience, consciously, its God-given sacral character. The root Catholic's faith in his Christian mission as an instrument of universal, incarnational self-awareness and his hope for some measure of achievement do not spark his impulses toward charity; rather, they flow from charity. His patience is most severely tested by institutional appeals to original sin, which seem to imply, in their fundamentalist way, that nothing ever can be done here and now, that man's corruption is unassailable; or as Bishop Dwyer explained with a touch of sarcasm: "So we are to achieve overnight that reconciliation of the sacred and the secular which has eluded every age up to now (and may, actually, be the Forbidden Fruit)." [4]

In a recent book two members of the Fordham faculty opined: "In twenty-five years, we shall not recognize the Roman Catholic Church in America." [5] That the process has already set in should be evident even to the casual observer. However a trip through the pages of the *National Catholic Reporter*—itself something new on the American Catholic scene—is even more revealing.

The *National Catholic Reporter,* a lay-published and -edited weekly Catholic newspaper, was born in October, 1964, in Kansas City, Missouri. The product has been— minor quibbling excepted—a positive source of joy to most

[4] See above, p. 137.
[5] Edward Wakin and Father Joseph F. Scheuer, *The De-Romanization of the American Catholic Church.* New York: Macmillan, 1966.

radical Catholic hearts. The journalism is excellent. Editorially *NCR* is four-square against the Vietnam War; for civil rights and social justice now; existential religion; the enlightenment of the American hierarchy; a meaningful liturgical experience and freedom of thought and expression in an open-style Church. Uninhibited by ecclesiastical censorship, it covers the Catholic newsbeat like a blanket. It also manages to retain a sense of humor, while sometimes scolding and sometimes kidding the pants off the American Church Establishment. A weekly feature, "Cry Pax" ("a column without rules"), consists largely of a priceless collection of fillers lifted from clerical sermons, episcopal rumblings, parish bulletins, and the like, accompanied by spicy editorial notes which remind the reader that even *aggiornamento* can be fun:

A recent issue of a publication called *Roses and Gold* from Our Lady of the Ozarks, published by the Oblate Fathers of Mary Immaculate at Carthage, Mo., contains this one: "Please publish my thanks to the Sacred Heart, the Infant Jesus of Prague and to the Blessed Mother for many favors received, among them the obtaining of auto driver's license for my nephew, who has very, very poor vision. His business was dependent on his ability to drive his car."

Mrs. L. S.

(*Residents of North Carolina are warned to watch out for a devout nephew with thick glasses. Residents of heaven are asked to stop kidding auto license inspectors.*)

Pastor's announcement at a parish PTA meeting in Omaha: "Feel free to come and discuss these matters with me and I am sure that in the end you will wind up doing what you were told to do in the first place."

From the parish bulletin of St. Joseph's church, Grafton, Wis., Feb. 26: "NO MASS STIPENDS: The answer is no scheduled Masses. We have exactly 33 stipends left. . . . If we have to use our own intentions, we'll also choose our own time to say the daily Mass. From the last four funerals we received

12 stipends all told. What happened to the rest? If you don't supply us with the daily stipends, there will be no daily announced Masses from Easter Sunday on."

(*No payee, no prayee.*)

From a September bulletin of Holy Name Cathedral, Chicago: "The most thrilling day in August was the 24th—the day of the installation of our new archbishop. We at the Cathedral were doubly blessed by being so deeply involved in the preparations for his coming. We watched the Cardinal red disappear to make way for Episcopal green. Do you know how many samples of green we looked at? Over 100 different shades and finally Monsignor Hayes picked the bright emerald green which is on the throne. Our rug man had to send to the East for the green carpet for the throne. . . ."

(*Isn't it wonderful to be a Catholic? We have such beautiful green thrones!*)

In addition to performing an outstanding reportorial service, *NCR* prints signed articles by religion commentators and scholars, Catholic and otherwise, from all the relevant disciplines, and it contains a generous "letters" section, open to the widest possible range of opinion, from grass-roots man-in-the-pew to learned academician. Many priests find this a convenient way of avoiding the ecclesiastical censor's ax, on the grounds that a letter (they are often extremely long) does not fall under the provisions of canon law requiring censorship of writings dealing in ". . . Scriptures, sacred theology, ecclesiastical history, canon law, natural theology, ethics, or other religious or moral subjects of this kind" (John A. Abbo and Jerome D. Hannon, *The Sacred Canons.* St. Louis: Herder Book Co., 1952, Vol. II).

The *National Catholic Reporter* is an important event in American Catholic life, chiefly because of its unique position as a Catholic newspaper fulfilling a commitment to publish all the Catholic news, in freedom. There is no dearth of Catholic newspaper-publishing enterprises. Every diocese in the country is involved in either the publication or circulation of a weekly Catholic newspaper. Taken as a whole it is a fairly large industry. But for the most part, the product is little more than a local bishop's house organ, controlled by reportorial and editorial policymakers trained to keep one eye cocked in the direction of the bishop. Although there is a current trend in such publications to report, side by side, conflicting points of view within the Church, to veteran Catholic press man John O'Connor, [6] the dialogue is phony:

It is an error, I believe, to subscribe to the idea of one "side" versus another—in the traditional military formations. This view tries for some sort of "balance"—a favorite word among the *timid*. This balance is reflected in the choice of safe personnel, in evenly stacking committees . . . or in selecting news for a diocesan organ based on so many stories for this side, so many stories for the other side. This gives the illusion of dialogue, but it is not. Rather than a side-by-side moving of the Church into the modern era, it appears to me that an advance guard of the Church has penetrated the modern world and is pursuing dialogue there. Much—undoubtedly most—of the pilgrim Church straggles behind, strung out like a wagon train. The differences among the disputants are surely a matter of point of view; some look backward, some see ahead, and most are just all confused by the clatter and dust around them. To proceed with the figure, this people on pilgrimage won't move without leadership—and the leadership can't be in the middle! This is precisely where much of the so-called leadership of the American Church has been and is: mulling around in the herd, clanking the cooking utensils and holding tight to the administrative reins when they should be out front—way out front. . . . The Church's vertical lines of authority aren't channeled for proper, open dialogue. You don't dialogue with an absolute monarch—and up until the present revolution that is what we have had. . . . I am convinced that the public issues of the Church deserve a public hearing. And even if I didn't, the editors of the wire services, the national news and picture maga-

[6] Former editor of *The Monitor* (San Francisco) and *Dialog* (Wilmington).

zines and the Madison Avenue book publishers do. The Church is news today, and I believe we should thank God for that. . . . I believe we must risk the scandal of controversy—precisely to avoid the "scandal of silence," the scandal of the pathetic gesture, the scandal of hypocrisy. Above all, we should avoid the scandal of the phony dialogue—confined to a policed press or to polite meetings in the chancery. We need the world's public opinion in the act, and the world needs to know our agony. ("Controversy Within the Church," *America,* April 9, 1966)

NCR has not failed to perceive (indeed to become part of) the "advance guard of the Church" penetrating the modern world in the pursuit of real dialogue, the impotency of a "leadership" caught in the "middle," and the "scandal of the phony dialogue."

"What, in the name of God, is going on in the Catholic Church?" "What the Hell is Happening in the Catholic Church?" The first quote is taken from the front cover of the *National Review* (May 4, 1965), the second from the front cover of *Ramparts* (November, 1967). There could be no more compelling evidence that *everybody* is asking the same question. In the following sections are samplings drawn from three years of the *National Catholic Reporter.* These should, at the very least, provide one with a long list of clues.

It must be immediately understood that the excerpts are highly selective, merely indicative of "where the action is" in American Catholicism today. This compilation, insofar as it represents earnest effort to break through (or break up) some of the Church's tired old structures, cannot be construed as depicting a microcosmic view of American Catholicism. It is not that. Neither is it a balanced picture of the *National Catholic Reporter*'s pages. Again, it is a sampling of "radical" or "left" or "root Catholic" thought and deed. It hardly requires the perceptive eye of a professional journalist to discern *NCR*'s objective, non-censoring reportorial policy. Archconservatives, too, make Catholic news. Hardly an is-

sue of *NCR* is without stories of some new word from the
Pope and from one or more bishops warning the faithful
against "grave dangers to the Church" flowing from the
"negative ideas" and "strange happenings" in the camp of
the prophets on the Left.

The positions emphasized in the following pages are minority ones. It is still considered "hard news" when a priest
talks back to a bishop (even over some relatively unimpor-
tant matter); or when another backs up pious expressions
of concern for his oppressed brothers—with his body; or
when laymen's groups worry over and experiment with the
manner in which they give communal witness to their religious commitments; or when a scholar manifests fidelity to
his work of probing ever deeper into the meaning of things.

In a way, these are "fringe" Catholics by Establishment
standards. Only the barest handful of the hierarchy manages
to now and then relate to—and on rare occasions even identify with—this group. At the other end of the spectrum
stands another vocal minority, more respectable in the eyes of
the Establishment. These are the "archtriumphalists," whose
posture is well put in a magazine subscription promotion ad
placed in *NCR:*

Just How catholic Are You Anyway?

TEST YOURSELF:

Do you believe the Catholic Church should change its position on birth control, abortion, divorce?

Do you want peace at any price in Viet Nam?

Do you believe priests should marry, nuns picket, students
strike?

Do you think the Mass should be jazzed up with jazz?

Do you think the "dialogue" should remain a tête-à-tête affair
between Liberals?

If your answer to the above questions is an unequivocal "Yes,"
you failed the test. We're sorry, but you're too catholic for us.
But if your answers were "No" or wavered around "Maybe,"
then you're the kind of Catholic we're looking for. If you want

to get in on some real dialogue—that gets right to the heart of the controversy in and around the church—then you should be reading: *Triumph*—The NEW, BOLD and BRILLIANT Catholic Magazine of News and Opinion.

In between, of course, there is the great mass of inertia, the pillars (as distinguished from the archpillars) just sitting around, waiting for nothing to happen.

A. IN AUTHORITARIANISM

Whatever one's vision of the Church and its mission, the need for a set of by-laws or structural guidelines, in the interest of a healthy, creative order, must be admitted. However, the existing body of ecclesiastical legislation—the Sacred Canons (now under official review)—is not only anachronistic, but also, in today's Church, an open invitation to the escalating "disobedience explosion," which regular communiqués from Rome and from local bishops interpret as "disloyalty" and "regrettable loss of respect for Divinely constituted authority." Much of the existing legislation has been—implicitly, at least—superseded by the decrees of Vatican II (for example, Canon 1325, which instructs Catholics to "guard against participating in debates and conferences with non-Catholics, especially public ones, without the permission of the Holy See. . .") (Abbo and Hannon, *op. cit.,* Vol. II). But despite the development of a new or revised code, it is the more basic concept of authority-in-the-Church-itself which is being called into question, and which brings about the kinds of tensions revealed in the following passages from the *NCR.* Such tensions have largely arisen between those who would no longer permit creative effort to be stifled by excessive authoritarianism and those who would preserve the institution of blind obedience.

DECEMBER 9, 1964—In an interview, Father Bernard Cooke, S.J., head of the theology department at Marquette University, discusses the problem of communication in the institutional Church:

Genuine communication takes place when the person who is doing the communicating is himself open to communication— when he lets people get at him. He has to say what he means, what he's really convinced of. That doesn't always happen in the Church. Some priests and religious are always *telling* people, but we never let them know who we are. There's a feeling that those in authority shouldn't really let others know how they themselves feel. There's a group mentality—a feeling that it's all right for those in authority to get to know one another, but that it undermines authority if the people are admitted to personal knowledge. . . .

Any time a leader opens himself up [he] faces the prospect of perhaps having to rethink his positions. [This is] necessary for any genuine sense of community. And it doesn't entail any loss of authority, if authority is understood as it is in scripture. If one studies the scriptural roots of authority, one sees that it is grounded there in the personal self-giving of the one in authority.

Community is never a static thing, rather, simply those who are communicating with one another . . . in an ongoing process. . . . Church authority is not domination, it is ministry. . . . To understand communication we should study the Incarnation, in which God communicated Himself to men. God didn't just come to the world and say what was wrong with it. He became a man and set out to transform humanity from within. You have to identify with a person to communicate with him.

December 23, 1964—Cardinal Joseph Ritter, Archbishop of St. Louis, "warmly received" a petition for an assembly of the clergy, religious, and laity, "aimed at the renewal of the Church" in the St. Louis area. He therefore announced the formation of a "Dialogue Conference," which would, he said, "seek representation, comments and ideas from every person and group in the archdiocese." The petitioners had informed the Cardinal of their three main objectives:

1. A fermentation of "Christian life coming from the free and open expression of public opinion reaching all levels of the archdiocese."

2. A "climate that will reassure all its people of a spirit of openness and concern."

3. "Personal involvement in which each member of this arch-diocese can feel that he is taking part."

The petitioners expressed the hope that such an assembly "could capture the imagination, stir the energies, and bring about the kind of involvement of Catholics on all levels that is necessary."

DECEMBER 23, 1964—Philip Scharper, executive editor of the Catholic book publishing house of Sheed and Ward, told an audience of clergy in Kansas City that the Church's outmoded "thought-model" of authority was responsible for her inability to respond to those "prophets" who would fulfill "the task of pointing to the sick spots—calling the Church into an area of thought or action into which she has not previously ventured." This failure, he said, was an abuse of authority. "When we think of authority in the Church, we usually see it in terms of a . . . pyramid. At the apex is the Holy Father, beneath him is the layer of curial assistants and the College of Cardinals, then the hierarchy of the world, their helpers in the priesthood, the religious, and forming the broad base of the pyramid, the inert mass of the laity." As a substitute thought-image, he suggested "a non-static pattern—a living, vibrant, electric series of concentric circles —like that mode when you toss a pebble into a pond."

Mr. Scharper also expressed his concern for communication failures within the Church:

Dialogue is a much abused word but one that helps us understand the kind of communication we need. Dialogue is not a monologue; dialogue does not exhort so it is not a sermon; it does not score points so it is not a debate . . . [it] is an authentic, human encounter involving at least two authentic persons who approach each other with love and respect, prepared to listen as well as to speak, to learn as well as to teach and prepared for the fact that after this exposure of myself I may never be quite the same. To enter into dialogue means to undertake risk.

Symbolically, Scharper would begin to construct a new communications system by denying Church authorities easy access to tape recorders:

When you turn on a tape recorder or a record player you know what you want to hear. The Council has made it clear that those in authority need also to be equipped with a telephone because when you pick up a telephone you don't really know what you are going to hear. And when one in authority picks up the phone, on the other end there may be a prophet.

JANUARY 6, 1965—When Father John Coffield withdrew from the Los Angeles diocese in protest over Cardinal McIntyre's suppression of priestly involvement in race relations activities, he told a press conference that the Cardinal had performed "marvelous work"—except in the area of race relations. This drew the following comment from columnist John Leo:

Father John Coffield, the latest priest to be hounded out of the Los Angeles archdiocese, has been for some years the key man among the small band of social-minded clergy in that underprivileged ecclesiastical territory.

He is an idol to the younger priests. Many seminarians regularly stayed with him each summer and conducted a kind of evangelistic work to the whole Negro population in the area. Mostly for his efforts on race, he has been called on the carpet by the cardinal more than 25 times, winning the titular presidency of what the young priests call the "Cardinal's Carpet Club." The club is sustained in part by a band of laymen who take notes on sermons and turn them into the chancery office, where they are rigorously examined for any taint of excessive apostolic fervor. If any is found, the priest is called in, and is warned, intimidated, threatened, or simply transferred. Even the mildest and most non-political reference to the Church's teaching on race has been known to bring a priest downtown for a tongue lashing.

As a result of his frequent "carpeting," Father Coffield has increasingly become a hero to those who understand what *aggiornamento* is all about, and a villain to those who don't. Some time ago, the cardinal tried to neutralize his priest's influence among the younger clergy by forbidding any young priests or seminarians to stay with him. But the clerics still crowded around, staying at the homes of sympathetic laymen near the rectory. . . .

Far from being radical, Father Coffield, in fact, seems rather conservative. In his press conference last week, he said that except for failure on race, the cardinal has done "marvelous work." But to place all the cardinal's non-racial policies under the title "marvelous," it is necessary to ignore most of what is going on in the archdiocese: the steady cancellation of speeches; the harassing of the colleges; the abuse of priests' rights; the long ban on dialogue Masses; the cramping of the human spirit at the unbelievable major seminary; the sustenance given the Far Right by the chancery itself—in short, the whole texture and quality of Catholic life in Los Angeles. Only the most charitable person can ignore the non-marvelous in L. A. today. The fact is that Los Angeles is the biggest scandal in the American Church, an open sore that will not be healed by looking the other way.

APRIL 28, 1965—Honesty in the Church discussed by columnist John Leo:

. . . if you are raised to think in simple categories of loyalty, obedience and authority, it is not easy to see where honesty fits in, particularly when it is those very categories that honesty is raising questions about.

There is in the Church a sort of "institutional-think" which is too often used to paper over cracks and deny the existence of problems which do not appear in ancient theological manuals. Those for whom institutional-think is strong do not seem to appreciate the rise of younger Catholics, clerical and lay, who take their thought processes from the culture in which they live, and who see no reason to develop a separate "Church" mentality to deal with their membership in the community of Catholicism. Among other things, they expect the same kind of straightforwardness and open dealing in the Church that they expect outside of it.

What the institutional mind fumblingly calls the "crisis of obedience" is to the non-institutional mind rooted in the problem of honesty. To the latter way of thinking, there is simply no more room in the Church for the selective frankness of Catholic discourse, the secretiveness, the refusals to meet real problems head on.

It is especially depressing that the new insistence on honesty appears to be largely unnoticed. Recently a well-known lay woman told me of a visit to her house by a priest she had known since boyhood. When the conversation got onto a controversial topic and the priest was asked his opinion, he launched into the official line, and was interrupted rather abruptly. "Frank," said the woman, "we grew up together—I *know* what you think as a priest; I want to know what you think *as a person*." What the priest said in reply is not recorded. But he had run flat up against a new-wave honesty-monger who demanded to know what he thought, after reading, reflection and consulting authority, and not just what he was told in the seminary.

There will be much more of this in the Church in years to come, and those who don't like it may just as well relax. It's coming anyway.

AUGUST 4, 1965—Columnist John Leo on Catholic internal criticism:

. . . Although the Church badly needs heavy doses of intelligent criticism at the moment, I think some unhealthy symptoms are developing among the critics. It seems to me that a good deal of the criticism is proceeding from an emotional base, and can be more easily explained in terms of personal problems than in terms of devotion to the Church. Some of it seems overly combative and shrill, and (worse yet) shows signs of hardening into a permanent pose of detached disgust.

It is easy to see why this might be happening—simply because the Church is so sluggish in reacting to sensible criticism. It is clear by now, for instance, that neither the Pope nor the American bishops are willing to do anything about Los Angeles, although the Church's moral disaster there has been documented ten times over. The kind of frustration that boils up out of a situation like this cannot be salved with a gentle reproof about styles in criticism. Even so, we have to be on guard that criticism does not harden into a posture of alienation. What the Church does not need is a set of sullen bystanders sitting on the sidelines and taking potshots at the Babbitts within.

One reason why there is so much steam to be let off is that there are so few channels for saying unconventional or unpopular things about the Church, however valid they might be. The outpourings in the letters column of this paper, for instance, are often the same sentiments that have been stifled before at several other levels. By the time the observations reach a paper willing to print them, the indignation level can be pretty high.

MARCH 2, 1966

Santa Monica, Calif.—Father William DuBay, proponent of a labor union for priests, has been relieved of his duties as a chaplain at St. John's hospital.

A week after he announced plans to begin the priests' union, Father DuBay was given 24 hours to move into nearby St. Monica's parish, where his duties are expected to be much more time-consuming.

Msgr. Raymond O'Flaherty, pastor at St. Monica's, said Father DuBay was removed because doctors and patients were dissatisfied with his work, and particularly with "excessive publicity" he has received recently.

However, both Father DuBay and a spokesman for the hospital, Margaret Doane, said they were unaware of any complaints.

Father DuBay on Feb. 14 announced he was starting the "American Federation of Priests." One of the union's goals was a "transfer policy which protects priests from arbitrary and oppressive transfers at the hands of chancery officials."

When he was asked if the move was an example of such an "arbitrary and oppressive transfer" Father DuBay answered, "Certainly."

AUGUST 24, 1966—From an interview with Bishop Victor Reed of Oklahoma:

"I have felt that this era in the history of the Church requires a greater degree of permissiveness than is ordinarily required. Because we are in a period of criticism of the past, and this criticism is meant to be constructive.

"And in order to accomplish this we must have a certain degree of freedom of expression.

"Now, I feel the purpose of criticism—we don't criticize just for the purpose of criticizing—is that we want to modify the structure of the Church—which is the result of the past experience of the Church—so that the Church may serve its purpose in the modern world, which is generally the same as it has always been."

What did he understand the Church's purpose in the world to be?

First, he noted, Vatican II was the first wholly pastoral council in the history of the Church, the first in which the purpose was to examine the service of the Church to others.

"Therefore," he said, "the Church has broadened its work into sociological areas which have long been neglected."

It is precisely this, of course, which is hotly objected to by conservatives in Oklahoma. The Bishop was asked what he would say to those who deny the Church should get "into sociological areas."

"The purpose of the Church," he said, "is to form the spirituality of the whole man, and man is a social being.

"I don't see how you can confine religion into a narrow field, particularly in these days when so much emphasis is being placed on this social relationship.

"All of society has become impressed with the importance of man as a member of society—of international society. . . . And all of these things have a moral and religious aspect."

Descending from theory, the bishop continued:

"My personal opinion of those who say we should not enter into social areas is that they're afraid of it—afraid for their own personal lives.

"The only people who talk this way, you know, are the haves, not the have-nots.

"I think it's a lack of confidence on their part in God, and also . . . some selfishness, a fear of loss.

"I think it also proceeds from a lack of appreciation of their responsibility to their fellow man, and how far this responsibility extends."

From a story by Ken Atchity: September 28, 1966

New York—Four laymen and a priest have announced the formation of an organization to deal with problems of freedom within the Church.

At a press conference last week, Eugene Fontinell, chairman of the executive committee, announced creation of a group called the Institute for Freedom in the Church. "The time has come . . . for the Church to make a positive contribution to the many battles for freedom which characterize our world," he said.

Other members of the executive committee at the press conference with Fontinell were William Birmingham, editor of Mentor-Omega books; Daniel Callahan, executive associate editor of *Commonweal;* Richard Horchler, program director of the National Conference of Christians and Jews; and Father William Clancy, provost of the Pittsburgh Oratory and former religion editor of *Newsweek.* Fontinell is chairman of the Queens college philosophy department.

The immediate incentive for the institute was last year's "Berrigan case," in which Father Daniel Berrigan, a peace activist, was suddenly sent on a mission to South America. At the time, New York Catholics formed a committee to sponsor an open letter to Father Berrigan's Jesuit superiors and the New York archbishop stating that it was obvious the priest was silenced for his criticism of Vietnam policy.

A request for signatures and money for an ad in the *New York Times* voicing a protest against Father Berrigan's treatment drew responses from more than 2,500 persons. The reaction prompted the directors to consider creation of a permanent organization.

JANUARY 4, 1967—Msgr. J. D. Conway,[1] canon law expert and widely read "Question Box" columnist, raked Establishment Catholic "pious hypocrisy." He told a hundred seminarians attending the second annual Midwest Seminarians' Conference:

---

[1] Now deceased. Prior to his death, Msgr. Conway's column appeared in more than forty Catholic weeklies.

We have been willing to pay unjust wages to maintain our schools and hospitals, ready to close our eye to social injustices rather than alienate wealthy donors, inclined to hedge on the truth that we may conceal flaws and failures. Most of us are less than honest, certainly less than frank; why are the children in our school taught half-truths and pious falsehood? Why do we seem to dedicate ourselves to the lifelong and fairly frantic task of covering up the failings of churchmen?

We seem to have developed an attitude of pious hypocrisy, which is strongly encouraged from on high, if not positively commanded. We are given to telling edifying little lies lest scandal erupt. We become experts in virtuous contortions, trying to defend the Sacred Roman Rota in all its decisions, the Holy Office in its persecutions and the chancery office in all its vagaries. Indeed, it has become the accepted opinion in our country that the chancery office is the last place from which you can expect the full truth.

I wrote a book of apologetics in which I deftly refuted a variety of standard accusations and arguments against the Church. I showed clearly that the Inquisition was advanced juridical procedure in its day, that the condemnation of Galileo was quite plausible, that celibacy was the glory of the priesthood in historical fact as well as in fervent ideal, and even that Spanish bullfighting was an edifying demonstration of courage and art.

My publishers submitted the galley proofs to a prominent Catholic scholar whose endorsement they hoped to use as an advertising blurb. He refused to have anything to do with it. . . . The book sold well, but I am very happy that it is now out of print. I don't even have a copy for myself. But unfortunately a paperback edition, only slightly revised, is still available. I will not tell you its name.

In this regard the council taught us much. I am thinking of the decree on ecumenism in particular. But by its own example it did not teach us enough. The re-shaping of tradition to make religious liberty emerge logically from it is less than convincing—not to say contrived. Our institutional apology to the Jews is less than half-hearted.

And there is a tendency to interpret evident duties as achieved facts, as in the opening words of the *Constitution on the Church in the Modern World:* "The joys and the hopes, the griefs and the anxieties of the men of this age, especially those who are poor or in any way afflicted, these are the joys and hopes, the griefs and anxieties of the followers of Christ."

How much does the grief and poverty, the anxiety and famine of the people of India concern the average Catholic—or the average priest? Ask a Negro in Watts what evidence he has seen of the Church's concern for his misery.

But I have particular reference to the explicit and stolid unwillingness of the Pope and the majority of the council fathers to openly discuss, or even to consider with any frankness, the two most critical and embarrassing of the Church's present problems: birth control and clerical celibacy.

I do not pretend that the council could have found a happy solution to either problem. But the official demand that eyes, ears and mouths be closed, that one even cease to think, is an attitude towards truth which threatens grave harm to the Church.

As priests we must keep constantly in mind that we find in the dignity of the human person the source of human rights. Our duty as priests is to serve human persons and to save them for eternity; and we can accomplish that only if we have a keen sense of justice and charity, of freedom and equality, and of human rights in general.

B. IN BIRTH CONTROL

No single problem in authority has shaken grass-roots confidence in the magisterium more than the birth control question. *De facto,* the Pope has been ushered out of Catholic bedrooms. One would be hard put these days to find a Catholic marriage counselor who still adheres to the hard-line blanket condemnations of artificial contraception made by Pope Pius XI and Pope Pius XII. But the present Pope seems to be following the historical pattern of unwillingness to right a wrong by a frank admission of error. Despite the advice of his special commission to the contrary, he thus far has refused to announce a reversal in thinking.

OCTOBER 28, 1964—Father John L. Thomas, S.J., sociologist at St. Louis University, warns that confessors have been "pinned to the wall" by penitents who ask for permission to use birth control pills. The confessor is "in a rough spot." He is unable to tell anyone to use the pill, nor can he forbid the practice if the penitent makes a conscientious objection. "If the Church refuses to come to terms with this thing, it will be making a very serious mistake. . . . We're waiting for something to happen."

OCTOBER 28, 1964—In a review of a new book, *The Experience of Marriage: The Testimony of Catholic Laymen* (Michael Novak [ed.], New York: Abbey Press, 1964), C. Q. Mattingly, managing editor of *Marriage,* discusses the personal statements of the book's contributors:

With many financial and personal needs unmet, Mr. and Mrs. F. turned first to rhythm, and when that failed them "to some method of birth control." And now? "It took awhile," she says, "to realize that I no longer needed to be afraid. I could relax and laugh and love as we had done when we were first married. I also realized that I had been living in a state of suppressed rage for five years, a rage at trying to conform to standards that were an insult to my intelligence and feelings." [1]

NOVEMBER 11, 1964—Following the publication of the book *Contraception and Holiness* (a collection of essays by eleven Catholics—including one archbishop—arguing for change in the Church's birth control attitude), there was an exchange between one of the book's reviewers and one of its contributors:

If the wishes of these contributors were to be carried out and if the Catholic Church were to teach that the practice of contraception between husband and wife were licit according to God's laws, this pronouncement would utterly destroy the teaching authority of the Church. The Church is irrevocably committed. . . . Ultimately, the entire structure of Church authority is liable to attack on the score of the premises of this book. . . . it skirts dangerously and ambiguously the question of morality-by-vote. Beginning with the blurb which castigates morality from on high to the repeated imperious calls for consultation with married folk and scientists in many fields, the book's impression seems to show that if enough people disagree with a moral pronouncement, their disagreement is enough to warrant changing it.—Rev. Francis L. Filas, S.J., chairman of the theology department at Loyola university.

Many of the distinguished theologians whom we consulted about this undertaking believed that pastoral concerns were pre-eminent and that the book should clearly underline the anguish experienced by many devout Catholics when faced with the need to effectively limit the number of their children and also to express their mutual love. It was recognized, of course, that no amount of personal suffering would justify even the slightest

[1] Cf. this author's review in *Ramparts*, August, 1965.

deviation from the absolute norm of morality. But given the in-certitude publicly expressed concerning the development of the doctrine of Christian marriage, it was believed that a clearer understanding of what the norm of morality really was could be brought about by listening to the views of married people them-selves. . . . All of the consultants and all of the authors of the various essays in the book were agreed . . . on one thing: that there was no clear evidence that the present teaching was irrev-ocable.—Justus George Lawler, professor of humanities at St. Xavier College, editor of *Continuum,* a quarterly review, and editorial director of Herder and Herder, Inc.

November 11, 1964—Four new Catholic books on birth control are reviewed by Father Robert T. Francoeur (then a candidate for a Ph.D. in biology at Fordham):

The one indisputable conclusion to which these four books lead is that traditional Catholic teaching about birth control is under challenge, and that the challenge comes from Catholics who are competent to offer it and who do so responsibly, out of concern for truth and with no wish to defy the Church's authority. It is simply a fact, and an important one, that those who support the views on contraception presented in these four books, and in similar works published elsewhere in the world, include some of the world's top theologians, *periti* at the council, bishops, arch-bishops and cardinals. . . . It is clear . . . that the new opinion is both weighty and serious.[2]

January 13, 1965—"The Church and Marriage," a pro-posed TV "Catholic Hour" series to be sponsored by the National Council of Catholic Men, was suddenly withdrawn "after protests from still unidentified Church authorities." The declared purpose of the series was "to provide a back-ground on the Theology of marriage . . . to report, rather than argue, the position of contemporary theologians," and to "clarify for Catholics the fact that while the Church's teaching on birth control is being carefully reexamined, there

[2] Less than three years later, Father Francoeur exposed himself to auto-matic excommunication by getting married.

is as yet no change in the church's official doctrine." The series was narrated by Philip Scharper, executive editor of the publishing firm of Sheed and Ward, and the script written by John Leo, *NCR* columnist and Associate Editor of *Commonweal.* A Vatican correspondent alleged that Cardinal Spellman was responsible for the protest which resulted in the cancellation of the series.

NOVEMBER 3, 1965—Jesuit sociologist Father John L. Thomas told an audience of priests, nuns, and laity at St. Mary's College, Kansas:

Courage is indeed required to admit the possible inadequacy of some aspects of the Church's past teaching on sex, love and marriage, as well as to tackle the arduous, delicate task of reformulating this teaching. Scholarly humility is also needed, for in seeking to interpret God's laws relating to human sexuality theologians must deal with a complex, emotion-loaded, universally puzzling, mysterious human phenomenon that has far-reaching implications both for the personal fulfillment of individuals and the continuity of society. . . .

Furthermore, theologians may not ignore the Church's past teachings in such matters, though an attitude of blind, uncritical adherence to traditional interpretations of sexuality would reflect culpable ignorance of relevant historical developments in doctrine, science and cultural systems.

What is at stake is little more than the relevance of the Church itself to the needs of modern man.

C. IN CATHOLIC EDUCATION

There is much sociological and other data now available to make a case for the early dissolution of the Catholic school system as we now know it. Studies have shown that traditional Catholic education in America has had no particular influence in shaping the "active participation" of Catholics (usually measured in such terms as Mass attendance, fidelity to marriage laws, parish support, and so forth). Moreover, some studies have indicated that the Catholic-educated person is less socially aware than the Catholic product of public schools—less inclined toward identification of religion with the important social questions of his time. To many it would seem that attempts to preserve the system intact will (1) continue to distract the American Church from its healing mission of reconciliation and (2) be economically impossible.

MARCH 17, 1965

Jamaica, N.Y.—Faculty members and students of St. John's University—largest Catholic university in the nation—have broken out in a long smoldering revolt over demands for more pay and more freedom.

The revolt erupted March 6 when 200 of 500 St. John's teachers walked out of the once-a-semester faculty meeting as it was barely getting under way.

Prayers had just been concluded at the meeting on the Jamaica campus when Andrew Robinson, associate professor of philosophy, rose and voiced "our outrage at and protest against the continued unilateral decision affecting members of this faculty."

Robinson is chairman of the campus chapter of the American

Association of University Professors. The association charges that the Vincentian-operated institution, headed by Father Edward J. Burke, has refused to increase substandard teacher salaries despite what Robinson says is a $2.5 million operating surplus this year.

Continuing his surprise announcement, Robinson told the faculty meeting the university had ignored the association's recommendations on salary increases. "In view of all this, I am instructed to move that this meeting be adjourned," he said, and the 200 teachers walked out.

One teacher was quoted as saying, "The trouble is that Father Burke not only treats the students like children, which they are, but he treats the faculty like children, too. That's what he has said—we are all children and he is the father."

The sentiments were echoed two days later when 500 students of the 13,000-student institution booed Father Burke's name at a rally backing the teachers.

The speaker was William Graves, honor student and member of the student council, who read a statement saying "Father Burke refers to himself as the father and to us as the children."

APRIL 14, 1965—An announcement by St. John's University that immediate pay raises and other benefits would be granted to its faculty in rebellion was labeled "a real snow job" by Father Peter O'Reilly, local chapter chairman of the United Federation of College Teachers. A St. John's administrator, Father Joseph Tinnelly, also announced the appointment of a special consultant to prepare a study of the entire problem of administration-faculty relations. Said Father O'Reilly: "We've been through that with Father Tinnelly. The result of Father Tinnelly's three-week study was his decision to make a six-month study. After that they may decide to make a five-year study." Said consultant Dr. John Merg, on leave of absence as president of Hunter College, "On more than one occasion during the past several years I've sounded off on Catholic universities and how they must become modern if they want to establish and maintain excellence."

OCTOBER 12, 1966—Two hundred and twenty Catholic college teachers have protested an order from Archbishop John P. Cody of Chicago on the grounds that it denies academic freedom. The disputed section of the order reads:

Notice is hereby given to the heads of all ecclesiastical entities in the archdiocese . . . of their obligation of first obtaining certification of credentials from the most reverend archbishop before extending an invitation, or honoring a request, by which an extern (outside) priest takes up residence or accepts any other commitment (pastoral, executive, academic, fund-raising, etc.) in the archdiocese of Chicago.

The protesters contend that this constitutes prior censorship of invitations extended to priests outside the diocese to speak on campuses in the archbishop's jurisdiction:

. . . University and college deans should not be required to secure the archbishop's consent when extending invitations or honoring requests relative to academic commitments. Because it requires that academic deans secure this consent, the decree gives the archbishop a power of prior censorship over the academic activity of both priest-scholar and university.

JANUARY 25, 1967—St. John's University (Jamaica, N.Y.) was preparing for a major teachers' strike called by the university's chapter of the United Federation of College Teachers. The union raised the following questions on academic freedom at St. John's:

Does academic freedom exist at a university that does not have contractual tenure for its faculty? . . . where there are no provisions for faculty control of curriculum, textbooks, or student activities? . . . when four chairmen of duly elected committees of the Faculty Planning Council are fired without stated cause?

Does academic freedom exist at a university when 100 members of the faculty of St. John's, who belong to the United Federation of College Teachers, find that their organization is denied the basic right to function on campus? . . . when the United Federation of College Teachers is not allowed to meet on the campus, distribute literature freely to the faculty, or meet with the administration to present proposals or gievances?

Does academic freedom exist at a university that has no established grievance procedures? And does academic freedom exist at a university when 31 faculty members can be fired three weeks before examinations without any specified reasons?

FEBRUARY 15, 1967

Notre Dame—Vast reforms in the operation of the U.S. Catholic school system are recommended in an international study of Catholic education. . . . The book, *Catholic Education in the Western World* . . . is a symposium edited by James M. Lee, head of the department of education and director for research on Catholic schools at the University of Notre Dame. George N. Shuster, assistant to the president of Notre Dame, wrote the foreword.

In a chapter on Catholic education in America, Lee, writing of financial mismanagement, especially in the elementary schools, claims that "millions of dollars are wasted every year by Catholic school administrators who have no budgets, who fail to utilize sound accounting and managerial procedures and who inadequately supervise plant maintenance."

Complaining that there is "no one stated purpose binding all American Catholic schools," Lee suggests the establishment of central agencies and the creation of a major coordinating body for the "orderly management" of Catholic education.

He says that Catholic elementary schools should be discontinued on the grounds that the attitudes and values of children of elementary school age are almost totally derived from parents, with schools providing little influence. "Specifically Catholic schooling is unnecessary at an age when school makes no deep value or attitudinal impact," he says. Lee suggests that the interest of the Church in forming the young might be better served by a system of pre-elementary schools.

He warned that Catholic colleges cannot compete with secular universities, and advised that they become "component" parts of secular universities. In this way, "Catholic higher education can come of age," he writes.

"Students would be enrolled in the Catholic college and would

be free to take their classes in any college within the university."
The Catholic colleges would have representatives on the secular
university's board of trustees, and would retain their Catholicity.

Lee maintains that "almost all Catholic colleges and a heavy
proportion of Catholic universities are woefully underdeveloped
in library facilities, outstanding faculty and plant facilities."

One way the schools might be improved, he says, is through
the reinvestment of money and personnel "to prune away those
branches of the Catholic school system which are inefficient when
viewed from the Church's purpose in operating the schools."

Lee believes that the Catholic school system should be seen
primarily as the concern of laymen, not clerics. But despite signs
of change, he said, "American Catholic education is heavily and
tightly controlled by religious. The day seems distant when laymen . . . will have a strong voice in, much less control of,
American Catholic education," he asserts.

Lee suggests, however, that the recent trend toward lay control of Catholic colleges and universities may well filter down
to the benefit of lower levels of Catholic schooling.

MARCH 15, 1967—A Jesuit educator, Father Neil G. Mc-
Cluskey, tells a University of Dayton audience:

The Catholic university must arm its professors of theology with
the same academic freedom that is accorded its historians, phys-
icists, and sociologists.

There is no more academic justification for the entry by a
local bishop or provincial into the university discipline of theology than there is for the local mayor or governor to intrude
into the field of political science.

New concepts and different interpretations by scholars are
put forth in the academic world to be examined, tested, proved,
rejected or modified by a peer group which can challenge or
approve because it has earned authority and competence through
scholarship and learning.

The Church no less than society itself needs a sanctuary for
thought away from outside pressures. Advance and development
of theological thought can never take place unless theologians are
free to move forward without external restraint.

Whatever the need that the bishop or provincial may have to

exercise vigilance over the purity of Christian doctrine taught in secondary schools and parochial schools, the autonomy of the Catholic university precludes such treatment. Theology is not Christian doctrine. Or if it is, then theology must drop its claim to be science and its justifications as an academic discipline.

In fact, theology then ceases to have a legitimate claim to be in the curriculum of the Catholic university or college. On the level of higher learning, the Church's official magisterium has only an indirect influence, that is, she speaks authoritatively to the consciences of her members holding elective office in political society.

Her influence in both spheres is indirect, not direct. And what of the risk to the purity of theological doctrine? The risk here is no greater than that taken by God Himself in creating thinking beings.

Father McCluskey's talk was obviously directed at a move by Archbishop Karl J. Alter to discipline four Dayton faculty members for teaching contrary to the "Church's magisterium." (The controversy centered around the teachers' views on contraception, abortion, purgatory, situation ethics, and papal encyclicals.)

APRIL 26, 1967—The summary dismissal of moral theologian Rev. Charles E. Curran from the faculty of Catholic University rocked the Catholic academic community and caused the school to shut down. From a story by correspondent Norma Krause Herzfeld:

Washington—Acting almost unanimously against the firing of a faculty member by its board of trustees, the students and faculty of Catholic University succeeded in closing down the university last week in an unprecedented rebellion against the rector, the trustees and the American hierarchy.

The Rev. Charles E. Curran, assistant professor of moral theology at the university's school of sacred theology, was fired last Monday, and agreed to wait 24 hours before making his dismissal public. No reasons for his dismissal were given to him then or later, he said.

Within the next 24 hours, the theology faculty had telegraphed all the trustees, asking them to rescind the dismissal immediately, and a mass protest rally of students, graduate students and faculty ended with a call for a general strike by the 6600 students "by Friday."

Another 24 hours saw the faculty members shut down their school of sacred theology and undergraduates and graduate students join the boycott. By Thursday afternoon, at an emergency meeting to which all full-time university teachers were invited, the faculty voted over 400 to 18 to cease functioning.

The trustees of the university—32 American archbishops and cardinals and 12 laymen, mostly businessmen—act for the entire hierarchy in overseeing the pontifical university which is chartered by Rome under curial control. This historic confrontation of the hierarchy by students and faculty over what they considered to be crucial issues of academic freedom and human rights apparently left no alternative for the trustees but to back down from their dismissal of the mild-mannered, 33-year-old theology professor.

. . . seminarians and student priests from the school of theology organized a protest march on the rector. Bishop McDonald agreed to see two student leaders. He conferred with them in the presence of the executive vice rector, the academic vice rector, the vice rector for business and finance, and his secretary, but gave them what they considered only a vague promise of some kind of hearing for Father Curran.

During the two-hour conference, about 1,000 students, both clerical and lay, stood outside the rector's residence holding signs reading "McDonald, Whose Side Are You On?" "Princes Persecute Me Without Cause—Psalm 119," "If There Is No Room for Charley in the Catholic University of America, There is No Room for Catholic University in America."

They sang "We Shall Overcome," and "The Times, They are A-Changing," with specially written words:

> "Come, cardinals and bishops
> Please heed the call,
> Don't stand in the doorway,
> Don't block up the hall.
> For he that gets hurt
> Will be he who has stalled.

There's a battle
Outside and it's ragin'.
It'll soon shake your windows
And rattle your walls.
For the times, they are a-changing."

D. IN ECUMENISM

While the intensity of effort—especially high-level effort—and the rate of progress in this field has not kept pace with the hopes and aspirations of the avant-garde, nevertheless it cannot be denied that significant advances have been made. The excerpts which follow are revealing of a relatively fast-changing situation. One has only to think back, say, five or ten years, in order to reflect on a time when current ecumenical events would not have been possible.

NOVEMBER 4, 1964—A Catholic layman [the author of this book] was reported to have preached the Reformation Day sermon at the Woodside Village Church, a Protestant congregation affiliated with the United Church of Christ. The service was described by the "venerable" associate minister as the "first Reformation Day service in all these years which I could celebrate." In his sermon, the preacher asked the congregation:

Is there a sound basis upon which you as Protestant and I as Catholic can rejoice together this October 25? If your answer is "no" we have made a travesty of the Gospel; we have blasphemed. If we do not desire to mock the Gospel our answer must be "yes." The Gospel supplies us with the basic motivation for ordering all our human relationships. Love is the answer. This is the only sound basis for rejoicing among Christians not merely this Sunday but every day of the year. . . . We must cease making war against mere caricatures of one another.

MARCH 17, 1965

Washington—The seven-member Bishops' Commission for Ecumenical Affairs took steps to plunge the U.S. Catholic Church into the mainstream of ecumenical encounter.

Under the guidance of Cardinal Lawrence Shehan of Baltimore, the commission briskly advanced Catholic involvement by approving nearly a dozen projects at a one-day session, March 10.

Results of the meeting as announced showed no noticeable dampening of ecumenical endeavors resulting from the recent letter of Archbishop Egidio Vagnozzi, apostolic delegate in the United States, warning U.S. bishops against "excesses" in interfaith prayer.

MARCH 31, 1965—Excerpts from "Uncommitted Believers, Committed Believers," a signed article by Rev. Bernard Cooke, S. J., an important American Catholic theologian:

I think we must ask ourselves whether the large-scale rejection of Christianity by intelligent and sincere men of our day is not a rejection of something which is usually less than Christianity. Must we not ask ourselves whether the men of today who feel that religion is an imposition on a genuine development of the human person—who feel that Christianity is an obstacle to genuine human freedom and development—are not to some extent justified by the fact that the forms of Christianity which they have encountered have been less than adequate in their expression of the Gospel?

If the atmosphere of western intellectualism has for a century or so been one largely devoid of any sense of the presence of the divine, is this not perhaps due to the fact that there is a protest of the truly honest mind to the caricature of the divine which is often portrayed by those who claim to be speaking for a God of Christianity? And to this extent is there not perhaps a vein of deep Christianity in the person who is classified as an unbeliever? Would this type of rejection occur if the fundamental intellectual and cultural heritage out of which these people have emerged was not itself one which had been touched by the deepest strains of the Gospel message of Christ? Has Christianity been rejected because of its Christianity, or because it has proved really to be a very insufficient expression of what the genuine article is meant to be?

To the extent that the position of these men with regard to Christianity is rejection of credulity and superstition it is really a genuine Christian attitude. To the extent that these individuals have by their historical and scientific studies forced us who formally profess Christianity to reassess our positions and purify our statements and practices, they have been part of the providential plan for the internal purification and development of the Christian mystery.

And I wonder, to the extent that they really have by their own intellectual honesty contributed to this process, if these individuals do not really deserve to be called Christian? And, if so, do they not form a body of very sincere and good humans with whom we, who more ostensibly profess Christianity, should seek reunion?

To put it even more bluntly, one would ask whether one can exclude from the lives and the witness to truth of these men the action of that Spirit who is the animating principle in the Church which is the body of Christ. Not that one can speak of these men as pertaining to the Church. This is the tragedy of the situation. But perhaps in their way they are contributing much more to the true manifestation of the mystery of Christ than very many individuals who with superficiality and complete self-confidence are giving a witness to Christianity which is really a caricature of the truth.

A Point which I think must be seriously considered by those of us who are involved in ecumenical discussion is whether or not the very problems which have produced the modern agnostic are not exactly the problems which historically have divided us who should form one community of faith. Underneath the multitude of confessional differences, divisions in practices of worship, even cultural alienations which split us off Catholic from Protestant, western Christian from Orthodox, there seems to lie one fundamental question: What is Christianity? What precisely is its role in history? How can it make claim as it does to uniqueness among the religious positions of mankind?

E. IN LITURGY

Catholics on the Left identify liturgy as celebration: of a commitment to life that, for them, is the difference between meaning and absurdity; of their eschatological hope; of the Word's presence in human history; of the Christian proclamation of universal brotherhood; of *the search* which is endless but never fruitless; of unabashed fellowship and communion; of the joy of repentance and reconciliation; of the communal commitment to bring a message of hope and love alive in the world of everyday human relationships, the world of work and study and experimentation and dialogue and confrontation and suffering and death. Catholics on the Left are more concerned with the "Why?" of liturgy than the "How to," which seems to be the major preoccupation of the bishops. There is a vast difference between true liturgical renewal and a liturgical revival based on the mere adoption of a new set of fixed rites and rituals. Thus far, true liturgical experimentation has not been endorsed by the hierarchy. As a result there is a burgeoning liturgical underground. It is here that the authentic Christian notion of liturgy as celebration is in the process of rediscovery.

NOVEMBER 4, 1964—Sister Corita, internationally known artist, and her associates in the congregation of the Immaculate Heart of Mary, have developed religious celebrations or festivals into "a high art." These day-long events, usually held at the Southern California parochial schools operated by the sisters, "feature puppet shows, plays, singing, dancing, banners and processional pieces, all created by the children and related in theme to the particular feast or season, such as Christmas, Easter, Advent or Lent." If biblical stories are enacted, the actual dialogue is either written or acted spontaneously by the children, who translate the essentials of the story into the vernacular, so to speak. A typical ending scene:

Mary: Well, Joseph, I guess I'll do the dishes now.
Joseph: O.K., Mary, I want to do some sawing before it gets dark. By the way, that sure was a good dinner.
Mary: Thanks, I'm glad you liked it. Oh, I think I hear the Baby Jesus crying. I'd better go and change his diapers. Don't forget to wear a jacket out in the workshop. You know, it's getting chilly.
           (*EXIT*)

At the Immaculate Heart College in Los Angeles, the annual Mary's Day liturgical celebration is held:

Many girls have bells and home made noise-makers which they sound in time to the beat of the live jazz band which is holding forth in the rear balcony. Then the band stops and gives way to a montage of tape-recorded sounds broadcast over a loud speaker. John Kennedy's voice is heard, almost as though he is right there speaking through a microphone. Little bits of his now-famous speeches are heard, faces stop smiling for a second, to remember. Eyes meet, noise-makers are silent. Then the "YEA, YEA, YEA" of the Beatles bursts forth with everyone echoing the raucous "YEA, YEA, YEA." This is followed by the rhythm of "He's Got the Whole World In His Hands" which starts everyone singing and clapping in time. Then carnival music, more singing, and every now and then the "YEA, YEA, YEA" of the Beatles. The auditorium is almost full now. Guests are seated and many people, accustomed to more sedate setting for Mass, are wondering how on earth the three-ring circus spirit will be toned down so that Mass can be offered. Then the priest enters and everyone stands with a flurry of bells and color. Father is dressed, appropriately enough, in bright red. He takes his place at the altar on the stage, joining the spectacle of color, flowers, pictures and words. Here and there quotes on the boxes stand out like neon signs, "Viva sweet love," "A Rose is a Rose is a Rose!" "YEA Love." All distractions have been silenced. The spirit remains but has been transformed and focused on the words of the liturgy. The dialogue Mass begins, with the celebrant speaking in a loud, positive voice. The congregation replies in like manner. There is no fumbling for rosaries or mumbling into prayer books. There are chants led by two young men. The celebrant says beautiful words about material and spiritual food, the joy of good food and communal feasting, and the Mass as the most joyful and sublime expression of the human need to "break bread together." At the appropriate times of Mass, the congregation ring their bells in joyful unison. There is a movement and color at communion time and then, all too quickly, the Mass is ended. But we have experienced something we shall not forget. We have truly CELEBRATED the liturgy. Some of us, for the very first time, have come to realize what the word "celebration" can mean when used to describe the Holy Sacrifice of the Mass.

JANUARY 27, 1965—Rosemary Lauer, well-known Catholic writer and academician, in an appeal for a "genuine liturgical prayer," describes certain American-as-apple-pie gimmicks that have crept into the liturgical life:

An announcement in a Chicago church that the seat collection is being increased to 25 cents, because "just as in any other business, a rise in over-head dictates an increase in the cost of the product," sounds very efficient, but slightly un-Christian. More Christian, however, than the installation of turn-stiles to take care of the seat collection at the entrance of at least one Ohio church some time ago. A good bit less distasteful, but still quite contemporary-American, is the electronic system in an upper New York church which lights up signs saying, SIT, KNEEL, STAND.

Also very modern and in the American Manner is the Joliet, Ill., pulpit which rises and descends like an elevator, making it unnecessary for the preacher to climb any stairs. But most hep of all is the taped Sacred Heart novena service conducted at a Milwaukee church—at least until a few years ago. The advantages were obvious; the priest "conducting" the service was free

to wander back and forth between the sacristy and pulpit while
the recording led the congregation in prayer.

It is still rather difficult to understand why a fellow spectator
at this phenomenon was not more shocked by the electronic reality than by a facetious prediction that the next improvement
would be a mechanical arm which would grasp the monstrance
and make the sign-of-the-cross over the people.

One can be grateful that these marvels of modern American
technology have not spread to many parishes. However, too
many parish priests, in their fervor for expediting things à
l'Americain, seem to confuse the sanctuary with the Indianapolis
speedway. The champion may well be the downtown Brooklyn
priest who said Mass (validly, in all likelihood), made the Sunday announcements, preached a sermon and distributed Holy
Communion—all in 25 minutes. As he left the sanctuary he very
understandably took a look at the clock in the rear of the church.
When one sets a record, one likes to know it.

FEBRUARY 9, 1966—University of Detroit students pick-
eted the diocese chancery office and circulated a petition, all
in response to the archbishop's ban on their folk song Masses.
The university's student counselor, Father Thomas A. Black-
burn, had this to say about the Detroit diocese ecclesiastical
officialdom:

Since school started I have called them, written them and in
every possible way asked them to come out and hear it, but they
have not done so. We think it is reverent and beautiful, and so
might they.

Those people downtown are living in a dream world. They
think these kids believe the Church and Church authority are
important. They couldn't care less about the Church and Church
authority or anything else, and the Church won't wake up until
they start leaving in droves. They don't understand that this is
a subculture. We're not saying that this Mass is a panacea, that
it's going to solve all the problems of reaching the college student,
because it's not. I doubt very much that many students will get
very excited about this—they couldn't care less.

When they asked students to picket the chancery one said,

"Sure, I'll go if I can picket to throw out the whole Mass." Another said, "In five years they'll be begging us to go to any kind of a Mass."

Those people downtown don't realize this. They're out of it.

JANUARY 4, 1967

Philadelphia—Father John F. X. Burton, a Jesuit High School teacher, has been expelled from the archdiocese for celebrating an unauthorized experimental Mass in a private home.

The 45-year-old priest, an instructor in religion at St. Joseph's College high school in Philadelphia, said he was removed from the archdiocese at the order of Archbishop John J. Krol.

He was notified of his expulsion December 27 by Father Edward J. Sponga, Maryland provincial of the Jesuits, and given 2 weeks to leave Philadelphia.

Although he had not received a new assignment, Father Burton said he expected to be reassigned somewhere in the Baltimore area. He said the order from Archbishop Krol specifies that he is never to return to Philadelphia for any priestly work. . . .

Father Burton was director of the Sodality at St. Joseph's College high school and also supervised a school-sponsored community action program that had involved several hundred Philadelphia high school students in interracial, ecumenical and catechetical projects in the city's poverty areas.

In 1966, he was cited by Temple University for his services to the poor in North Philadelphia.

In a farewell letter prepared for distribution to friends and associates in the Philadelphia area, Father Burton said: "I have no intention of becoming discouraged, although I am considerably disappointed by this turn of events and would ask you to carry on the fight to rid the archdiocese of the cant, dishonesty and irrelevance that weighs as a heavy burden on so many of us who would bring the Church in Philadelphia within the mainstream of contemporary Christianity.

"I do not leave with any bitterness or pique, but only with bewilderment at the absence of true leadership and compassion on the part of the local hierarchy."

JANUARY 11, 1967—An unsigned editorial describes a recent liturgical event experienced by the writer:

We're thinking of a Mass we witnessed not long ago, offered in a private home one evening by a missionary priest and a group of about 20 persons, mostly teenagers but including younger children, parents and a couple of grandmothers.

First the group gathered in the entrance hall of the home, purposely left in semi-darkness, to recite the *Confiteor*. Those who wanted to do so acknowledged their faults publicly, asking forgiveness of God and their companions; and absolution was given.

Then we moved to the living room and most of us sat down, some on the floor, for the service of the Word. If memory serves, parts of the service were read by girls; nobody thought much about it. After the epistle and the gospel, there was discussion, lasting perhaps an hour—too long, some of us felt, but rewarding. The priest set a tone that encouraged both teenagers and adults to speak up, giving their own responses. Some of them took exception to the ideas offered by the celebrant, and on reflection he agreed with some of their criticisms.

For the service of the Eucharist we gathered in a semi-circle around the dining room table. In other circumstances, one speculated, the priest might have used the vernacular; he dropped a broad hint that if anyone should ask to receive under both species, he would not feel able to deny the request. But the Canon and Communion were quite as usual, except that the bread the priest consecrated—a single unleavened loaf, which he broke and distributed at Communion—had been baked by the mother of the host family. Unfortunately there had been no time to practice singing and no accompanying instrument was available, and so only one hymn was sung, a conventional hymn of thanksgiving after the last blessing.

When Mass was over, coffee, Cokes and cookies were served, and there was more discussion—going on, in fact, till the priest "hid himself from the multitude" by going upstairs to his bedroom.

According to Father Annibale Bugnini, who explained the latest liturgical declaration in a press conference last week, celebrating the Eucharist in a private home in this way "minimizes and weakens the sense of the church as a meeting place for the people of God in its wider meaning." Further, "it would attenuate greatly the universal, communitarian and fraternal aspect of Communion in the faith and in the charity which must animate our full Christian assemblies."

With all due respect, but with the candor that seems needed, we suggest the possibility that Father Bugnini quite literally doesn't know what he is talking about.

SEPTEMBER 13, 1967

Trenton, N.J.—A priest and 20 Catholics who have been holding around-the-table home liturgies for 10 months have announced they will form an experimental parish against the wishes of their bishop.

Both the priest and the layman who is the informal head of the group said they are bringing the underground community into the open as a "religious form of civil disobedience" to protest what they say is the too-slow pace of renewal.

Both said too that they didn't consider they were separating themselves from the Roman Catholic Church, and added that they would recruit up to 40 more adult Catholic members for the parish, called CLEO (Catholic Laymen's Experimental Organization).

The priest is Father George J. Hafner, 40, an assistant pastor for 13 years, who is currently at St. James church in Jamesburg, N.J. He said he will leave that assignment to serve as the new group's priest. . . .

Father Hafner said the group was also concerned "over the Church's failure to meet the real problems of the day." He said CLEO has plans to work on a war on poverty project and added that members will be active in civil rights and peace efforts. He said the new group will try to work through civil institutions, rather than start its own Church programs. . . .

Father Hafner said a few people first began to meet in August of 1966. They wanted to push for renewal but recognized they were too small and inexperienced, and became a study club instead, he said.

After two months, they started having Masses at the meetings and they have continued to do so. The group has met every other week. Membership eventually grew to 30 adults.

Father Hafner said the Masses are "probably close to what a lot of underground communities are doing." He said members usually are seated around a table.

They sing songs in a contemporary idiom, and have readings from the Bible as well as from newspapers, books or other contemporary sources. The homily is an open discussion. There are extemporary prayers.

Father Hafner said leaven bread—"usually little buns"—and individual glasses of wine are used. He said he says an "informal consecratory prayer" and then passes them out and each person communicates himself.

Father Hafner . . . said these home liturgies were a key factor in the formation of the group. . . . "The experience of such intense community gradually formed the members of the group in the conviction that this type of Christian community life was the kind they were seeking."

In June, Father Hafner said, CLEO considered joining the National Association of Laymen, an independent lay organization seeking a voice in Church affairs, but decided against it. "We just felt that we would get in the same old power struggle, playing the diplomatic game of trying to get permission to take off the maniple (the napkin-like vestment formerly worn on the left forearm)," Father Hafner said. "We just decided that—just like the Negro situation—we just can't wait forever while people make minor changes in the law."

Father Hafner said Bishop Ahr turned down the request to approve the experimental parish because it would upset too many Catholics. After that, the priest said, the group met Sunday, August 27, to decide what to do.

Father Hafner said that 10 adult members decided at that meeting they do not want to continue without approval and are dropping out. The rest favored announcing what they were doing and seeking new members, he said.

OCTOBER 18, 1967

Trenton, N.J.—Bishop George W. Ahr says he has ruled out any possible approval for an unauthorized floating parish because its founder, Father George J. Hafner, gave a talk in which he said the Church is corrupt.

Bishop Ahr, 63, took the action in a letter dated October 5, the day after Father Hafner's talk to 200 persons at the Newman Club of Monmouth College in Long Branch, N.J.

The events shattered a temporary truce that had been worked out between the bishop and the Catholic Laymen's Experimental Organization which has been holding unauthorized home Masses for almost a year. The bishop had agreed to reconsider his rejection of the group after its members said they would halt the Masses. The truce lasted less than a week.

Excerpts from Father Hafner's talk at Monmouth College:

The entire Christian Church has become corrupt. I can speak with assurance only of my own Church, the Catholic Church, but many from other denominations have told me that the same state exists in their Church as in ours.

Corruption is a strong word but I believe that it is time for strong words. A Church is corrupt when it has been turned away from its original goal and purpose and so modified that it serves its original purpose no longer. This is certainly the case in the Catholic Church.

The corruption can be seen in the building of marble palaces for the men who claim to be successors of the Man "who had not whereon to lay his head." The corruption can be seen in the political machinations for position in the Church by men who claim to be the guides to sincerity and truth. The corruption can be sensed in the superior, lordly air which surrounds the visit of a bishop or a cardinal.

The corruption can be observed any day in the towering structures called the "house of God" which dominate the slums of our large cities. The corruption can be experienced any time one takes part in the mechanical ritual of precisely executed ceremony of the Roman ritual, so completely opposite the simple meal of brotherhood established by Jesus. . . .

We must repeat once more that the superfluous wealth of rich countries should be placed at the service of poor nations, the rule which up to now held good for the benefit of those nearest to us, must today be applied to all the needy of this world.

I am sure that the Pope is fully sincere in his desire to help the poor. We are told he was deeply moved by the conditions he saw in India. Why then does he live in a royal palace, dress in outlandishly lavish clothes, allow himself to be carried in a gilded chair and maintain a retinue of servants that no millionaire would have?

Why does the Vatican continue to hold its assets in the Italian banks estimated at close to $10 billion which could feed most of the poor of Italy. Why does the Vatican maintain a medieval city-state in the middle of the city of Rome with all the implications of being a state separate from the real world?

It is time that the whole monument to medieval Christendom be turned into a museum and the visitors' fees to be used for the poor. Let the Pope adopt the simple clothing and manners of modern man. Let the vast bureaucratic system be decentralized and only truly central issues handled in Rome.

Nor is the corruption in the Church limited to the Vatican. Look at the building programs going on in any diocese in our county. In our diocese $16.5 million are about to be spent on four high schools for our white middle class children while Negro and Puerto Rican children in this same diocese will continue to receive inadequate schooling, live in inadequate housing, be deprived of opportunities for betterment and bitten by rats.

Look at the rectories in which our clergy (the servants of the people of God!) live in luxury. Hardly a house in the community can be compared to the rectory in wealth and opulence.

One more area. This year in all likelihood the Catholic Church in the United States will spend more than 50 million dollars in church refurbishing. The liturgical renewal calls for a renovation of churches. Most bishops insist that the redecoration of the "house of God" be done with fitting dignity. Therefore, nothing but the best will be used in most places.

Our own cathedral is about to be redone to suit the new liturgy. It will surely cost over $100,000. While the work of renovation of that building goes on so that "devout" Catholics may worship more meaningfully, the poor will still be starving and living in degraded circumstances less than a block from the cathedral door.

What in God's name are we talking about when we ask for more *meaningful* services if the gospel is preached and the Catholic populace comforted with the sacraments while Catholics remain free to ignore the crying needs of their neighbors! How can we speak of preaching the gospel at all when the very place in which it is preached denies the whole meaning of the message! . . .

I have become fully convinced that no temporary measures, no gradualism, no revision of ceremonies, no new organization within the Church will meet the crisis which is so suddenly developing within the Church.

This past summer one half of all the seminarians in our diocese quit. Everyone knows that nuns are leaving in droves—and not the mean or problem-type nuns either—often the best and most dedicated women of their community.

Priests are quitting in great numbers—I believe the opposition to celibacy is indicative of the frustration and despair that a man feels in the welter of red tape and institutionalism which restricts him as he tries to be of service to his people.

Catholics, young and old, are just quietly absenting themselves from church because they find it totally unrelated to their lives. I have received literally hundreds of calls and letters from people who have said that they have given up the practice of their religion or were just about to do so because the whole business is so meaningless.

The result is building like a gigantic ocean swell and the Church is calmly putting up a picket fence to solve the problem.

F. IN NUNS AND THE PRIESTHOOD

The ferment is having profound effects on nuns and priests, a ferment ranging from discontent and disenchantment to renewed vitality born of a feeling of liberation. The discontented and disenchanted are leaving in larger than ever before numbers—or hover on the verge in a touch-and-go ministry. The newly liberated are either seeing their ministries in a new light or are beginning to find room to openly proclaim what has always been in their hearts. As a group, nuns appear to be running far ahead of priests in terms of outward signs of true renewal. Most priests seem to be doing business as usual.

January 13, 1965

Cincinnati—A nun-missioner issued a call for Sisters to "leave the security of our 'safety islands' and step out into the traffic of renewal."

Sister M. Joseph Clare, member of the Movement for a Better World staff in Washington, D.C., told about 600 nuns at a workshop that "some of us may be knocked down in the process" but the risk has to be taken if Religious hope to "grow with the Church."

To develop a "keen sense of the Church," nuns occasionally may have to abandon "pet projects" to fill new needs, said Sister Joseph Clare, of the Sisters of St. Francis of Mary of Joliet, Ill.

She suggested that it may be better to help thousands of Catholic students on a secular college campus than, for instance, to be a member of the staff of a small parish school, when the needs of the total Church are assessed. She advised nuns to make themselves "available to the poor and lonely," and to look for opportunities to engage in adult education as well as teaching children.

Sister Joseph Clare called for "re-evaluation of religious life" within religious communities and for opening up of channels of communication between Sisters and their superiors.

Some of the silence of religious life could be put aside in favor of healthier "dialogue" between members of a community, she suggested.

APRIL 28, 1965—A letter to the editor:

A few thoughts on priest-Sister relationships:

What a sad comment on our corporate Christian maturity, when "love of God" bars in-depth communication with the dispensers of the Mystery of Christ—and this, in the name of "virtue" and "prudence."

How we could grow from genuine interpersonal relationships! But first we must realize that it is only as human Christian religious, and in that sequence, that we encounter each other. We must be willing to truly know one another and just as willingly be known, all of which require time and a greater measure of freedom. That warmth and genuine affection may enter a priest-Sister relationship is simple testimony to the human element which MUST exist: Christian love of neighbor (I presume this still includes priests and Sisters) has never presupposed denatured beings!

I can't help wondering how many Sisters would have missed Christ completely had He appeared, for the first time, in our decade, wearing clerical black and a Roman collar. A more honest Christian viewpoint on human relationships in general would be of salvific import to us all!

> Sister Mary Bohlen, O.S.F.,
> Naperville, Ill.

MAY 5, 1965—In a speech to some 1,500 Milwaukee area nuns, Rev. Alfred McBride, O. Praem., of St. Norbert's Abbey (De Pere, Wis.) discusses convent life:

The technique of secrecy. Communities which function on the "I love a mystery approach" are doomed to fall. The hiding which is so prominent in religious houses can only lead to suspicion and cynicism . . . it destroys the openness which is essential to community. Secrecy spawns intrigue and is a persistent threat to honesty.

The failure of confrontation. Fraternal charity has often degenerated into a bland charade in which more reasons are adduced for avoiding the genuine solution of personal differences than for true and courageous "laying it on the line." The failure to confront produces a polite system of coexistence rather than community. It issues in the somewhat humorous situation where the party line inexorably drones on "we are a community," while implicit policy tersely cautions "don't communicate!"

Make convents into homes not houses. The spartan barracks-like atmosphere of many religious dwellings strips them of all human warmth. The proverbial scrubbed look of many convents may solicit a wistful sigh of envy from a housewife, but there is the uneasy feeling that Lady Macbeth walks the halls at night. Not many people feel comfortable in the antiseptic atmosphere of an operating room . . . convents . . . should not be baptized West Points.

Apply the principle of participation. The local convent is presumably a community of adults—if all decisions and solutions are centered in only one person, then the intelligence, experience and creative power of the rest of the community is untapped, ignored, frustrated and eventually atrophied. . . . In every other area of modern life the crossfire of community exchange is a normal and accepted procedure. I see no reason why it cannot be part of religious life.

JULY 5, 1967—From a story by correspondent Margaret Martin:

Shreveport, La.—Twenty members of the Daughters of the Cross announced last week they are leaving the order to establish an experimental lay community in Milwaukee this summer.

The 20 include an assistant principal of a Shreveport high school, two grade school principals and the mistress of novices at the motherhouse.

Their departure will leave the Shreveport-based order with 60 nuns, most of them working in Louisiana.

The nuns applied for a dispensation from their vows and will return to their legal names. They will not wear a habit. They will live in small groups in apartment houses and share their earnings to support themselves.

Some will be in non-teaching fields, but most will stay in teaching, which is the order's primary apostolate. Several have applied for jobs in the Milwaukee public schools. . . .

Some of the nuns said they felt that the restrictions of convent life prevent them from mixing more with the secular community and with their pupils.

The 20 range in age from 24 to 54. Six had not professed final vows, and one has been a member of the order for 37 years.

Although they are the first Daughters of the Cross to try experimental community living, several other orders have lost members to such experiments. One of the largest previous groups to leave an order was made up of 10 Sisters of Notre Dame who left Cleveland last year to form an experimental community in Pueblo, Colo.

JANUARY 20, 1965—Among those Catholics raising the question, "Why not women priests?" is Mary Daly, an American, holder of a doctorate in sacred theology from the University of Fribourg:

One can only hope that it will be given fair consideration and that those who are too prone to give specious arguments will think seriously of all that is involved.

In an age in which there is a crying need for priests in many countries, it is possible that the exclusion of women from Orders will have tragic consequences.

In any case, the ambiguity concerning the status of Catholic women—an ambiguity in which anachronistic ideas and practices meet modern realities in head-on collision—cannot continue without increasing harm to women as persons and to the Church as a society.

Urged to speak and to lead in public life, but condemned within the Church to silence befitting their predecessors of nineteen hundred years ago, Catholic women feel the forces of contradiction and look hopefully to the future. The anti-feminist tradition within the Church is having a hard time finding firm legs to stand on. The props offered in the past by existing social conditions, by false biological and philosophical theories, and by anti-feminist legislation have melted away.

FEBRUARY 10, 1965—Two Catholic priests, one a psychotherapist and the other a psychologist have written a book entitled *Psychological Aspects of Seminary Life* (by George Hagmaier, C.S.P., and Eugene C. Kennedy, M.M.; University of Notre Dame Press, 1965). The seminarian "grows totally or not at all," they suggest:

One of the aspects of family life which should *not* be brought into religion is a perpetuation of the parent-child relationship. Seminarians are not children, and the rector and faculty should not perceive themselves as parental figures. Staff and students are equals in many respects, and in some intellectual, spiritual, and psychological matters the young may occasionally outrank the old.

The emotionally insecure adult needs to have other adults dependent on him, such as the rector who is reassured as to his own worth and supposed autonomy only when his most whimsical and autocratic demands are met with immediate and unquestioning compliance. Infantile personalities invested with authority all too often reproduce others of their kind. There is an axiom in psychology which holds: treat an adult as a child and he will act as a child. This is the reason, perhaps, why Cardinal Suenens suggests: "An adult cannot renounce the right to obey as an adult."

Yet many seminarians have no choice. They are, year after year, "to be seen but not heard." It is not surprising, therefore, that later on, as pastors and superiors, they exercise the same autocratic, blindly demanding, and at times even arrogant sway over their subjects or curates. They "give as they got," because unhappily they know nothing else.

MARCH 24, 1967—A letter to the editor:

The practice of giving stipends for Masses and for the sacraments of baptism and matrimony has always been a cause of embarrassment to me and, I believe, a source of cynicism among both Catholics and non-Catholics, and as I look back I cannot recall a single instance of a Catholic publication candidly discussing or explaining it. If my thoughts are the result of an idiosyncracy peculiar to me then they need not take up your time. If, however, there is a wider interest, then you could do both priests and laymen a service by publishing a discussion of the practice.

The Mass stipend seems to encourage and to thrive on a superstitious attitude toward the Mass which reduces the Mass to a fetish that gives the owner a magical power over salvation. People who are calloused to the needs of others while they are alive attempt to insure salvation by setting aside a sum in their wills for their own departed souls.

Another aspect that might be considered is what does one who pays a Mass stipend really get. I do not believe that most people know. Does he corner the graces emanating from Sacrifice? Or is he merely remembered by the priest and congregation in their personal prayers? If it is the latter, should one have to pay for prayer?

You may find my use of the word "pay" offensive; however, when there is a rate schedule and a feeling on the part of most people that they must give something, isn't it a fiction to characterize the stipend as a gift? It does not appear that the priest is praying for the soul or intention of a benefactor who has remembered him. On the contrary, he appears to be praying, and in a manner agreed to beforehand, because he has been paid to do so. If he does not, the "benefactor" feels cheated. There certainly is not much spontaneity on either side in such a situation.

The aspect of the market place becomes more evident at baptisms and weddings where we even abandon the language of gifts and cautiously inquire, "How much are you supposed to pay Father?" or "Did you pay the priest?" It is difficult to see how the priest's character as Christ's representative can keep from suffering if he is reduced to selling sacramental services. I feel certain that American priests do not refuse to baptize or to marry people who are unable or who are even unwilling to pay. However, there must be some disappointment in the former case and some ill-feeling in the latter case on both sides which does not enhance the priest's pastoral effectiveness.

If the cause is economic, perhaps we should stop deluding ourselves into believing that a priest can live on $150 a month and start paying him a decent salary.

In going on at such length I probably have demonstrated my ignorance on the subject, which I readily admit. I have done so merely to suggest areas that might be profitably discussed. Well, you have listened to me; now I would like to hear from you.

William M. Barvick,
Kansas City, Mo.

Editor's note: Readers' comments are invited.

JUNE 16, 1965—A letter to the editor:

It is a sad, sad sight to see a man become walled up within himself because of the decision made in the exuberant generosity of his youth. How many priests are thus imprisoned by a decision prompted by an immature idealism?

To be productive of any good, celibacy in the Church must be voluntary. It would be cruel and unjust to force this "martyrdom" upon any man. We readily assume that celibacy in the clergy is voluntary because it is taken only after some seven or eight years of preparation and it is taken in a public manner. From a legal point of view, this assumption is valid. But what about the psychology of the situation?

In order to take on a lifetime burden freely, there must be clear knowledge of what one is doing. An infant, obviously, cannot marry. By the same token we must question whether or not a man of 25 can determine what he will voluntarily be accepting at the age of 50. Just how knowledgeable is the sheltered levite in the matter of matrimony? His years in a parish, if he is lucky enough to get a pastoral assignment, will later convince him that he knew very little about parental life at the time of his ordination.

Celibacy—in order to be Christ-like, in order to be truly productive within the personality—must be continuously voluntary. It must be freely accepted each day. When it is only tolerated because there is no other way out, or because rejection of it will mean excommunication, a scandal in the community, and a broken heart, then there is no meaning left in it, no purpose for it.

Some may say that the same reasoning that would permit priests to abandon celibacy would allow for divorce and remarriage for reasons of unhappiness. But the parallel is not exact. There is nothing in the nature of celibacy that demands that it be permanent. In fact, novices take it only for short periods of time. Also marriage brings with it interlocking responsibilities toward one's wife or husband, sons and daughters. In celibacy a man stands alone.

Basically, I would conclude that if there are reasons to dispense a Brother or Sister from "perpetual" vows of chastity— then the same reasons for freedom apply to priests. In a situation where a priest no longer *voluntarily* accepts his celibate state we run the risk of his decline into a state of moroseness of mind or actual perversion of body. It is much more humane to give the alternative of a dispensation from celibacy, for "it is better to marry than to burn."

It may take a century before we achieve a married clergy in the West. Until then, charity demands that we give an alternative to excommunication or embitterment, namely, a dispensation from celibacy for the priest who no longer can freely accept this way of life.

Southern *Sacerdos*

AUGUST 4, 1965—From an editorial on celibacy:

There is no point in concealing our own opinion, or in inflating its value. We think modification of the discipline on celibacy is advisable. This is, however, a properly tentative conclusion. We are not so tentative about the need for study and discussion. Finally, there are hard-nosed types who say that the authorities in the Church will not take another look at celibacy until or unless forced to it by the pastoral necessity of filling empty pastorates. We hope they are wrong, that the matter can be studied on its merits.

In our opinion it would be an acceptance of personal responsibility for those who agree with these views to make known their judgment of the matter to their bishops. The same is true (we admit with some reluctance) of those who disagree.

MAY 4, 1966—Students at St. Charles Borromeo Seminary, Philadelphia, evaluated their institution in a report to be delivered to Archbishop John J. Krol. In their study, the students found St. Charles deficient in every area of training for priestly service. The report followed by three weeks a thirty-student walkout protesting a fellow-student's expulsion from a scripture class.

Excerpts from the report:

In general the students are conscious often not only of a lack of fraternal charity in the student-professor relationship, but also the actual presence of a mutual spirit of antagonism. Student initiative is frequently judged as student aggressiveness and insubordination. A spirit of intellectual inquiry is often dealt with as a symptom of arrogance or intellectual pride. . . .

There seems to be no agreement within the official seminary mind of what the priest of today is supposed to be and to know, or how he is to be trained. . . .

Students have "a feeling of academic inferiority" because of the seminary's lack of accreditation, and that "this sense of inadequacy . . . is reinforced by the attitude of some professors who feel that many of the students would not be successful in a college or university environment, and who teach accordingly. Hence, a real sense of challenge never arises. . .".

Many faculty members lack knowledge of the "actual mentality of the students." There is an "absence of certain fundamental competencies, both in the subjects they have been assigned to teach and also in specific training and pedagogical method" among faculty members. . . .

Too often emphasis was placed on "the negative approach of seeking out error, rather than a positive one of searching for the truth," and . . . academic freedom was hindered by some professors who assumed the role of disciplinarians.

Library facilities suffered from a lack of qualified personnel and a "dearth of well-chosen books currently in demand."

A student survey showed that "only 10 to 20 percent of the books in the seminary collection would be of any conceivable use to the students in the present curriculum."

The students recalled that *The Egg and I,* a humorous account of life on a chicken farm "was once shelved under agriculture, and a book on politics called *The Changing Tides* was shelved in the geography section."

The present system of discipline fails to create an atmosphere in which the individual can exercise his individuality without being thought of as a threat to the common order. The seminarian learns early to begin to submerge his personality in order to serve the smooth functioning of the system desired by the authorities. . . . Initiative should not only be allowed, be granted grudgingly by authority; rather it must be demanded from those who are to be the leaders of God's people.

OCTOBER 5, 1966—A letter to the editor:

Many priests who have married and many priests who will marry in violation of the law may be guilty of violating a commitment to the priesthood but not to celibacy. The Church recognizes that a commitment made without awareness of circumstances is not binding. For example, a person who makes a "holy commitment" in marriage to a blood relative is no longer bound to this commitment when this circumstance becomes known (Canon 1076).

The priest who accepted celibacy at the time of his subdiaconate could easily lack awareness of the circumstances and therefore feel free to marry without breaking a commitment to celibacy. For example, as a seminarian he is conditioned to think that celibacy will allow him fuller freedom to serve God and the Church and that if he were married his field of service and effectiveness as a priest would be restricted. After functioning as a priest for a few years he discovers that 99 per cent of the priests he knows could still have done what they did and continue to do what they are doing with a wife. He discovers that he himself would be much more effective in his priesthood with a wife at his side rather than a pastor over his head. Existentially he realizes that the conditioning he received was false. The reason motivating him to accept celibacy was not valid. Ergo, he concludes that there is no violation of a "holy commitment" to celibacy if he should marry or has married. His conscience is free of guilt. He feels no need to subject himself to the indignities presently required for a priest to get permission to marry.

There are other reasons why a priest may feel free to marry without violating a "holy commitment." For example, a priest may follow the following course of reasoning: Celibacy is a

charism, a special gift of God for the sake of the church. (*Cf.*
Decree on the Ministry and Life of Priests, Ch. 3, p. 16). As a
charism it cannot be induced or demanded by ecclesiastical legislation. Prescribed by law it is envisioned as a deprivation of right
and a matter utterly outside the limits of ecclesiastical jurisdiction. The officers of the Church have transcended the scope of
their authority to "preach the gospel" (Mark 16:15) in making
it a necessary step to priesthood. Accordingly it is a law that
has no right to exist, a bad law. And so, a priest, realizing he
does not have the charism of celibacy, feels free to marry without violating a commitment to celibacy like the Southern Negro
who does not break a commitment when he exercises his right
to vote after failing to do so for years because of a misguided
cultural pressure.

In the light of the above thinking it would be more accurate
to say they were not breaking a commitment but pursuing a
right.

Unfortunately, in pursuing this right they have had to give
up the exercise of their priesthood. Perhaps there is a failure
in commitment here, but perhaps not. Their marriages could
be regarded as an eloquent and courageous condemnation of an
unjust law and a call for immediate reform. Are there not times
when a flight into Egypt is justifiable until the Herodic system
is dead? Then will the celibate priests and the married priests
live together in freedom and mutual respect exercising their sacred ministry.

(Rev.) Frank De Witt,
Chesaning, Mich.

JUNE 28, 1967—A letter to the editor:

I am a middle aged priest. During the past couple of years it
has become gradually more clear to me that I can't continue the
celibate life. It is humbling to me to admit that I have to put
down the crown of celibacy because I am not called to it. Nevertheless, I'm strongly convinced of my priestly vocation. To me
it would seem a grave act of treason were I to abandon the
exercise of the priestly service.

Neither in the gospels nor in the epistles do I find any indica-
tion of a contradiction or incongruity between the priesthood and

the married state. Nor can this be found in the history of the first centuries of Christ's Church.

In scripture, celibacy is presented with great delicacy as a very special charism or calling. However, it is not necessarily related to the priestly calling. I found, rather, some very serious warnings against taking this privilege lightly, as in St. Paul's: "Better to marry than to burn."

The vocation to the priesthood is, to my mind, a serious and special calling from God and scripture is the Word of God. For these reasons I feel compelled in conscience to continue my priestly mission and at the same time to marry, that is: I need to be married *in order* to live up to my calling as a priest.

Would there be anybody who is willing to help me find a way to work this out in such a manner so that I would not be excommunicated by the ecclesiastical authorities? Would there be any bishop willing to override a man-made law in order to give more freedom to God's designs?

Although this is a very personal problem, I know I'm speaking also for you, tens of thousands of fellow priests, who are in similar straits. Some of you have already decided for one or the other side of the dilemma. You have either given up your mission as a priest, leaving you with a bitter taste of frustration and dissatisfaction, or you held on to the practice of your priesthood in spite of constant struggle. In this case you are left with the bad conscience of having ruined the life of the woman most dear to you. Others of you have resorted to some sort of concubinage, causing you and your partner the excruciating pains of constant qualms of conscience.

I call on you, my fellow priests, to do everything possible to live up to your conscience, be brave and fight for this inalienable right.

Purifying changes, as history indicates, have usually originated in the grass roots. Hierarchy has recognized and legalized these changes later.

Christian obedience is not the blind obedience exacted by authoritarianism, which disregards completely personal conscience and responsibility. I wish to recall here, for clarification, the trial of Adolf Eichmann.

Christ demands love. From love springs an obedience which is a personal response requiring the full use of free will and intellect, thus enhancing the importance of personal conscience.

Our Church is losing ground and vocations to a large extent due to lack of enough dedicated and happy priests, and because of many embittered priests. Millions of people are as sheep without a shepherd. Must this continue in order to sustain a restrictive, man-made law?

Name withheld

OCTOBER 25, 1967—From a story by William J. Mitchell:

Notre Dame, Ind.—Slashing away at a Church he said has "kept men guilty, frightened, docile, loyal and silent," Father James Kavanaugh renounced his priesthood before 400 persons at the University of Notre Dame, Oct. 15.

He claimed, "the institutional Church is dead," and suggested, "the Bishops at the synod are wasting their time."

Author of the best-selling book, *A Modern Priest Looks at His Outdated Church,* Kavanaugh said, "I will resign my priesthood. I'm tired of beating my head against the wall."

He explained the rationale behind his resignation: "I plan to formally disassociate myself from the priesthood as a means to express my utter rejection of the refusal of the bishops to put Vatican II into effect."

He said, "I hope to give others the courage to do the same."

Blasting everything from Church doctrine and the sacraments to religious celibacy and hierarchical authority, he said, "Your institution can go to hell! I want no part of it. I don't find it in the gospels."

G. IN THE WAR ON POVERTY

Self-examination as "Church of the poor" is one of the Catholic Left's principal preoccupations. There are few hopeful signs, however, that the institution as such is taking itself seriously in this regard.

NOVEMBER 11, 1964—From an editorial on poverty:

Christ did not say that the Church was like a field set apart and divinely protected from the existence of evils and problems. He did not say that the Church was above mundane matters; it would be planted in the earth, in dirt. He did not envision the Church as static, complete or perfect; it would be a tiny, dynamic element mingled with other elements and making them different through its presence. The Church, then, must be involved in all aspects of human life, must be concerned about the realities of poverty and nuclear war and family life, about governments and economics and underdeveloped peoples. The Church must be in the world. . . . Christ immersed Himself in the problems of men and shared in their joys; He was wonderfully human and it was through His humanity that He reached the world and was its salvation. The Church—its bishops, priests, religious and laity, collectively and individually—cannot ignore or hold in disdain the common clay of human affairs; it was in such clay that 2,000 years ago the seed of life was planted.

DECEMBER 9, 1964—Columnist John Leo described the scene as Cardinal Spellman dramatically opened a package containing a fancy leather case, at a New York luncheon. The

package contained Pope Paul's $80,000 tiara which he had
announced as a gift to the poor:

The cardinal obviously enjoyed the drama of the occasion, including the tale of how he had smuggled the tiara through customs. . . . Most of his guests were properly overcome . . .
touching it reverently and in general displaying the sense of
awe appropriate to what the cardinal has called "an object of
veneration." . . . the cardinal explained that the tiara was a gift
from the Pope to the American Church. No reporter was crass
enough to point out that the tiara had already been announced
as a gift to the poor, which the American Church is not. . . .
The tiara is now on display in St. Patrick's Cathedral, near the
wax dummy of Pius XII with the big emeralds on its hand.
After New York has paid its respects, the tiara will be sent on
tour so that everyone will have a chance to file by it reverently.
. . . Then it will be deposited in the Vatican Pavilion . . . before ending its days in the National Shrine in Washington,
which as anyone who has seen both the Shrine and the tiara
can testify, is even more appropriate. . . . I confess an inability
to understand how the Church can seriously attempt a campaign
against poverty, as it did at the council, while the Pope has an
$80,000 tiara gathering dust in the attic, and while the cardinals
sit pondering the question in ermine and silk outfits that *Time*
magazine tells me are worth $3,000 each. This is why the
Pope's recent announcement about donating the tiara to the
poor struck me as a moving and telling gesture. . . . It seemed
to subtly suggest a whole new tone for the Church in its attitude
to worldly riches and in its traditional fascination with pomp
and golden "objects of veneration." . . . But now it appears . . .
the Church is not divesting itself of anything at all . . . the
Pope's magnificent gesture now looks a bit shabby. The lesson
it was intended to impart has been neatly undercut . . . [and]
the most disturbing aspect to me was that in the name of poverty
the Pope should send an expensive tiara to the richest nation
on the earth, the very week that he was departing on a pilgrimage to one of the poorest. The Pope has spoken movingly of his
intent to make the trip to India in the spirit of Gandhi. If he
had instructed the men around him to ship the tiara to India

(instead of, say, the white papal auto that was shipped there for his own use) he might have made a profound impact on India and the world. Certainly it would have been somewhat closer to the spirit of Gandhi. But instead of being divided and sold for the benefit of poor Indians, it is being kept intact for the alleged edification of rich Americans. So goes the opening skirmish of the war on poverty.

FEBRUARY 10, 1965—From a story by A. V. Krebs, Jr.:

San Francisco—The Rev. Ronald A. Burke, the Gilroy, Calif., priest whose activities on the community's Interfaith Migrant Committee were the center of a recent controversy, has received the John F. Kennedy Human Rights award of the Santa Clara County Catholic Interracial Council.

Father Burke had been co-chairman of the Migrant Committee until last November when his term of office expired. His pastor, the Rev. John T. Dwyer, directed him not to accept another term as co-chairman. Catholic growers had launched an economic boycott against St. Mary's parish in protest over Father Burke's activities.

The CIC citation praised Father Burke as the citizen of the community who "best challenged the conscience of the community to recognize right as well as reason and to avoid shame as well as violence, to the person who best accepted the truth 'that here on earth God's work must truly be our own.'"

Father Dwyer, in admitting Sunday collections dropped during the Father Burke controversy, stated: "Father Burke's term of office expired at the very time this dispute arose. I suggested that he not seek reappointment because I felt this was an area where a layman's participation was better, particularly in view of the Vatican Council's statement on the role of the laity. Archbishop McGucken backed me up in my belief that a layman can do a better job.

MARCH 9, 1966—Cardinal Joseph Ritter of St. Louis has asked all of the assistant pastors under his jurisdiction to notify him if they wish to serve in poor inner-city parishes.

"I realize this is an unusual request, but these are unusual times. Unusual opportunities present themselves. Priests now involved in performing service in poor areas 'are doing wonderful work,' " said Cardinal Ritter.

APRIL 20, 1966—A correspondent reports on the current activities of Father Philip Berrigan:

Baltimore—In the year since his sudden transfer to a Baltimore slum parish, Father Phil Berrigan has managed to stir up city hall enough that West Baltimore is no longer being written off as an area where nothing can be done.

The Josephite, a campaigner for Vietnam peace, nuclear disarmament and civil rights, was transferred abruptly to St. Peter Claver parish April 24, 1965, reportedly because his foreign policy views clashed with those of some residents of Newburgh, N.Y., where he was teaching in a Josephite seminary.

Since the transfer, his activities have been shaded by a cutback in speechmaking and by the full reported controversy concerning the Latin American assignment of his brother, Father Daniel Berrigan, S.J.

During the first six months at the Baltimore assignment, Father Berrigan directed a survey of housing conditions, helped line up more than 100 frightened residents to file formal charges against landlords and leveled a series of charges against local officialdom. The charges began with the suggestion that the "city administration seems to exist for landlords rather than tenants," and ended with the warning that West Baltimore might be in for an eruption similar to the one in Watts.

In the last three months the action he stirred up has begun paying off for West Baltimoreans. Building inspectors have shown up at dilapidated buildings. Landlords have been appearing in housing court. Pressure for reform of local housing laws has taken on a new urgency. . . .

FEBRUARY 8, 1967

An article critical of U.S. Catholic missionary efforts in Latin America has erupted in a dispute between Cardinal Richard Cushing of Boston and the author Msgr. Ivan Illich.

In Boston, Cardinal Cushing made an unscheduled appearance before 2,000 persons at the Catholic Inter-American Cooperation Program (CICOP) conference to label the article "a colossal lie."

In Cuernavaca, Mexico, where he is director of the Center of Inter-cultural Documentation which trains Latin American missionaries, Msgr. Illich told the *N.C.R.:* "If the cardinal has said that, then he has not carefully read the article or else he doesn't know the facts."

Writing in the January 21 issue of *America,* the Jesuit weekly, Msgr. Illich argued in an article entitled "The Seamy Side of Charity" that:

—U.S. missionaries, wittingly or not, often work to support U.S. political and economic interests in Latin America.

—They help to perpetuate the status quo in a social and economic system that desperately needs changing.

—They carry "a foreign Christian image, a foreign pastoral approach and a foreign political message."

FEBRUARY 15, 1967

San Antonio—Two priests punished for entering the Brownsville (Texas) diocese to aid striking Mexican-American farm workers pleaded last week that needs of people be put before Church protocol.

The priests are Fathers William Killian and Sherrill Smith. They and three other San Antonio priests were arrested near Rio Grande City February 1 as they tried to encourage lettuce pickers to strike.

When they returned to San Antonio, released on $100 bond, Father Killian, editor of the archdiocesan paper, the *Alamo Messenger,* and Father Smith, archdiocesan director of social justice, were ordered by Archbishop Robert Lucey to spend a week at a Jemez Springs, N.M., retreat house.

The other three priests, who went without permission but not in disobedience of a direct order to stay home, were not punished. Fathers Killian and Smith admitted disobeying the archbishop's order and said the punishment was just.

MAY 10, 1967—From "An Open Letter to the Pope," by Donald McDonald:

An "example" is now needed in the world community, an example to verify the moral-philosophical truth that the generosity which the rich must show to the poor is not an option, it is an obligation.

May I suggest that as an earnest [expression] of your own and the Church's deep commitment to this moral truth, as expressed in your most recent encyclical, *Populorum Progressio,* and as a follow-up to that encyclical, you make the following proposal to the world community:

The Roman Catholic Church will contribute one-half of its wealth to a World Fund to be administered for the benefit of the poor and underdeveloped peoples of the world, on the condition that each nation in the world agree to contribute two percent of its Gross National Product to the same World Fund for the same purpose for a period of the next ten years.

By this act, the Church would demonstrate concretely and generously to the world that its concern for the poor and the destitute peoples is sincere, that it is real and that it is deep.

I feel confident that such a generous action on the part of the Church would generate similar generous actions on the part of other churches, and on the part of national governments throughout the world.

I feel confident it would also inspire individual men and women, believers and unbelievers alike, to make substantial sacrifices of their personal possessions in order to make personal contributions to the World Fund.

It would also enable the Church to "travel light" on its pilgrimage through time, unencumbered with much of its present material possessions which, as you know, have been the cause for criticism directed against the Church not only by those who are not Catholics but by those Catholics who believe it unseemly for the Church of the Carpenter of Nazareth to present such a lavish and luxurious exterior to a world which measures sincerity as much by one's actions as by one's words.

I make this suggestion mindful of the fact that the Church's charity on behalf of the world's poor has been magnificent and that much of it has not been conspicuous or even visible. I am also mindful that the accumulation of the Church's wealth has been an accumulation over hundreds of years, dating back to a time in history when it was virtually only the Church which was in a position to perform the essential custodial function of preserving intact the artistic and intellectual heritage of mankind. . . .

JUNE 7, 1967

Rochester, N.Y.—Bishop Fulton J. Sheen has announced a plan to tax all new construction in his diocese to help "the poor of the diocese and the poor of the world." He also said part of the diocesan development fund will be turned over to the poor. The tax will range from 1¼ per cent to 3 per cent, depending on the cost of the building. It will be levied on all new buildings and additions—churches, schools, rectories and convents—which ordinarily require chancery approval.

The purpose of the tax, said the bishop is two-fold: "To cut down on extravagances in building, but also to make the local Church conscious that it is part of the Mystical Body throughout the world."

He also told pastors that the annual Christmas collection—until now considered a gift to the pastor—must now be deposited in the general parish fund.

Bishop Sheen said the tax—levied after discussions with the diocesan advisory council—was being made "in consonance with the encyclical, *Development of the Peoples*," which states that the "advanced nations have a very heavy obligation to help the developing nations."

H. IN PEACE

For the Catholic Left the Nuclear Age has brought home with precision the idiocy of embracing war as an acceptable human institution.

FEBRUARY 17, 1965—Two Catholic priests—Daniel Berrigan, a Jesuit, and his brother Philip, a Josephite—and Dorothy Day, publisher of *The Catholic Worker,* signed a declaration pledging complete non-cooperation with the American prosecution of the Vietnam War. The declaration condemned the "suppression" of Vietnamese aspirations for political independence and economic freedom, and the "inhuman torture and senseless killing" in Vietnam. "Positive steps must be taken to put an end to the threat of nuclear catastrophe and death by chemical or biological warfare. . . ." It also acknowledged the signers' understanding that they were liable to prosecution under the Universal Military Training and Service Act which prohibits advising persons who face the draft to refuse service.

At a press conference in New York City, Father Berrigan elaborated on his position:

All that we can hope for is that through this action we can test the commitment of the Church—and others too—to the principles made explicit by Pope John XXIII in *Pacem in Terris,* perhaps particularly his statement, "It is hardly possible to imagine that in the atomic era war could be used as an instrument of justice."

We haven't yet said anything seriously critical of the immoral buildup in Vietnam. Rather than rock the boat—or rock the military—we seem willing to witness, even support either by silence or through actual personal effort, the incineration of millions of people.

He said his first hope was that "a few exposed actions—such as this public declaration—might awaken a few people," but added he feared relatively few Catholics were yet ready to make that response.

Our basic Catholic attitude seems to be "believe in Christ and be a good citizen." We don't seem to realize yet that it is not always possible to do both, that there are times when we are called to say "no" with our whole soul and body.

MARCH 10, 1965

New York—Priests, nuns, ministers and a rabbi were among 125 persons who took part in a one-hour sidewalk vigil March 3 protesting American military participation in Vietnam.

The demonstrators, mostly non-Catholics, stood along Broadway south of Times Square holding placards in the silent protest. In later comment, they criticized the renewed air attacks on North Vietnam and what they considered the American government's unwillingness to negotiate the crisis.

The participants included three priests and three nuns.

The priests were Fathers Peter Riga of Buffalo, Philip Berrigan of Newburgh, N.Y., and Thomas Cowley, an English Dominican in the United States on a research project. The three nuns, all from the College of New Rochelle, N.Y., were Mother Amadeus, the superior, Mother Mary Berchmans and Mother Mary Alice, director of students.

Father Riga called his participation "a last resort in protesting a seemingly hopeless situation." He cited Pope Paul's appeal for "use of the United Nations in promoting mediation of disputes and restoration of peace."

Father Riga also charged the United States had lost a sensitivity to people's desire to be free of oppression. "We have lost by aligning ourselves with a succession of governments which simply do not represent the people of South Vietnam."

MAY 5, 1965—Father Philip Berrigan, outspoken civil rights advocate and critic of U.S. policy in Vietnam, was ousted from the faculty of the Epiphany College Seminary (Newburgh, N.Y.). The seminary administration had apparently yielded to outside pressure which included threats to withdraw financial support of the institution. Very Rev. George O'dea, Epiphany superior, said that he had warned Berrigan to stop speaking about the war in Vietnam. But after the admonition, Berrigan said, in a speech to the Newburgh Community Affairs Council:

Do you honestly expect that we could so abuse our Negro citizens for 340 years, so resist their moral and democratic rights, so mistreat, exploit, starve, terrorize, rape and murder them without all this showing itself in foreign policy? . . .

Is it possible for us to be vicious, brutal, immoral and violent at home and be fair, judicious, beneficent and idealistic abroad?

The same government was involved and it reflects the moral and social caliber of its people, the same cross section of government and military personnel which works abroad as representative of the larger community in America.

Berrigan's removal, said O'dea, was "for the good of the order."

MARCH 29, 1967—One bishop, eight Catholic college presidents and 800 other Catholics sponsored an ad which condemned certain aspects of American Vietnam policy. Appearing in eight weekly newspapers, it "emphatically and unambiguously" denounced:

"Indiscriminate bombing, which grossly destroys any sufficient distinction between combatant and civilian;

"The horrible destruction of human life by means of napalm and fragmentation bombs;

"Depriving the populace of necessary food supplies through crop destruction;

"The torture of prisoners in any form whatsoever."

The statement in the ad also held "that immoral acts on one side do not justify immoral acts of retaliation on the other, and as Americans and Catholics we feel it necessary to call attention to our own responsibilities."

The co-sponsoring bishop is Auxiliary Bishop James P. Shannon of St. Paul and Minneapolis.

OCTOBER 25, 1967

In Detroit, Father Maurice Geary, a Roman Catholic representative in the local Clergy and Laymen Concerned About Vietnam organization, announced that two churches would be "sanctuaries" for men who refuse to take part in U.S. military [involvement] in South Vietnam.

Invoking the Middle Ages' right of sanctuary, Father Geary said the government would have to raid the church buildings to arrest Detroit area non-participants who seek refuge there. The churches are St. Joseph's Episcopal Church and Christ Lutheran, a Lutheran Church in America congregation.

He made the announcement on behalf of The Resistance, in which Clergy and Laymen Concerned is a participant. "Our civil disobedience is a form of religious obedience," said Father Geary.

(Father Geary, an assistant at St. David's Church, has been temporarily moved out of the parish by the archdiocese following "tensions" between the priest and his pastor.)

NOVEMBER 1, 1967

Baltimore—Father Philip Berrigan and artist Thomas Lewis fasted in a Baltimore jail after they and two others were arrested Friday for splattering blood on Selective Service records in a protest against United States involvement in Vietnam.

The blood, poured into about 16 file drawers in a Selective Service office in Baltimore Customs House, was reportedly drawn from the demonstrators themselves.

The demonstrators issued prepared statements saying in part:

"We shed our blood willingly and gratefully in what we hope is a sacrificial and constructive act. We pour it upon these files to illustrate that with them and with these offices begins the pitiful waste of American and Vietnamese blood 10,000 miles away."

The four demonstrators also called on others to "continue moving with us from dissent to resistance." They emphasized they were not trying to avoid detection nor to escape but were ready to "submit to apprehension and the consequences of our action."

Friday afternoon the archdiocese of Baltimore issued a statement saying the chancery office had no prior knowledge of the action. It also said it would have disapproved had it known.

As of Friday, both Father Philip Berrigan and his brother, Father Daniel Berrigan, poet and chaplain at Cornell University, were in jail and fasting. Father Daniel Berrigan, a Jesuit, was arrested with several Cornell students at Washington, D.C., demonstrations when their permit to demonstrate expired at midnight, October 22. He and the students declined to post bail and began a protest fast.

I. IN RACE RELATIONS

While many Catholics, lay and clerical, have been part of, and even have helped to shape, the American racial revolution, it is nevertheless a sad fact that mainstream Catholicism is basically as racist as mainstream America.

NOVEMBER 4, 1964—An editorial questions the "neutrality" policy of Cardinal McIntyre, Archbishop of Los Angeles, in the California Proposition 14 issue:

The question at issue is not merely political but also doctrinal, having to do with the nature of man and society; and what laymen who understand this are asking is not that the cardinal issue orders to voters, but that he tell Catholics what the Church teaches. . . . If the request sometimes is expressed in inflammatory language, that is regrettable. But it is also understandable, because a question of justice is involved, the justice due to Negroes and to persons of other minorities, for whom passage of Proposition 14 will mean the destruction of a liberty only recently acquired. . . . It is understandable also in the light of the cardinal's very vigorous leadership of a recent political battle to protect the tax exemptions of Catholic institutions; the cardinal has never explained why his scruples about the sanctity of the ballot did not operate when the issue concerned the welfare of Church institutions. . . . we cannot admire the cardinal for imposing his own "neutrality" on his priests, many of whom experience a most serious conflict of conscience because they are prevented from saying what they know needs to be said to the white people of Los Angeles at this time.

NOVEMBER 4, 1964—In Philadelphia, the Catholic Inter-group Relations Council lodged a protest with Archbishop Krol over the summary transfer of a priest out of the archdiocese because he took part in civil rights meetings. In a letter to the archbishop, the Council stated: "The jurisdiction of the archdiocese in this transfer is not questioned; but the extraordinary action of the archdiocese in ousting this young priest from his post at La Salle [College] has been a setback to the Church's work in Philadelphia for interracial justice and to ecumenical cooperation for this cause." The letter added that the action "disturbed non-Catholics, Negro and white, who worked with Father for interracial justice and love and who were encouraged by his presence and his spirit. It has taken from the Church in Philadelphia a priest willing to speak and act for human rights and for the divine worth of the poor and oppressed at a time when most of our priests in their sermons are silent on these grave and controversial moral issues." The priest, J. Clement Burns, O.P., had been warned by diocesan authority to stay away from civil rights demonstrations or meetings if he did not wish to be transferred out of the jurisdiction.

JANUARY 6, 1965—At a press conference, Rev. John V. Coffield, a Los Angeles pastor, announced his intention to go into "self-imposed exile" in Chicago, thereby making "the strongest protest I can make" against Cardinal McIntyre's social policies. Coffield indicated that he had often been reprimanded by McIntyre for his outspokenness on civil rights questions. "A Buddhist monk could use self-cremation as the strongest form of protest," but "it isn't open to me." He professed his love for "the Church that is trying to silence me. I want to be obedient to her, but the clear law of obedience is that we are not to obey when we are certain that to do so would be sin, whether the command be given by mother or father, priest, bishop or cardinal. We can sin by silence as well as by action." Father Coffield revealed that during the Proposition 14 campaign he had been ordered to leave California by the Cardinal and was not permitted to return until after the voting. "I want to have no part in the continuing evil of silence. I was hopeful that silent acceptance of the injustice to me and my parishioners would help defeat 14. I was wrong. I should have fought it openly." McIntyre had told him that in speaking out against racial injustice "I was not doing my duty, that I was not behaving as a priest should. . . . I feel he does not know how deeply hurt the Negro people are by this thing, and how deep-rooted is their determination to correct injustice, but when I talk to him about it, I don't get very far. I hope he becomes better informed on the race question." He agreed with a reporter that "Cardinal McIntyre is not in the 20th century."

MARCH 31, 1965—An editorial deplores Archbishop Toolen's response to the Selma crisis:

Archbishop Toolen is 79 years old, and nobody wants to be harsh to a man of that age. But this man is the spiritual leader of all the Catholics of Alabama, charged with the duty of telling them the meaning of Catholic Christianity. In recent weeks the people of Alabama have had put to them in the clearest terms a choice between justice and injustice, between the continuance of repression and the beginning of liberation. A man who joins genius with sanctity has led the Negroes of Alabama in relentlessly pressing the choice to the conscience of the state and nation.

In these circumstances Archbishop Toolen went before the Friendly Sons of St. Patrick and confused the issue. "There is too much politics in the whole thing," he said. "The question seems to be who will get the Negro vote." The Sisters and priests who gave witness in Selma to the reality of human brotherhood, he said should be "at home doing God's work." Dr. Martin Luther King was accused of "trying to divide the people."

The archbishop defended the white people of Alabama because "they have led in the defense of their country in war." He implicitly degraded the Negroes of the state by saying that "we are trying to bring them up to the standards they should have." As if paternalism were not bad enough, he fell into demagogy: "Do we need crusaders to show us how to run the state of Alabama?"

However obviously deplorable such statements are, it would not be necessary to deplore them publicly if the issue at hand were an abstraction, or if it touched only Catholics. But the crisis in which the archbishop has taken a hand is one involving concrete human rights which an oppressed people are on the verge of attaining after centuries of denial. He has diluted the worth and power of the witness given by Catholics who came to Selma and Montgomery. He has confirmed some of his flock in their preference for tribal values over Christian truth.

We find it possible to understand and forgive Archbishop Toolen's failure, just as we forgive ourselves for failures no doubt as serious and indefensible. But the failure has to be labeled for what it is. And it ought to have consequences. Cardinal Shehan has repaired some of the damage by his blunt statement of a very different view; the whole Church in the U.S., for that matter, has this time borne its share of the burden. But the Catholics of Alabama are still not receiving from their own pastor the bread of truth they need but the stones of equivocation and half-truth. The compassion one may feel, and should feel, for the personal limitations of a man faced with a task that is beyond him does not cancel the need to call for a remedy.

APRIL 7, 1965

Wilmington, Del.—Baltimore's Cardinal Lawrence Shehan has again defended out-of-state priests who took part in the Selma and Montgomery, Ala., civil rights demonstrations.

During a press conference March 26 Cardinal Shehan said the gathering of clergymen of various religious faiths in Alabama "was instrumental in developing the ecumenical spirit and strengthening the spirit that has manifested itself more in recent years."

A priest has a right to participate in such demonstrations because he is a citizen and doesn't lose these rights when he becomes a priest, the cardinal said.

He added: "It is true that a bishop could have forbidden priests to go to Selma but short of a prohibition—and I haven't heard of any bishop outside of Alabama who forbade priests to go there

—I would think a priest has a perfect right to participate in a peaceful demonstration."

MAY 19, 1965—Another Los Angeles priest has been transferred for violating Cardinal McIntyre's rule against speaking publicly on race relations.

Father Phillip E. Berryman said that members of his all-white parish (St. Philip the Apostle, Pasadena) had complained about a sermon he gave at two Masses on May 9. "I figured that in conscience I just couldn't preach for two years in that parish without ever speaking on race." Among the points made in his sermon:

Endorse the cause of Negro freedom in your heart;
Pray for this freedom;
Examine your own attitudes, to see if you harbor prejudices or hatred;
Don't be afraid to take a stand in conversations with your friends;
How do you think Christ views our silence?
Consider the possibility that God might want you to work with responsible groups for the elimination of discrimination.

Father Berryman was moved to a girls' academy with no duties except to say Mass and hear confessions.

JUNE 30, 1965—Father Maurice Ouellet was ousted from his pastorate of Selma's "Negro" Catholic parish. His dismissal, said reporter Jerry DeMuth, marked the end of "a four-year ordeal of balancing the demands of his conscience and those of obedience to the Church through its Alabama representative, Archbishop Thomas J. Toolen." Father Ouellet commented:

Whenever any civil rights activity starts or continues they write letters and start calling the bishop, believing Father is behind it all. Everything in the diocese is against him: some white priests say we've done so much for Negroes. But hell. Negroes don't want this—a plantation system. I've heard churchmen say, "We take good care of our Negroes."

I could be a white priest who works for Negroes or a priest working with people. But I feel I can only be a priest working with people. Then I become one with the people. I feel what they feel, know what they know.

The Church has an air of respectability. It didn't want to get down in the gutter with people. But the Church exists for the people, not the people exist for the Church. The Negro is the Church. If you feel like a Negro, you're compelled to push the Church. Then you'll end up with a bandage on your head . . . figuratively speaking.

Probably the hardest thing for me, I had to decide what to do. I could not help the Negro by committing suicide or by fighting the Church. I had to impart to Negroes the mind and spirit of the Church.

Whites say to me, "Well, Father, you come from the North. You don't know these Negroes." But they (the Negroes) take me into their confidence. I know how they act. When they talk to a priest, they can talk freely. They don't have to follow the old pattern. Some will say to me, "I want to vote, but I got five children to feed."

Whites believe the Negro is satisfied. Even the Church felt this. But they sure as hell weren't.

When some hear of my speaking on this occasion this evening they will say, "Why doesn't that Catholic priest mind his own business." This *is* my business! I am a shepherd and among this group are to be found some of my sheep. I would indeed be a sorry shepherd if I did not attend my sheep. . . .

God did not tell Peter to remain in his church and concern himself only with the purely spiritual matters of his people; rather our Lord very simply entrusted to him the care of His flock.

AUGUST 18, 1965—A letter to the editor is a portion of Father James Groppi's response to critics of "civil rights" priests:

"The priests should be obedient to all laws," is what they tell us. Usually this attack comes from one who is not involved in the civil rights struggle. We are accustomed to hearing this attack from the rectory priest. Any man who has studied the plight of the *Black Man in White America,* and then throws up his arms in disgust over the violation of a traffic law to point out a social injustice, is beyond me. Where is the criticism of the Church and the priests who have closed their eyes for decades to the violation of our constitutional laws? Looking at this whole affair in the light of just and unjust laws, in my judgment, is erroneous. What the priests were doing in reality was giving witness to the fact that there is a constitution in this country, and that those in authority are not enforcing the meaning of that constitution, which calls for equality of treatment for all American citizens. To criticize these priests for the violation of a traffic law in a minor way and then to disregard the purpose of the demonstration, and the toleration of the hideous violation of our constitution in the past, is hypocritical.

> *(Rev.) James E. Groppi,*
> Milwaukee, Wis.

JANUARY 26, 1966

Baltimore—Cardinal Lawrence Shehan, Archbishop of Baltimore, defied an anonymous threat on his life and became one of the highest ranking American prelates ever to appear before a government body to appeal directly for enactment of specific legislation.

The cardinal spoke before a public hearing of the Baltimore City council to try and persuade that body to enact an open occupancy bill which it has twice before defeated by narrow margins.

Only an hour before Cardinal Shehan was scheduled to speak, the chancery office received an anonymous call warning that the cardinal might be shot if he appeared at the city's War Memorial Building to testify.

When he arrived, the cardinal was accompanied by two uniformed policemen and the legal counsel for the Baltimore diocese, Francis X. Gallagher.

The cardinal's appearance before the City council underscored the archdiocese's determination to join with other faiths in leading the drive for fair housing legislation in a city that is more than one-third Negro.

When Cardinal Shehan stepped before the microphones to deliver his appeal, he was received with hisses, boos and cat-calls. Twice during the brief speech Cardinal Shehan had to pause to allow the echoing jeers to settle before he could continue.

Many members of the heavily Catholic City council were visibly shaken by the reception given the prelate who appeared at the hearing in the simple black suit of a parish priest.

FEBRUARY 2, 1966

Milwaukee—A Catholic priest was one of 11 civil rights demonstrators convicted of disorderly conduct in charges arising out of a civil rights demonstration.

Father James E. Groppi, 34, curate at St. Boniface parish, three other clergymen, four lay men and three women were each fined the maximum $100 and costs by County Judge Christ T. Seraphim, February 1.

The demonstrators were arrested December 6 at the construction site of a new public school. They were among 20 demonstrators who formed a human chain blocking an opening in a fence surrounding the site.

They were participating in a demonstration sponsored by the Milwaukee United School Integration Committee against the city school system. The demonstration protested that the new MacDowell school would have a predominantly Negro student population.

Police said the demonstrators prevented a truck and workmen's entering the site. They said when police ordered the demonstrators to disperse or face arrest, the 11 remained in front of the opening with their arms interlocked. Father Groppi and two others who testified admitted that they refused to move.

MARCH 29, 1967—From a story by Dan Patrinos:

Milwaukee—Two white priests in a largely Negro parish gave Palm Sunday sermons criticizing Archbishop William E. Cousins for statements in a controversy over the use of Church money for civil rights.

The parishioners applauded. The church is St. Boniface, an

inner-city parish. It has many white friends from throughout the city who attend Mass there.

The priests said neither of them had planned to say anything on the subject. One, Father James E. Groppi, the civil rights priest criticized by the archbishop, said he was moved to say something while listening to the reading of the Passion.

The parish's other assistant pastor, Father Michael T. Neuberger, spoke out first at the 10 a.m. Mass. He said he was "ashamed of and for" the archbishop's statements that no money from the diocesan charity fund was used to support civil rights.

At the noon Mass, Father Groppi defended his civil rights activities and his role as adviser to the Milwaukee Youth Council of the NAACP.

Father Groppi told the congregation that the archbishop had told him that he had poor public relations in his civil rights efforts. "I suppose," he said, "I have hurt and touched white sensitivities. If people are going to be disturbed by what I say, that's why I say it. I'm tired of this negative peace."

He said he would continue to "tell you now and always the way things are—the black man is being cheated. If that's bad public relations, it's too bad. I'm going to say it again and again."

A full page newspaper advertisement in six suburban newspapers touched off the controversy. It was placed by unidentified groups claiming to represent Catholic laymen.

Appearing just as the annual archdiocesan Catholic Charities and Development Fund was to begin, it asked whether money from the fund was financing civil rights demonstrations. The archbishop called the ad an appeal to racial bigotry.

He also responded by calling an emergency meeting of his priests. At the meeting and a press conference the archbishop said "not a dime" from the fund had gone to civil rights activities. He criticized Father Groppi for having a "chip on his shoulder" and said the priest didn't speak for the Church on civil rights.

From the pulpit, Father Neuberger asked: "If Father Groppi is not the voice of the Church in civil rights, then who is? Where is the voice of the Church in this city. . . . If Father Groppi is an extremist—and I disagree that he is—then he is that way because of the silence on the part of the Church."

AUGUST 9, 1967—From an editorial, "Is there a way out?" :

. . . The power of persuasion has reached its limits. But the Churches have another resource that has not yet been deployed in full measure, in anything more than token measure: their wealth. If the Churches—and by that we mean those in the Church structures who control or help control the use of Church property and income—cannot hope to persuade, they can act for themselves, and thereby become persuasive.

Those religious bodies, Jewish and Christian, whose leaders have grown to understand the agonizing scope of the race problem and its central significance in determining America's mortal destiny, are both numerous and rich. Their wealth is relative, and much of it—especially their current income—is allotted to good and necessary works of religion. But in the very words they themselves have uttered, and in view of the national mood, the mood in the ghettos, in the suburbs, for relevancy, their hope of bringing religion from the periphery of life to its center, in their honest repentance for the past sins committed by religion itself against the poor and oppressed, in their acknowledgment of the debt they have contracted to God and man for at least permitting and at worst conniving at the national crime of racism . . . for all these reasons, and because in this country religion is free to be its best self, the leaders of organized religion could now radically review the uses to which they put their wealth, in whatever form it may exist. There are buildings that need not be built, conferences that need not be held, programs that can be postponed, good works that are not good enough, in the context of today's necessity, to justify their cost.

Let them then, each according to its own structure, commit themselves together to raising a sum on the order of one billion dollars, the entire amount to be raised or pledged in one year, and all of it to be devoted, in alliance with government but independently of it, to the most effective and fundamental means of restructuring our society. Let them consider it a tithe offered to God, a tax imposed by themselves in a nation that frees them from taxation, a sacrificial offering for their own failures, a gift not to the poor but to the whole people who need to be redeemed. Let the poor have the strongest voice in its control. Let that sanest of radicals, Martin Luther King, head the cabinet that determines its use. Let none of it be spent for the benefit of any Church. And when the deed has been done, let there be no pride that it was done.

If this is a dream, it is better than the nightmare vision we have seen in Detroit. If there can be a more realistic hope, a more fitting response, a more creative and substantial gesture we have not heard of it. It is words on paper now. Any churchman who commands respect and has power of decision could put it on the path to fulfillment and change history.

OCTOBER 25, 1967—A story by Jerry DeMuth:

Chicago—Father James E. Groppi, adviser to the Milwaukee NAACP Youth Council, said Thursday that if half of its members left the Church because of its involvement in civil rights it would be "fine and good."

"They shouldn't have been there in the first place," he said at a meeting sponsored by the Catholic Interracial Council of Chicago.

Father Groppi spoke at a South Side public school after the Chicago archdiocese blocked several attempts to have him speak at a Catholic church in a Negro neighborhood. The archdiocese also publicly disowned the talk as not sponsored by the archdiocese.

The priest, who serves as assistant pastor at St. Boniface church in Milwaukee, spoke before 600 persons. He told them the Church shouldn't care about white sensitivity but should concern itself with the sensitivity of "the poverty-stricken people in the black ghetto."

"The role of the priest in the ghetto is to be with his people and speak out very strongly against the secondary status blacks are submitted to. This is the role that Christ played."

Father Groppi said that the Church must be active in civil rights because it "hits at the very core of justice and brotherhood."

Praising black power, he said it is "good, it's Christian, we need it. Black power is what's going to save America. It's not only going to save the black man, it's going to save the white man. It's a redemptive force in our country."

He defined black power as "where the black man finds his identity, his manhood." He said it meant political and economic power.

"Communication isn't meaningful unless both sides sitting at the table have power," Father Groppi said.

Father Groppi said that he uses non-violence as a tactic and accepts the right of self-defense. "We're non-violent to a point," he said and referred to a case where he claimed police kicked a 12-year-old girl in the belly. "If that ever happens in my presence," he said, "and I have a baseball bat in my hand, someone's going to get it. You can call it what you want, but I call it Christian self-defense. Our attitude is this, if you attack our women and children, then we're going to use self-defense. This is the last test for this kind of protest. I very honestly don't know where we go from here. If non-violence hasn't moved white conscience by now, I don't know if it's going to move it in the future.

"We still sing 'We Shall Overcome' in Milwaukee," he said. "Maybe we should sing 'We Shall Overthrow.' We also sing 'Black and White Together' and 'God is on our Side.'"

At a news conference the priest commented, "Many black people have already given up. Perhaps the next step is guerrilla warfare, I don't know."

Father Groppi also criticized Catholic schools for being divorced from the Negro community. And he added that using the Catholic school as a "gimmick to bring people into the Church" is unchristian. "The school must be social-action oriented from the first grade up," he said.

He referred to teaching Negro history, going out on picket lines, going to council meetings when votes on fair housing are made and going to court when a slum landlord is brought to trial. "Until Catholic schools teach social orientation, they might as well close their doors," he said.

J. IN DIVORCE

The whole question of church legislation against divorce and remarriage is under serious examination. Already this stirring up of the question is effecting real-life change. It is no longer uncommon for priest-counsellors to turn "situationalist" in cases where ecclesiastical law will not or cannot provide a remedy for a divorced Catholic who desires to remarry "in the Church." In such cases many priests are looking beyond canon law into the equity of a particular situation, and advising that remarriage should not be an impediment to continued participation in the Church's sacramental events.

MARCH 8, 1967—In an essay entitled "How Indissoluble is a Catholic Marriage," Professor Louis Dupre, philosopher and theologian at Georgetown University, examines the traditional theological arguments which stress the permanent character of marriage and takes issue with some of their foundations:

I do not intend to deny the relevance of the sacramental aspect of marriage to its indissolubility. But I do say that the sacrament alone is not a sufficient ground for this indissolubility. Nor do I believe that any of the exceptions to the indissolubility of a marriage between non-Christians would not apply to the Christian marriage.

I reject the thesis that only the union in faith fully realizes the marital union. Faith gives the marital union an added dimension, it makes marriages more sacred; but it does not make it more a marriage. Those bound in a sacramental union have more reason to live up to the obligations of marriage. One might even say that their marriage is more indissoluble, but only because the natural obligation of marriage takes on the additional character of a religious commitment, not because its nature makes it more difficult to dissolve.

The marital obligations of the Christian are essentially the same as those of the non-Christian, although the former has stronger motives to fulfill them. It would be mistaken to ignore the natural features of the marital contract because of the sacramental dimension. The Pauline privilege itself must be seen in these terms: any contractual commitment must remain subordinate to a person's supreme commitment. That the same supreme commitment does not exist for the non-Christian does not make the Christian's right and obligation purely supernatural. Nor does his supreme commitment place him entirely outside the contractual situation, for no valid contract can stand in the way of man's highest duty. In that sense the Pauline privilege is perhaps not as unique as we have traditionally believed.

However important faith may be to the Christian idea of marriage, other elements are even more essential to marriage itself. A refusal to let one's marriage partner live in religious peace undoubtedly jeopardizes the sacramental aspect of marriage. But adultery—or more specifically, infidelity so profound or so prolonged as to constitute desertion—strikes at the heart of the marital contract itself, without which there would be no sacrament. Marriage, even on a natural basis, is much more than an ordinary contract. Yet, as Pope Pius XI reminded us, its commitment is still basically a contractual one. We should not overlook then, an essential principle of any contractual commitment: if one party violates the basic obligation of the contract, the contract is discharged. He loses his rights, and the other is freed from his liabilities.

K. IN CHURCH AND STATE

A Church that relies upon special State favor (a tax-exempt status, for example) for the sustenance of its institutions will always be party, in some measure, to the *quid pro quo* of political life. The Church must always stand ready to address itself to the political power structure without fear of economic reprisal.

MAY 10, 1967

Washington—The possibility of congressional or court study of the tax-exempt status of business income to American churches was suggested last week in the *Washington Newsletter* of the National Council of Catholic Men (NCCM).

The publication described the issue as "the newest battlefield in the ever-fermenting church-state controversy in America."

Describing the situation as one in which an American religious institutional structure may be gaining the whole world but losing its soul, the report said the occasion is "a bone in the throat of not only professional atheists but also to men of faith."

According to the newsletter, the matter is "of deep and growing concern among those who love the Church and recall with trembling repeated incidents in history when that Church nearly strangled itself in worldly involvement."

At issue is the fact that churches of almost all denominations in this country have large business holdings totally unrelated to their primary mission as churches. Cited as examples of such business operations were one of Washington, D.C.'s plushest apartment buildings, a night club in Hawaii, and office buildings and hotels in major cities, among others.

The NCCM Newsletter suggested that churches be required to pay taxes on their unrelated business income, just as other tax-exempt organizations now do on income derived from activities "secular to their primary purpose for existence." "To require churches to pay taxes on their corporate profits would remove the undemocratic advantage which they now enjoy in competing with corporations and small businessmen," observed the publication.

The significance of the situation can be seen in the concrete reality of the average citizen making contributions to those churches out of pockets more and more emptied by rising taxes. Equally ironical in the face of rising business failures among small businessmen who also contribute to churches (along with their corporate big brothers) is that some of their competition comes from businesses owned by churches—businesses often operated with non-union labor.

L. IN THE YEAR OF FAITH

JUNE 28, 1967—Father Walter J. Burghardt, president of the Catholic Theological Society of America, raises some questions on the significance of the Church's "Year of Faith."

Chicago—I suspect that a year of faith is a good thing, that is, concentration on faith is a good thing and perhaps called for because of the challenges to faith in our time. There is a crisis of faith, even within the Church, very widespread.

The question how can a human being believe in our time is not just something that's outside the Church. It's in the Church, in fact it's in the seminaries.

I suspect it goes back to even more fundamental questions: Who and what is God, and how does a human being get in touch with God?

The younger people especially are not at all impressed by, say, some of the older ways of making contact with God. For example, the order and beauty of the universe. It doesn't sit well with these people at all.

It may be because . . . in the modern world they're so much more conscious than we were or even are that man manipulates nature. They can't see God in nature because nature is more and more man's creation. . . .

If you're going to limit the Year of Faith to gathering in churches to recite the Nicene Creed. . . . Repeating anything that has been repeated for generations is not going to do anything effective to anybody—I don't care whether it's the Nicene Creed or a Mother Goose rhyme. Once it's something that is simply constantly repeated you have a problem.

The thing is first of all to deepen one's understanding [of] what is meant by a thing like the Nicene Creed. For example, they will complain, and I think rightly so, that saying that the Son is consubstantial with the Father just doesn't grab them.

Now, do you simply go off to something else, or do you at least see whether there is something in that which if deepened, if put in modern terminology, if explained properly, can be made more relevant? The tendency nowadays is to say that if I don't find it meaningful, why, I simply drop it.

We theologians feel that in anything like the Nicene Creed, in a great deal that is traditional, we feel that there are values which ought to be preserved and that the main problem will be translating it.

EPILOGUE

Anyone who would attempt to celebrate signs of authentic Christian witness in a book called *The Catholic Left* should be aware of the probable consequences: exposure to charges of simplistic thinking or oversensitivity. "After all," I heard a Catholic archbishop once say, "we are born into this world with original sin on our souls. Therefore, we should not expect too much of ourselves. We mustn't be too hard on ourselves. Trust in God and Holy Mother Church. Social problems have a way of working themselves out." In the political order, how very often one hears the accusation made: Obviously he is lacking in ability to understand how enormously complex this world of ours really is; his mind becomes boggled; he reaches for easy answers. Yet, is it not true that the person so indicted might well be a man who not only has the ability—and stamina—to deal with complexity, but who refuses to let it overpower him, who refuses to use it as a crutch to justify apathy, who sees the urgent necessity of men simply being men to one another, as institutions and laws and hierarchies tend more and more to knock the life out of life.

The archbishop's security blanket—original sin—binds him to blind servitude to customs, habits, and to the past. He nestles in as *victim,* rather than *fashioner,* of his environment. His morning alarm is not the daily call to *metanoia* (see Chapter 3). He wakes up still saying his "night prayers": Now I wake me up to sleep. He lives with the Establishment, never challenging "the art of the possible," constantly challenging the God of History.

The mass media can always be counted on to adulate those political leaders who are most adept at trading off human dignity for personal political security. Anyone who takes the *Reader's Digest* seriously knows that President Johnson's personal political future is a high priority variable which must be thrown into the hopper whenever an attempt is made to re-evaluate our Vietnam "commitment." And anyone who takes the Gospel seriously knows the things that are Caesar's are not necessarily identifiable with the things that are Johnson's.

When questions and answers cancel themselves out man will have digressed to a lower level of being than that envisaged by Christianity's notion of recapitulation in Christ. Very practical men are at work on this problem. It must be assumed that the Rand Corporation has a set of projections based upon the survival of only two human beings: one male and one female. (And, no doubt, one apple tree.)

When Christians run out of questions—important questions—concerning their own meaning as a human assembly (see Chapter 2), they will have nothing left to sustain them but apples.

When Christians cease to be men of roots, they will have capitulated to the faceless liturgy, properly celebrated only by robots. (See Chapter 3.)

As long as Christians in America continue to denigrate, dilute, and by-pass the wisdom in their own Life Manual (see Chapter 4), a great future for violence in this country can be safely predicted.

If Christians refuse to challenge the dehumanizing defense of colors and other abstractions by means of the institution called "war," all other Christian references to a reverence for life will serve only to expose more clearly their self-contradiction (see Chapter 5).

American Catholics who condone universal economic inequity, oppression, and injustice (and happily reap the benefits therefrom) in the name of America First will continue to lend their baptized voices to the chorus of Establishment epithets ("simplistic," "naïve," "idealistic") directed at the Peter Rigas of our generation. (See Chapter 6.)

There is a progressive irreverence for life and human dignity in the institutionalized Establishment which cannot be reversed by benign notions of political and social evolution. The case for slow and steady progress has been destroyed by the Hydrogen-bomb Age.

Have we gained or lost in the last forty years? Americans might well compare their own country's socioeconomic "gains" against a loss column which includes the Bomb and the things we have already done with it, the four decades of war—cold and hot—and the present status of American race relations. Is the net result a plus or a minus?

The kind of computer that would belch out an easy answer to this question will never be made. But the question is nonetheless real. It will never be answered, yet it must always be asked. And value judgments will be made by people who take it seriously. And these will be signs of a healthier, more authentically Christian, more basically human attitude toward presence, mission, and involvement in the total human community. And, therefore, signs of hope. Revolutionary signs of hope.

I have hope—but then, I am a simple man.

JAMES COLAIANNI says that he "was destined from time zero to write a book entitled *The Catholic Left.*" Time began for him in Paterson, New Jersey in 1922. After a parochial school secondary education he studied at Seton Hall University and John Marshall Law School. Admitted to the New Jersey Bar in 1949, he practiced in that state until 1952. About ten years ago he became intensely interested in theology, so much so that eventually he decided to give up law and New Jersey and enroll in the Institute of Lay Theology at the University of San Francisco. After a ten-month course at the Institute, Colaianni became a Lay Theologian in Mt. Carmel Parish. During his sixteen months there he also studied journalism at Stanford and began writing for the Catholic press. Distressed by the conservative approach to activism he encountered in his parish, he joined the staff of *Ramparts* in 1965 as Managing Editor. He was later promoted to Assistant Publisher and Religion Editor, but he left the magazine after the now famous control dispute of 1967. Colaianni, married and the father of six, has recently returned East, specifically to Washington, D.C., where he has been appointed Executive Director of the Liturgical Conference. The author of this book is also the editor of the forthcoming *Married Priests, Married Nuns.*

DATE DUE

MAY 4 1971		
AUG 15 1972		
APR 29 1975		
MAY 1 4 1982		
GAYLORD		PRINTED IN U.S.A.